These are the strangers who met together

to work out their problems . . .

CLAUDIA — product of a prim New England background, she finds she has married a homosexual and realizes she cannot remain his wife or keep his child.

BOB — overprotected by a real "mom," Bob is superior and aggressive in all his relationships.

EVE — the only child of a man who thought siring a boy showed virility, but "anybody can father a girl," she turns to promiscuity.

JOHN — he discovers at a very early age that his father is a transvestite, and has been unsuccessful in his human relationships since that time.

MOLLY — her miserable, jealous childhood has driven her to sex relationships which she bitterly resents.

MOE — the death of his young wife has shattered the foundations of a life carefully built on the barren legacy of a brutal, loveless boyhood.

BETTY — hopelessly ambivalent in her attitudes to both parents, Betty is looking for guidance toward a normal life.

TOM — viciously bitter and resentful, he hates men, women, children and — most of all — himself.

Later joined, following the death of one of the above, by . . .

ABBY — a beautiful mulatto who had been a foundling, Abby comes to the group when she finds that she has unwittingly fallen in love with her own brother.

WHEN THE TROUBLED MEET

("*Fortunate Strangers*")

FORTUNATE

STRANGERS

by

CORNELIUS BEUKENKAMP, Jr., M.D.

F.A.P.A., F.A.G.P.A.

Diplomate, American Board of Psychiatry
Certified Psychoanalyst and Immediate Past President,
Association for Group Psychoanalysis and Process

NEWCASTLE PUBLISHING COMPANY, INC.

NEWCASTLE PUBLISHING COMPANY, INC.

EDITION 1971

ISBN 0—87877—000—

To the Loving,
May their yearning for a second chance
be fulfilled

PREFACE

This is an actual human experience. It is woven from the threads of events in the lives of people who have existed but whose identities have been changed. There is one exception—the therapist, the weaver of the tale. His identity remains unaltered in order to provide a reference for authenticity. These ventures find their way into an area of group psychotherapy.

The earthy language and unbridled behavior of the participants may warrant a note of explanation. Within the confines of the therapeutic setting, the therapist, without specifically saying so, had encouraged this release to facilitate reaching higher levels of maturity. It was his belief that otherwise their repressed anger would remain as a barrier against further growth. However, he did point out the unfortunate results that might come from contact with one another, or from such modes of expression, outside the group.

After these ventures came to fruition, the need to record them became evident. The value was to convey a different perspective—one involving a new concept of human relatedness.

To reach a wider audience, a nontechnical approach was used.

CONTENTS

WHEN THE
TROUBLED MEET
(*"Fortunate Strangers"*)

1. *The Participants Gather*

"I just don't know any more. I've made such a mess of things." Her words churned deeply. She had reached a point where she had ceased to mean anything to herself. Nodding, I urged her to continue. "I was so sure that I had been a good mother. Until now I had always believed that all would be right if one lived a clean, moral life—this was the way I was raised. But now I'm lost and confused."

Opposite me sat a woman who, three months before our present meeting, had abruptly entered my office accompanied by her husband. This time she had come down alone from a little town in the austere hills of New Hampshire, our first meeting since those staggering days—days that had centered around her daughter's lacerated life. In the interval, she had built up such agitation about those events that she could rest no longer. With this burden, it was hardly a mystery that her torment had driven her to return. At that first meeting she had found comfort in me, but there remained too many unspoken words. Even now, as she spoke, the words could not relieve her suffering. They did disclose that she was perplexed not only as a mother, but in her understanding of herself. Yet her drive did not mask her traditional family background—where femininity was held as a brittle state requiring considerable protection. She was a pretty woman who looked older than her forty-seven years. Her dress was dark blue and loosely covered her capable straight frame. As I looked into the pain in her face, I could feel the self-hatred that raged within.

This moved me. It was not difficult to understand her. But this meeting was not that simple. I knew and appreciated how hard she had tried. There could be no denying her motherly devotion. Instead, it seemed to me that her difficulty was that, not being able to accept the normal impulses in life, she had recoiled from them with excessive conscience.

Despite this recognition, my feelings toward her were still in discord. I admired her courage but the influence she had had upon her daughter, Claudia, was another matter.

Claudia had changed my perspective concerning human relatedness as no other person had. And as her mother sat silent and broken before me, I could feel Claudia peering over my shoulder. It was not a position of comfort. I was caught in the crosscurrent of one of life's most fundamental struggles—the mother-daughter competition.

Nonetheless, I resumed our conversation. Before long the impasse ended. She seemed aware of my efforts to reach her even though her anxiety continued. Our emotional contact was a slow one, but its effect lifted her despair. This development brought with it a recovery of her feelings of worthiness. Experiencing this with her, I felt it safe to give her a clear picture of Claudia which I had not been able to do at our previous meeting. She followed my explanations well, even though the concepts were contrary to her own moralistic judgments. I was attempting to make her see that her life with her daughter could not be reduced to such convenient simplicities. Rather, I stressed that behavior, regardless of its expression, was an act of survival. Extreme actions were only the outgrowth of drastic threats to a person's existence. Often these threats caused responses with little or no conscious knowledge in the mind of the threatened person.

My viewpoint was freely accepted by Claudia's mother. I had expected her to have more difficulty in changing her way of thinking. Her accord let me offer her further reassurance. I told her about Claudia's profound effect upon the lives of many. And as I spoke, the words evoked the associations of the past—a recall kin-

4

dled by this renewed contact with Claudia's mother. These memories turned to that day when my actual involvement with Claudia began.

My part in this recall was as a psychiatrist. Claudia's first words had come over the telephone. She had made a long-distance call. Her vocal bravado concealed some of her panic. Nevertheless, it had managed to seep through. Her utter frankness impressed me. She spoke to me as if I had been her lifetime confidant. I had not been prepared for her call and, more importantly, her candid comments. Usually, new patients waited until they arrived at the office, and then, after making a careful study of me, would decide whether or not to reveal their problems.

But then again, Claudia was so different in many ways. She possessed a personal magnetism that even crept over the long-distance telephone wires. She poured out her intimate secrets so freely that I found myself struggling to keep pace. Despite this, it was her simplicity which made me sense that an unusual relationship would develop between us.

It really was not complicated—just rare that two people, without stopping to think about it, were unreservedly accepting each other. A small-town girl, distressed and the current and chief object of gossip, and a strange man, about whom she had but hearsay knowledge, had formed an alliance.

I knew then, as I know now, that I was not pitying her. Nor was I aroused to anger over the cruelties that she had experienced. Instead, her trust had stirred my desire to be the kind of person deserving of such a trust.

I don't know whether it was my imagination or not, but even then, on the telephone, some transformation seemed to have occurred in Claudia. It did not seem to be the lessening of her panic —but was more like the relief a person feels when at last he has spoken freely and a resurgency of self-respect follows. We ended our conversation with arrangements for an appointment.

When we finally met and each time thereafter, there was an air of anticipation about her. She was a wistful thing, weighing hardly a hundred pounds. Although she was twenty-two years old,

5

she did not look it. She was caught in a maze of probing, futile questions: "How do I look?" "Maybe I shouldn't have done that?" These took precedence over all other inquiries. Despite an outward calm there was a spiral of unending, rising tension within this slender, only child. Her features often spoke more clearly than her words. She had a gentle face, with soft, pale skin stretched tautly, drawing her lips almost imperceptibly tight. Thus Claudia, anxiety ridden, came daily to encounter the workaday world.

Often, in our random conversations, she spoke of an envy of young, attractive women. Later, I was to speculate on the meaning of this envy, but the solution was not simple. Hidden in this narcissistic identification was a horde of archaic fantasy-material—a rich fantasy stock pile, charged with a never-externalized quantum of energy. With our proximity to this energy, it became obvious why she held it in bondage. She thought of these women as representing the accepted and understood daughters that she longed to be. The resultant resentment had at its core a murderous hostility.

It was in this connection that Nature, with its infinite wisdom, had indeed been clever in the personality mantle it selected for Claudia: It could little afford to allow her to jeopardize the world. A hate, whose intensity could turn iron white, roared and bellowed within her, with her mother as the object of its force.

The tigress mother was an unceasingly virtue-driven, self-denying, God-fearing matriarch. The linoleum on her kitchen floor was spotless. Her empty milk bottles glistened at the rear door. Dust knew no space in her hallowed, glorified dormitory, which supposedly represented the warmth of a home. Never would she dare permit her brain a moment's idle rest. Dark shadows of evil might emerge from forbidden sexual thoughts and burst into hideous view.

The tiger of the jungle, to stretch a point, was a non-self-winding alarm clock. Each day was ticked off in the same stereotyped, harmless orbit, starting and ending exactly on the same point of the perimeter, the only difference being a lapse of twenty-four hours. Claudia's father was friendly, courteous, and always tipped his hat to the ladies. To him, this only child was a complete mystery. The mystery had started when she was three. One rainy afternoon, she

6

had asked him if she could prance about the house in a pair of his old shoes. Scatching the back of his bald head, and sticking one thumb in the bottom pocket of his vest, he had succumbed to confusion and was unable to come to a decision. Nevertheless, this represented for him the nearest brush with a concrete opinion or position in his entire fatherhood.

Claudia, at the time we made our first appointment, had not only left her parents' home in New Hampshire, but had returned to her apartment in Manhattan. It had been here, two years earlier, that she had been married and had even known motherhood. Her marriage, which had reached coitus as few times as there are days in the week, failed in its inception. The father of her daughter, at the time of his paternity, was more dedicated to enriching his life through experiences with men than with women.

(I have since learned what this man accomplished with his life in later years, including the fulfillment of the role of a healthy father in another marriage. This will remain, in my mind, as one of the finest achievements I have ever known. He had been born and raised in the severest of ultramundane environments—a brothel. His mental health today stands as a proud monument to the mutually creative enterprise of himself and his psychiatrist, a valued friend of mine.)

Claudia's first few sessions with me dealt with how she felt upon discovering her husband's problem. It was as if it proved to her the fear she had long harbored—that anything she tried would fail or else she would manage to destroy it. The crisis came when she looked at her infant daughter and saw her as the symbol of all this futility. She felt that she had no choice—the child was given out for adoption. In this emotional state, she returned, with the instinct of a wounded homing pigeon, to her birthplace in New Hampshire.

Now, as the weeks went by, her trust in me turned into a confidence that allowed her to feel "the worst was over." She had accepted that there was at last one person with whom ugly destructiveness would not occur. It would be safe to say that not only did we like each other but we were as casual and comfortable with each other as any two people could care to be.

7

Yet, strangely, it was at this juncture that I had a strong realization. Several other of my current, young adult patients had shown comparable progress, and then, for some unexplainable reason, each had leveled off to a plateau. Claudia was fast approaching a similar stage. If possible, I wanted to avoid such a development for her as well as to resolve this difficulty confronting the others. It was clear that their potentials for growth had not been brought to sufficient fruition. These facts and circumstances led me to study their individual backgrounds and responses to treatment carefully, hoping to find a meaningful pattern.

These pursuits produced some high lights but not a decisive answer. The patients had been coming to my office once or twice a week, six months to a year. One was a secretary, another a mechanical engineer, a third a psychology student, and so it ran. Most had spent their lives in New York City or its environs. Their families were the kind who sometimes had had difficulty in making ends meet. Their formative period occurred in the Franklin D. Roosevelt era and they were influenced by the liberal, socially progressive ideas of those days. Indeed, they were bright, but unfortunately this had been a hindrance rather than a help. One, in addition to Claudia, had been married, and all had had more than a passing acquaintance with what Dr. Kinsey termed "outlets."

Each, not unlike Claudia, had been suffering from what might be thought of as a vacuum—a vacuum created by being unable to communicate with other people. While their symptoms and problems varied considerably, they shared an emotional loneliness. This loneliness both drove them toward and repelled them from people. It was creative and destructive. Often, in fact, it was difficult to separate these two elements.

However, there was much more involved than the emotional loneliness. Specifically, as I had been listening to each of them speak, I began to realize that the difficulty was not limited to a circumscribable area that they could focus upon, but rather to several. I appreciated the difficulties confronting them, but still, I could see no way out.

My own fine teachers had instilled a credo in me. Love and understanding, in an atmosphere which attempted to bring meaning out of confusion, formed the basis of psychological therapy. I believed I was giving this to the best of my ability. Then what was wrong? Why were they failing to make sufficient progress? I could have closed my eyes and said that this was simply their multiple confusion, but in my heart I knew this was not true. Certainly, my well-trained, more experienced and equally dedicated teachers could be wrong—but I doubted it. Perhaps I was not listening to my patients with enough comprehension.

Here was the clue. In their verbalizations to me, there was, with their inept blind fumblings, a message. Granted, it was not clear, but oh so vital! What they were saying, so difficult to sense, came from their deep desire to have a second chance in life—not just another opportunity, but a special kind of experience. An experience offering duplication, as well as a re-enactment, of a living-through process. ("Living-through" is an experiential process in which the past is acted or reacted upon as if it were the present.) I began to feel their need to have the scope of their fantasies meet with reality without causing embarrassment or further confusion.

This reasoning led into this mental imagery: If each of these young people could have all the related areas with the others brought together, the blending might make their own lives take on a more comprehensible meaning. This process could be compared to seeing a jigsaw puzzle fall into place after a struggle with each individual piece. Of course, there was one major difference—unlike working with the jigsaw puzzle, they would need, in working this through, to start from an unconscious level.

I was not sure, but I had a strong feeling that the lack of such an opportunity was responsible for their stumbling blocks. My precise clue had come from their attempt to seek a different outcome, both for themselves and "the others" of whom they spoke. The repetitive, incomplete pictures they had presented had produced a sub-threshold impression upon me. Thus, in thinking about the problem, a question arose. These patients talked a great deal about other people in their lives. Maybe the reason for the failure of further growth during therapy was nothing more than an absence of these "other people." The more I thought about this, the more troubled I became. I realized that I could not bring these "other people" into my office simply because my patients had talked about them. This would have been impossible and impractical, as well as harmful to their therapy.

Then I suddenly realized I could bring all of these young adult patients together, and permit them to serve as the "other people" in each other's lives.

At this point, my experience with group psychotherapy was limited. For several years, I had helped alcoholics in their organization, Alcoholics Anonymous. This had served as a valuable background. Further, while still in psychiatric training, I had used this group-psychotherapy technique in a mental hospital with some success and gratification. The literature available on the subject, although not abundant, was dynamic and illuminative. Yet, in essence, though this literature had been helpful, the necessary guidance to the specific problem facing me remained unclear.

Fortified to this degree, I decided to bring eight patients together. Actually, bringing them together was no easy task. One by one, I cautiously approached them. The approach was an unfortunate one; unfortunate, in that my caution was accurately perceived and responded to as my insecurity. My lack of greater maturity in this situation was not without its blessings. It revealed, immediately, what was missing in our respective relationships—a relatedness in the presence of "the other people."

Actually, it had taken me some four weeks to prepare these patients for the initial group session. Their resistance had been severe. Now the moment was at hand. And so, on a spring evening I waited with some apprehension in my office in New York City as they began to arrive, one by one.

Before they arrived, I had decided to remain at my desk in my inner office, feeling it wiser not to join them until they all were present. However, I did not want them to feel that perhaps they had made a mistake in their schedule and therefore I left the door between the two rooms open so that they could see that I was waiting for them. By doing this, I also felt that the later arrivals would not feel too uncomfortable on seeing only strange faces.

The first to arrive, quite in accordance with his need to be leader, was Bob. In fact, it seemed, as he selected a seat in the rear of the room, that he was availing himself of the ideal vantage point in order to examine the others upon their arrival.

This smart, natty-appearing psychology student was about five feet, ten inches tall. His one hundred fifty-two pounds were sparingly distributed upon his thin frame. Black-rimmed glasses dominated his high-cheekboned face. His appearance usually brought a response in women that would stir them to take the initiative. And although he was hardly an Adonis, there was a sexual appeal about him that drew women closer.

An introspectiveness had been nurtured by his mother's concept of him. To her, he was an invalid. Until he was ten, she had actually pushed him about in a wheel chair, using the excuse that he was a sickly boy. In reality, his physical state had been no different from that of any healthy child who was thin, angular, long-waisted and somewhat on the aesthetic side. Unconsciously, he had taken what he thought to be full advantage of his superabundant maternal attention.

Bob's manner of speech was like that of many glib New Yorkers. His grammar was acceptable, but his sentences were loaded with clichés. He overused metaphors and overaccented endings of sentences. Often, he repeated the last words of sentences for emphasis. All of this underscored and revealed his insecurity. More often than not these characteristics caused others to misunderstand and to become annoyed with him. They would often feel that he was preaching to them, rather than talking to them.

His interest in education was an unconscious striving—a striving for self-medication. The fear of others, with its bedfellow, grandiosity, unconsciously integrated itself into the form of a self-curing psychology student.

Bob's behavior, in the early days of his individual therapy, was in keeping with his self-curing enterprise. He would sit back with his legs crossed at the knees and pontificate. As he spoke, completely unaware that he was talking to himself, by identification, he would seemingly be giving advice to others, which was in fact his own medicine.

The other people in his life fed his grandiosity. They, comparatively speaking, were naïve in the ways and language of his highly organized defenses. His intellectual dexterity made it nearly impossible for the others to reach him. His emotional denial of them was too erudite for their perceptive capacities.

There was an emotional hunger within him despite this integrated rigidity. And the choice of the word "hunger" is not accidental, for this drive was toward mother. The crippling dependency upon his mother had, in effect, been his principal mode of human contact. His resulting alternatives were but two—intellectualism and "momism."

I realized that it would be some time before he would discover and feel himself to be an emotionally secure human being. He would need to find some woman who would love him without her maternal needs interfering.

Bob's father, as one might easily imagine, was mostly characterized as a passing shadow—asthmatic, frequently unemployed, alone. Tragically, he outlived his wife.

Bob, at our initial meeting, had entered my office in an Oxford-grey suit of "Ivy League" cut. He had treated me with a passive, cold respect.

Our formative period had passed as a pleasant, uneventful, casual, friendly gentlemen's chance meeting, gentlemen who were obliged to share quarters on a lengthy train journey.

When the issue had arisen over his entrance into the group, Bob had been disdainful. His objections were numerous. However, at the basis of his resistance was his fear of exposure. Not that he had anything to be ashamed of, in reality, but rather he felt vulnerable when dealing with more than one person at a time. As a result of my encroaching on this vulnerability, there were many arid interludes between us before Bob forgave me for including him in what he called "an earthy, ruffian gathering."

What I saw when Molly first appeared was a rawboned, cynical, full and firm-bosomed young woman. Had she been a boy, any high-school football coach would have converted her into a fullback at once. Her ostentatiously messy dark hair, and the badly applied lipstick on overly thick lips, immediately conveyed her message. She was distressed. Her lack of entity struck one with such impact that, silently and inwardly, I often felt her feelings to be perpetual sobs.

Tears, we all have experienced, but Molly went beyond simple crying. She started with dry eyes, and ended with convulsive gasps.

She had been born in a tenement on the lower East Side of New York City, with five other siblings. Her father's favoritism for her eldest sister bordered on the line of overt sexuality. For tasting this most forbidden fruit, her sister knew the inside of a state mental hospital all too well in her adult years. The product of an Irish father and a Jewish mother, Molly's father's rejection of her had driven her toward Judaism with a vengeance.

The session we had soon after our first meeting will remain permanently in my memory. With a kind of rancid frenzy, she described to me, with all its odors and grunts, a scene between her parents when she was twelve years old. Alternately, between sobbing and hysterical laughter, she told of her father's animalistic approaches toward her mother. This had occurred during her parents' callous oblivion to her presence in the dimly lit bedroom they all shared. Somehow she staggered to the finish of the story and never told it to me again.

There was a nebulous strength in Molly, despite her disheveled external appearance. Her panacea for her neuroses was writing —not any sort of writing, but poetry. Her lines lacked agility and their meaning was obscure.

This ambivert and her psychiatrist had a relationship which can best be characterized as electric. It was always charged with anxiety, and like alternating currents, this anxiety fluctuated back and forth between hate and adoration. Never was I held in a single continuous emotional position for any length of time by Molly. The only consistent thing about her feelings was the guarantee that the whole gamut of human reactions would be covered. I was left feeling very much "non-related to" by her. It made no difference that I received an endless flow of emotions. It was not a realistic me she was seeing. What she was doing was treating me as an inanimate object rather than as a person. I did not take these responses personally, as I sensed that these were the manifestations of what is known

13

as transference (a state in which an entire series of earlier experiences are reactivated, not as past events, but instead, within present relationships). The nature of this protectional system (throwing out, upon another, feelings and ideas that belong to oneself) harbored a danger—a danger that Molly held in abeyance with the denial that I was animate.

Next to Molly sat Eve. Her training in social work had taken her from her parents' Back Bay Boston home. New York City gave Eve the freedom she craved. She was rich, spoiled and tremendously alluring—a nymph, with long dark eyelashes, she possessed a childlike charm although she behaved like an adolescent. Men were things to be played with; this and only this was her creed. Her hate, interlaced with love, was something which struck sheer drama wherever she went. So disarming, so fraught with manipulations, was dear Eve, that her men always had more than they could handle.

This pixie, with her wiles and talents that included a high I.Q., was my last selection to join our group. I had many reasons for making her a member. We needed another female to even matters up a bit; her age and college-educational level dovetailed well. These facts, of course, important as they were, did not constitute the real basis for my selection. Socially and culturally, she was a misfit for the group, yet she belonged. Mundane items such as these have proven themselves to be of secondary value in this clinical orientation. In essence, the issue was transference.

Candidly, in Eve's transference to her therapist, she had seen him as "D-a-ddy"—not any father, but the biggest, nicest, warmest, most ideally perfect protectionist any little girl could dream of. Of course, she had practiced the range of her manipulative repertoire upon me. But I, with equal determination, mustering up every ounce of brain power at my disposal, was attempting not to be hoodwinked.

The crowning moment in the beginning phase of her individual treatment had come soon. On that particular day, early in the evening, she entered my inner office. She wore a black ensemble simply oozing eroticism: a scoop-necked dress, with skin-tight glisten-

14

ing sleeves traveling to the ends of her wrists and a bodice cut to give her breasts every emphasis without being offensive. Her normal voice was deep and rich. Now, it seemed soft. "Doctor"—she spoke, as if I had never heard the word in my life before—"I wish you to—that is—if you care to—permit—my parents to visit you." I was suspicious, and I did not answer immediately. This is the psychiatrist's greatest tool. However, this time, she too was silent, and a deepening pensive mood grew. After what appeared to be an eon, I spoke. "Eve, why do you want me to see your parents?"

Her answer was clear and sustained. "I don't know, but it seems there is a strong need in me to have you see them." As she spoke, the anxiety in the room lifted, as a morning fog is burned off by the sun. Her former façade of seductiveness was now gone.

My caution had been unnecessary. This was her way of saying, "You are really the man whom I have come to trust and respect—this is my only hope." Sensing her grasp at normality, I agreed to see them.

Eve's father talked incessantly; not of Eve, of course, but of himself. He spoke of his business, and his interests. It soon became obscure to me where his ego boundaries began or the confines of his business started. He was well liked by everyone. He saw to it that I was duly impressed with this identification badge of security. "A man has to be well liked in this world to be a success—especially a businessman like me," were his repeated words. Repetition was no small property of this well-meaning little boy in man's clothing. His bravado and digression left little room for thought while one was with him. Despite his aggression it would be misleading to say that he followed the "dog eat dog" philosophy sometimes prevalent among modern businessmen.

His relationship to his wife, who sat next to him in the interview, was not unique. She gave him his necessary primitive food. This sprang from an uncomplicated maternalism—love of a little boy. From this "momism," he was able to bounce from female to female, denying his sexual insecurity with each leap. (Eve had previously told me that her father's sexual insecurity produced a few "tender" gifts, including a mink coat to his most devoted paramour, his wife's closest friend—an occurrence of no rarity in our culture.)

A castration fear externalized itself in his relationship with Eve. Apparently, the cliché, "Any simp can have a girl child, but it takes a real man to produce a boy," was involved. A man like Eve's father, whose masculinity would have been bolstered by the birth of a son, repressed this idea into his unconscious. With its return to conscious behavior came his confused attitude toward his daughter. He treated her as if she were his son. Actually, he had inculcated this axiom into his fantasy—the fantasy of the ideal, spoiled little boy he could have been.

In turning my attention toward Eve's mother, whenever I was permitted to do so, this is what I saw: A pleasant, overfed and slightly resigned woman, quizzically taking in the goings-on. The mileage through life had taken little toll. She, too, had played well at this childish game of make-believe marriage. I believe she knew her position was mother surrogate. Still, there was an exception to this maternal imagery. In her efforts to obtain her wants, the key to a man's heart was not turned by his gastric juices at all, but rather through "letting the little boy make mud pies." Mud pies, of course, he made quite well. In the meantime, she buzzed from one do-good enterprise to another, always with one eye on the society column. She was sure that she had kept up with the "cultured things in life." Need I stress that this constant activity repressed the cogent fact that her mud-playing husband was the prototype of her alcoholic father?

Eve's inculcated attitude toward the male of the species was obvious. Mother taught daughter well. Men should be treated as necessary evils. Beguile them, seduce them and smother them with praise, for little boys need ample room in their gadget-play.

On Bob's left sat John, a lean, twitching boy with a humid handshake, the voracious intellectual of the group. Although working part time, he was basically a perennial student who refused to grow; he lived within a shell. A child, who denied his personal responsibilities, he was a lost figure. I never saw him in a suit that fitted. His palms were constantly in the ends of his sleeves. His coat fell off his thin shoulders in billows. His face was dominated by a perpetual frown.

John had many characteristic movements. His body seldom went into locomotion without an abrupt start. Wherever he was, his head moved from side to side like a spectator at a fast tennis match —the piercing eyes darting about.

He felt that people should be unconsciously able to understand each other's thoughts and feelings. Of course, this was particularly true if the subject were himself. His understanding of personal communication was identical to our present-day comprehension of flying saucers. Actually, John was not as disturbed as all this would indicate. It was just that his life had had so few guideposts.

Guideposts in life are a broad and generic subject. Children are, like the rest of the human race, members of the primate genus. Primates have many outstanding characteristics. High on that list is the need to learn by imitation. The setting of examples serves as a prototype for children. Identificational guideposts are one of the more underrated aspects of normal human psychology. To become masculine, boys need men as fathers; to become feminine, girls need women as mothers. The relationship between John and his father was attenuated, not due to the lack of quantity, but of rather more importance, quality. The fine father-son camaraderie was missing.

When John was about eight years old, he arrived home unexpectedly one day. He had a cold, and the nurse had sent him home from school. John's father, a night watchman by trade, despite a master's degree in history, was going through his daily ritual. It must have been one or one thirty in the afternoon. John, unusually quietly for him, had gone directly upstairs, looking for his mother to put him to bed, as the nurse had instructed. Finding no one about for the moment, he wandered into his father's bedroom. His eyes became fixed in stupefaction. His father was standing in front of the dresser mirror. The lingerie he wore was lacy and ornate. A delicate, pale, well-powdered face was receiving an artistic stroke of lipstick. A hysterical cry, as feminine as that of a woman in labor, left his father's throat as he swooped down upon the boy and scratched face and arms in one uninterrupted motion.

17

It is not my feeling that any single event in a child's life can cause him to be maladjusted. But is there one among us who could honestly say that such a bedroom scene with his father would not seriously damage a child's masculine guideposts?

The other significant person, during Johnny's formative years, had been his mother. A tender, goodhearted soul, she bore life's load like a burro. Heavy-laden and traversing a rocky terrain, this confused woman agilely held the line of family balance. John was an elder son by three years. His mother's adoration of her two boys was complicated by endless toil. Daily, she had hovered over them with bustling meticulous care. Mending their torn clothes, preparing three hot meals a day, and keeping them away from the "bad boys" of the neighborhood, she had managed to neglect herself completely. She had, through constant activity, succeeded in preoccupying herself to the point of denial of self-awareness.

How harmful to her self-appreciation was this tenet that "My boys are my everything." As a girl, still in her teens, she had been a beautiful Venus. A young goddess, surrounded by roses and flattery, met a Grecian god (Narcissus). The touch which Venus received was John. Dripping with guilt, she had to beg the self-styled god to leave his bachelor bliss. Overcome by feelings of ruinously lowered self-respect, his insensitivity to her further increased her deepening emotions of unworthiness.

With this picture of John's family, one can readily understand that John and I had a difficult time of it. His resentment of all authority was as tender as an area ripe with boils. My encounters with him sometimes made me feel as if he thought I were treading upon this area with heavy boots.

Betty was at the distant end of the sofa, a big smile serving to hide her inner tensions. She was the most talented individual of the selected group. When we first met, she appeared as a bobby-soxed, lost child, who had come to New York from Washington, D.C., in an attempt to escape her family as well as seeking therapy. Her ambition was to become a commercial dress designer. Betty spoke of her family as being strait-laced, conservative and puritanical. Sensing that her immaturity was preventing her from attaining her goal, she realized it was necessary to leave home. The reason why she had had to uproot herself was not in sharp focus, but she was firm in her conviction.

Betty's attitude toward men was this: She knew that all men were either devils or gods or both, because her mother had cautioned her accordingly.

Of equal significance were her feelings toward herself. In contrast to the many witticisms we have all heard at one time or another concerning "double lives" and "two heads," Betty was a trio. The weakness of her own self-identification had necessitated this trio. In Betty's mind, with utter unawareness, she was her father, her mother and herself. As confusing as this sounds, it was not strange. The process of imitation, which was discussed a while back, is latent with intrigue. Our earliest route of perceiving and understanding is through the oral cavity. Recall your observations of the infant lying in his crib. His struggle to put everything in his mouth is amusing. Do you realize that this is his attempt to discover the world? This process of learning, coupled with our primitive need to imitate, results in a psychological process known as orality. In this orientation, the human being, regardless of his chronological age, evaluates and understands all experiences through the mouth—*i.e.,* oral psychology. It is characteristic of these individuals to prefer to have things "happen to them," rather than to "do things," in keeping with the "infantlike" psychology.

From this, you can understand how Betty, in attempting to reach reality and normality, had swallowed the images of both of her parents, because of her own weak ego-structure. (Ego-structure is that part of the human being's personality, partially conscious and partially unconscious, which refers to the self.) In so doing, she was unconsciously, in both action and thought, a trio.

This trio and I, surprisingly enough, got along rather well. All was fine as long as I knew which role of the trio was being projected upon me. It was not an easy task, for it led not merely to charged circumstances, but to an item of lasting importance, which will be discussed later. Its germination contained the intimations of things to come.

Betty's older sister was not unlike the mother. These two

women were close to God, and distant from their husbands. In Betty's mind, there lurked a suspicion concerning these two marriages. On one occasion, this feeling was expressed. With a creeping loneliness in her voice, she had said, "I feel these marriages existed in heaven, but never in bed." It is not uncommon for little children to deny with vigor that parents ever did "that terrible thing."

In contrast to this naïveté were Betty's views on sexual morality. Determined, as though she were the combined Chiefs of Staff of the nation's military forces at war, she remedied the unpardonable state of virginity at the first drop of her handkerchief. Such a tenacious drive, without the apparent desire for pleasure, could not escape my interest. Slowly and indirectly, in our individual sessions, I had attempted to elicit pertinent and collateral material. At all times, she had been most co-operative and friendly in our discussions. Measure by measure my efforts came to nil. Even with all the information I had about Betty, I was unable to put it into a meaningful pattern. Yes, she wanted love, marriage and a home, but these seemed vague as she spoke. Each "romance" appeared to have the essential emotional ingredients, yet they contained no more love than my tax payments. This dilemma baffled me. The meaning of these communications escaped me. With reflection, it struck me at last: her older sister had a history of a premarital pregnancy. This had almost "killed" mother. The daughters' wishes to engage in excessive sexuality were now seen in a new light. In Betty's case, the evidence had expressed itself in various forms. Dream material, intense fear of pregnancy, as well as her poor judgment and management concerning contraception, made her unconscious desire clear to me. Her real goal was to gain what every little girl needs so badly—her mother's love. However, due to her unconscious identification with her mother, the pursuit had become enmeshed. That is, she and her mother shared one and the same unconscious wish. And when Betty had said that her mother's marriage was made in heaven and not in bed, this became my integrating clue. Betty's excessive sexual behavior was merely carrying out her mother's unexpressed wish. Since Betty had swallowed her mother's image, these unconscious, unexpressed wishes were being released by her. This explained why her sister's behavior had almost "killed" mother—seeing her child carry out her own inhibited impulses.

Betty's sexual activity had been nothing more than her desire to have her mother's approval and love by performing that which her mother could not do herself. This concept was further supported by material she revealed later.

To John's left, in motionless silence and without visible signs of emotion, sat Moe. Fundamentally, he was a regular, good-natured fellow. In spite of his extensive self-appreciation, and an embittered attitude, he was likable. Beneath the bitterness lay a warm kindness. As one of eight children, Moe had known little warmth. It almost seemed that his gentleness was present in counterpoise to the indoctrinated hate. His daydreams were abundant with self-idolatry. But, as though to maintain balance, he participated in life with an active sense of humor.

Moe had been an athlete and looked the part. Basketball had been his forte. While he was at college, I remember having seen him play in Madison Square Garden. Not that he had been the star, but rather, the faithful playmaker. A six-foot-two frame, jet-black curly hair and heavy ash-grey beard, made him conspicuous at a great distance. Now, his gait was sluggish: his shoulders drooped, and his eyes hugged the ground. His playing days, both literally and figuratively, were over.

When Moe was seventeen, he had met Ruth, who, despite her teen years, had been a wonderful oasis in his life. How much more appropriate it would have been had she been named Bathsheba, for her loveliness was poetical. Rich chestnut hair set off a clear white skin and moist full lips. Their love bloomed amidst the crowded tenements of the Bronx, and it had made little difference that the tranquil lakes of their imaginations were in reality bleak concrete.

Then—it was May 1950—Moe had been drafted. Ruth and he could wait no longer. A three-day leave from San Diego, and she had become his wife, in Nevada's blazing Las Vegas. It was but a four-weeks-older groom who left on a Navy destroyer for Korean shores. Three months from the day they had wed, Ruth bled to death from the toxins of conception.

On a cold dreary dawn, "the skipper," with bloodshot eyes, had broken the news to Moe. Weary, having slept only between passes of shrieking jets, they stood face to face, both ill at ease. Each was wondering what to expect from the other. "Son," the captain started, with a long pause following, "I don't know how to say this"—another long pause—"your wife has been ill."

"I didn't know!" and then, quickly recovering, "Sir," in a quieter voice. As bewildered as he was tense, Moe waited for further details.

"Yes," the skipper continued, "she passed away yesterday."

Back in his bunk, and quivering with grief, Moe buried his face in the pillow. The captain's words, still resounding in his ears, had, in one second, plunged him into emptiness.

After his discharge, Moe had drifted aimlessly for months. As if by accident, he had come into our lives with a beaten hound-dog look, his tail between his legs. He joined us physically, but his spirit was elsewhere. We were never sure of his thoughts and feelings. Reward was ours, however, whenever he was finally capable of sharing them with us. The strange admixture of a loathing aversion to reality and a keen sense of it inevitably moved us when he spoke.

His father had owned a bakery. The members of this ceaselessly active enterprise were, primarily, his children. Remember, from your own childhood days, "the old lady who lived in a shoe"? These kids lived in the bakery. Unlike the old lady—Father did know what to do. He had no labor problems. His contracts were all in blood. The unwritten code was no work, no eat.

This man walked through life with brutality as his companion. He knew people, but cared or felt little for them. Seldom was he defeated; and yet, he never won. Like the cynic he was, he knew the price of everything and the value of nothing. Living only during respites between dodging creditors, he managed to accrue a potbelly and a sizable fortune. In spite of this fortune, his wife and children continued to walk about the streets in threadbare clothing. Often, in fact, he had been so successful in concealing his profits that his bankruptcies were his greatest windfalls.

Moe lived in sheer terror of this man, whom he was forced to accept and call his father. Even as a boy of six, playing ball out of doors, he would run and hide in someone's basement when he saw the familiar hulk swaggering up the street. The razor strop and those "ungrateful brats" had more than a nodding acquaintance. The time Moe, working as a delivery boy, had spent a fifty-cent "tip" from a kindly, childless woman is illustrative. Happy, as if he had inherited the world, he had gone and sat in the bleachers, to see his heroes, the Yankees. When Moe had returned home, gleefully, there stood the tyrant. Crack went the razor strop. What right had he to steal money from the cash register? No amount of reasoning could induce this crazed bull to believe that a lonely woman could have given anything to his ungainly calf.

The cow of this herd was characteristic. Her lot was to bear and raise offspring, and at the same time keep peace in the home. "Sure," she reasoned, as once or twice a year she accompanied her husband to the movies, "those women have fun, but that's only in the movies." She knew there were a few real women who had fun, too, but everyone knew where they would wind up.

An aura of greyness surrounded Moe's mother: her hair, her skin, her clothes and her life.

Moe and I were practically friends before we knew each other. How or why, I am not completely sure. When we were together in individual sessions, we must have sounded like bluejays. Sports, jokes, politics, religion—on and on we went. The sessions had hardly begun before they were ended. He needed a father, and I had a wonderful son—a son of whom I was proud. I have a son at home, but this was different. How different, it is hard to say. The age disparity between these two sons was not the striking differential, rather it was the thirst of the patient: he was so dry. Moe was so "short-changed" by his own father that he appeared to be making up for lost time. Never was a moment of our valuable time idly wasted. As he once jokingly said about himself, "I have to talk so much, when I'm with you, in order to get my money's worth."

At this moment Claudia arrived. She was wearing a scarlet jumper and white silk blouse. These colors impressed me as fitting her psychological paradox. The clashing of the angry red with the peaceful white appropriately represented her divergent inner struggles.

Hardly had she seated herself then she began chitchatting. Of course this was an anxiety release for her. And while the attention of all those present was upon her, it gave Bob the opportunity to examine all the others with less detection.

I found myself noting his need to control the environment by exploration of its characteristics. He appeared so adept with this procedure that the others were totally unaware of its presence.

Claudia had waited for this occasion eagerly. When I had introduced her to the idea of group psychotherapy, her response had been the least resistant of all. Despite her holding the center of the stage, I could see her craning her neck in my direction, impatiently waiting for me to join the group.

Her beckoning glances increased my desire to get started, for I felt some misgivings at not introducing the group members to one another. But I resisted, remembering my previous decision to avoid an uneven beginning. Futhermore, not wanting this to turn into a social gathering, I felt that customary propriety would defeat the aims involved in this form of psychotherapy—it would probably delay the emergence of their repressed anger. Also I reasoned that in the absence of a statement on my part concerning their mode of expression, I would not be setting up a hampering influence.

Last to arrive was Tom. He occupied the most distant seat from my inner office and scowled at the others. As I looked at him I could not help but think that man at his normal best is defective yet does not seem to resent it—but Tom did. Tom resented everything. He hated me, men, women, children—and himself most of all. This hatred of himself was an ingenious device. Nobody, absolutely nobody, could say anything terrible about Tom which he had not said "better." If your disposition was at its worst, and you were in your ugliest mood, Tom could outdo you. Tom was the person who invented the dyes out of which they made the "blues."

During World War II, we all remember the emergence of the "Sad Sack." Compared to Tom, the "Sad Sack" was Mercury.

How he came into therapy is a story in itself. One day, a rainy one, when he was attempting to outdo the weather, his sister could stand him no longer. My phone rang, and answering it, I heard, "O.K. now, damn it, tell him!" A female voice ordered this emphatically.

Then, a long pause, and finally the lowered, muttering tones of a man's voice, "If you're not too busy, Doc, I want to ask if a guy like me should see a doctor like you? You see, Doc," his voice droned on, "my sister, who does the cooking, says that if I want any supper tonight, I've got to see a psychiatrist first—so will you see me, Doc?"

I didn't want the boy to go hungry, so we met.

That first session, and those that followed, were all the same. He would trip over the doorsill when he came in. As he sat in a chair, the weirdest and wildest collection—pieces of string, bent fishhooks, crumbly, dirty pieces of paper, nuts and bolts—would spill from his bulging pockets. I once asked him if he believed in collecting things. His reply was that he tended to be on the saving side, "Because, after all, you never can tell when you'll need them." He also proceeded to inform me, "There isn't anything like it—having things immediately available when you need them—especially if they are in your own pocket. And," he went on, "really, Doc, you know it!" With the nearest thing to a smile that I had yet seen on his face, he finished on a philosophical note, "You can't depend on people."

This knowing smile, which he shared with me, was a cue. It revealed so much. In one brief instant, I had been privileged to look in! Here, the source of the difficulty was exposed to me. His *modus operandi* was simply this—I, Tom, who feel so superior toward people, best not to let them see my contempt for them. I need them not; I use them not; I am I. His external decorum served still another function. It relieved him of the guilt he would otherwise have experienced. Specifically, this narcissism, if externalized, would render him hostile—hostile because, by contrast to the frailties of others, he would outshine the world.

His narcissism extended as well to his external mien. For, if you recall, he was even superior to "Sad Sack." He would not allow anyone to be better than he, not even at being miserable.

Such extremes bespeak still other extremes. What are these other circumstances? How did they influence Tom? Why did he no longer communicate with others? These questions are easily propounded, but are not readily, if ever, answered.

A family picture, which included a series of dilemmas, contributed, no doubt. He had two brothers and three sisters. These children had been ushered into the world by strangers. Why strangers? Just because a man and a woman agree to share the same house, they are not necessarily friends. Such were Tom's parents. His father had his own life, his mother went her way. Seldom did the two paths cross.

His parents' marriage was not the end result of discord. They had simply never established "diplomatic" relations. Unfortunate people as these were, they do not represent an unusual situation. In fact, the deficiency which all of our group had in common, though in varying degrees, was the inability to love. Indeed, it takes considerable energy for people to have a mutual investment. It takes time for roots to intermingle. The case of love at first sight is but the case of immediate emotional response. True love, of which I am sure no one can speak as a complete authority, happens otherwise. It comes with long-standing, repeated deposits and withdrawals. As with all bank accounts, they stand or fail with the depositor. The deposits need deposits to be added.

What are the deposits? In one overly condensed concept—relatedness. Relatedness—regardless of its size, nature and direction—with enough frequency and consistency, will create a dividend: love.

This love is most often confused with its precursor—need. If need dwells persistently, then love will not be the dividend. The relentless demands of need destroy both parties. The donor becomes depleted, the recipient immobilized with guilt. Hate rules the servant, revulsion dominates the master. Obviously, then, the danger in the scope of need is large.

We can all ask ourselves this question, at some equivalent point of our relationships—when need flies out of the window, will love fly in?

26

2. *The Lonely Meet*

Appropriately enough, on this particular evening, it was wet outdoors, and the temperature was on the chilly side. April in New York, eight lonely people sitting in an open circle about to be with their psychiatrist, and all seemed in balance.

For those of you who do not know April in the city of New York, may I explain? Early April is cold. It knows neither winter nor summer. There are whispers of promise in the air, but growth awaits.

This relationship between the environment and its people was revealed in the uneasy tone which prevailed. The attitude of these silent patients, if put into words, could have been, "Doctor, do something for us." Their wish to have me present them with a magical cure was fervent. Their deep longings to be fed, like the infant who makes a minimum contribution, were clear.

With a sense of excitement I watched them in the large, comfortable, adjacent room. Its high ceilings and soft green hue, with its subdued lighting, gave the impression of a homey, middle-class, English living room, rather than a doctor's office. The chairs had been arranged in a circle, with three of the seats joined in the form of a sofa. By coincidence, Tschaikovsky's "None But the Lonely Heart" was playing on the radio.

Although each had been in the room innumerable times before, they sat as if it were their first visit. Curiously, I noticed that the seat they had left for me was the one which separated the two sexes. The women had chosen to consolidate on the sofa. The men had sat in the individual chairs, forming an equal half of the circle, as if in morbid fear of the females.

Now the time to join them had arrived. A wave of high exultation rolled over me. I felt like the bather, ready for his first dip of the season in the ocean, having a memory of knowing how to swim, but not having performed the exercise in some time. The anticipation of the surge of the water, and its coldness, brought forth beads of perspiration. I halted a moment at the doorway and then entered the room. With an uneasy smile, I spoke, yearning for a fluidity to develop.

"May I have the pleasure of introducing you to one another?"

Immediately, they all rose. The introductions went well and without a fumble.

"Ah," I said to myself, "glad that went so well."

Upon returning to our seats, I continued.

"Well, we all know why we are here. It's my feeling that the less said by me as to how we should proceed, the better. May I say merely that we are here for no one's benefit but our own. This is not a philanthropic society, but rather a laboratory of human emotions, which will give you a chance to see yourself in action, to see how you affect others, and how others affect you. So, won't you please begin with anything you wish."

A slight adolescent giggle seemed to puncture the air, from the feminine half of the circle. Stony silence encompassed the masculine half. Immediately, a frozen state of silence developed. Implied was the attitude, "Oh, no you don't, Doctor. We came here to be treated by you. You're not going to get out of your responsibility that easily." They looked at one another anxiously, each measuring and sizing up the others from ever-increasing degrees of insecurity. Courage seemed to wane as the moments passed into minutes.

Many things occurred to me. Here sat nine human beings, eight fermenting with unrest. I, the ninth, was desperate to have some interaction occur. After all, they knew only me, and I was their one tie to familiarity. They trusted no one else, and now I was encroaching upon this trust. My reasoning and planning had been to follow this course—that if they were to become united into a group, and this group was to be democratic, the leader should not be the dominant force, as it would inhibit the process. Of course, this unwittingly produced a state psychologically resembling infancy—early infancy in the sense that we know only one parental image, and are dependent upon it for complete and total sustenance.

These conditions were indeed challenging for Bob. He had known them well. You will recall that his chief mode of human contact had been an overdependency upon his mother. Thus, with an accomplished approach which belied his insecurity, he began to encounter this first critical theme. Gesticulating, he dove in, and expounded upon how vital it was for all of us to develop relationships with one another. And the more he talked, the less sincere he was. In the meantime, the rest studied and compared one another nervously.

Among Bob's many points was the one which revealed his prevailing unconscious attitude toward me. He had openly praised me at considerable length for bringing the group together. However, it failed to conceal his disturbance at having to share his therapy with the others. "The idea of having me, a professional person, grouped with these atrocious, sick people," had shown through and had been gathered by many of the diligent listeners. It was my feeling that although they sensed his loathing, they were so glad to have someone "take over" that, for the time being, they did not seem to mind.

Gradually, the motive of his subtlety in damning me with faint praise had crept through his external façade. And it became clearer as the session wore on that my placing him in the group had been responded to as if I were refusing to recognize him as the preferred child. Yet, his unspoken feelings had contributed the contagious spark that ignited the other members' emotions. In essence, it was an emotional force that started the conversion of the individual patients into a real group.

Beginning cautiously, the others started to take issue with Bob. It was their disguised way of expressing interest in joining the fight against the symbolized, unyielding parental figure. If ever I learned from experience, it was on this occasion. I saw disagreement designed to serve as acceptance; acceptance to join forces. They rallied as one against that which they had consolidated into the image of me. Not I as myself, but as all parents rolled into one. It was their day—indeed a choice opportunity—a chance to release the anger they felt concerning inane parental bunglings—bunglings which had been committed in the name of, "I'm only doing it for your own good."

Although I had never spoken these fateful words, I was treated as if I had. By the middle of this first session, the clamor began. It kept getting louder and louder. Each one, in or out of turn, "screamed" vociferously, overlapping as they went on. Their laments poured forth with memories of parental misrule. Yet, consciously, they did not know that I, the host, was serving as a displaced target.

The sounds of their expressions had jogged my memory. A clear picture of the pediatric service in a general hospital flashed before me. As feeding time would approach in this nursery, one infant would awaken the others, the whole group's wails increasing to a crescendo. And who could deny that our initial session was as if that scene were being duplicated and re-enacted with a spontaneity that was contagious?

On it went until the end of the session. They were spent. Then, without revealing the meaning of their behavior, I bade them good night, at the same time conveying to them that I felt they had made an excellent beginning. To have given them interpretations at this juncture would have embarrassed them and destroyed their courage for the battles that lay ahead.

After they had all left, I returned to my inner office to review the happenings. It was then that another parallel dawned. Their behavior had been like the first round of a professional prize fight. The only difference had been that there were eight combatants instead of two. Each of these patients, like heavyweight contenders, had been feeling the other out. Each, carefully, had avoided real contact, and had merely tested the strength and weakness of his opponents.

This testing period continued roughly from six to seven sessions. They met twice a week in the evening for an hour and a half. I, serving only as a catalyst, and similarly experiencing a new kind of anxiety, watched a torrent of emotional behavior break forth.

It had started during the eighth session. Bob had successfully implanted the "let's hate our parents" theme and it had bound them together. All of them had been out to seek revenge and demand love. Curiously enough, Bob remained unaware of what he had caused. Of equal interest was the fact that they had carefully avoided open conflict with me until then.

Molly was the individual who had been most infected with the indoctrination. Whether or not this was related to Bob's doings or her own well-placed hatred of her father, or both, was difficult to say. With abundant motives she was the lead-off hitter. "Say, Doc, who the hell do you think you are, anyway?" she complained. "We're paying you money for this farce. Here we are coming to you for help, and what do you do? . . . Nothing. You don't say a word. Why, you don't even protect us from one another."

"Yeah," spoke up John. "What a racket. He gets eight of us together at once, when otherwise he would only be seeing two patients. He'll be getting rich, and we'll be getting more and more miserable."

Then Moe began, "Really, I'm not mad at the doc, but honestly, what the hell goes? Here we've been sitting around talking to one another, and as far as I can see, nobody gives a damn or says anything back."

Betty, silently staring at me, had a knowing look on her face. She seemed to be thinking, "Well, what did you expect? He's a man, isn't he—they never give you anything, anyway."

Eve, of course, was above all this commotion. She considered these people as belonging to the dregs of the human race. Her condescension expressed itself as she filed away at her long fingernails. On occasion, she would stretch out her arms and admire them. This feminine gesture was filled with disdain and vanity.

Tom trudged in late, as usual. He was muttering something about those "stupid subway guards. Those bastards gave me the wrong directions." After a few minutes of listening to some more of

Molly's, "And if you, God damn you, Doc, don't do something about this . . ." he growled, "Nah, why don't you go soak your head, Molly?"

I had often suspected that Molly would rather fight with a man than eat. In situations like this, she played her role to the hilt. She snarled back, "Do you think, Doc, I'm going to put up with the likes of that? Why, look at him! He's a jerk, and you know it."

At this point, the "heat" in the room was becoming disturbing. I did not feel displeased. To me, this exchange spoke of promise— of human relatedness. It was Bob who was in distress. No longer was he able to sit back passively. Gone was his composure. His study of the habits of the "human species" had been interrupted. Sitting up and leaning forward, he began to "operate." I had the distinct impression that his own cunningness was endangering him. "You know," he began, these words representing his introduction to every occasion in which he felt insecure, "it seems you people do not understand each other. A little more tolerance is what is needed. Now really, Molly, so what if Tom does have his faults, haven't we all? After all"—and he was at his seductive best—"you're bright and charming." It made little difference to him that her hair was unkempt, as usual. Nor did her repeatedly disheveled picture, with ill-fitting stockings and their crooked seams, disrupt his hucksterlike maneuver. His reinforced attempts to calm the others converted his approach into that of a slick swain. Beaming, he continued, "Molly, you know that actually Tom doesn't really dislike you. He only believes he does. I'm sure in time you two might even grow to be friendly." Turning toward Tom, he finished his contrived emotional effusiveness. "Tom, really you're a nice guy. I wouldn't let Molly's words set so deeply, if I were you. It seems to me, fella, that people are always misunderstanding you. I know what it is to be misunderstood. And you're so right about those damn subway guards."

The more he spoke these condescending words, the more control he was able to gain over himself. Calculatingly, he had succeeded in removing the attacking drive of the patients from the therapist. He unwittingly had disclosed, in this behavior, his unconscious need to punish me, but not to destroy me. And now the punishment had gone far enough. The threat that I might be destroyed by the others, whom he had unconsciously aroused, had to be diverted, for his need of me was great. Masterfully, at the critical moment, he had again gone into action. What had appeared to be done from a superficial level of benevolence was actually a powerful, subtle control. It had outflanked all obstacles appearing in the roadway of his life. The pattern had stemmed from what he considered to be taking revenge on his overpowering mother. His connivings had rendered his emotions poverty-stricken. A loss of spontaneous living had resulted from his preoccupation. (Preoccupation to a psychiatrist means the involvement with one's narcissism and the gains for this self-love.) Such a limiting existence had to be maintained at all costs. And as a result, any women who came into his life were inevitably exploited through the guise of a mother. For it was a fact, his mother had been a vicious cat who had snarled and bitten the imaginary enemies of her favorite kitten—himself.

Yet all of Bob's repressive activity had not been a complete success. Tom and Moe were irritated by Bob's behavior. Though silent, they were restless with intolerance. Molly had shrugged her shoulders, as much as to say, "What's the use?"

Gazing with a cold, fishy stare, John was dissecting Bob with a silent query, "What sort of a specimen is this, anyway?"

"Glad that's all over," was Eve's response. She reacted as one who had been exposed to an open garbage can.

By contrast, in the ninth session, Claudia appeared oddly. All that had occurred had had little effect upon her. Her silent communication had been, "I couldn't care less!" Yet, something new had caught my eye concerning her. While these isolationists had merged into a group because of their hostilities, she had remained alone. She had been busy—busy changing her life. Not to just any new life, but to one of a particular glamour girl. She envisioned for herself a special kind of charmed existence. To become like Eve was her object, although I doubt that she was aware of this at the time.

She now wore her hair as Eve did—bangs and shoulder-length page-boy cut. Her cosmetics were changed to conform to her idol's. Strangest of all to me in this unconscious duplication were her mannerisms, and, in particular, her voice. The few words she had spoken were perfect reproductions of Eve's voice. At one point, when my eyes were cast in Eve's direction, I was amazed to see her lips immobile.

The province Eve had with men, her artistry and frank outspoken admission of her actions, produced a vicarious life for Claudia. With each episode that Eve would live or relive in the group, there would be Claudia, a half step behind, behaving as though she were the principal figure. This identification, as her individual sessions revealed, was her desire to be the understood and loved daughter, which in her mental imagery she thought to be.

When the group learned Claudia's story, they overcame their initial shock and slowly appreciated her repressive ways. They did not sit in judgment of her for having abandoned her child. They could easily see and understand why Claudia admired Eve. Incapable of having a life of her own and feeling like an ogre, what choice did she truly have? Her right to live could not be denied.

Claudia remained absolutely immune to the group's references to her "empathy-show." Life had returned, and it was of little consequence that there were some incongruities present. It was just "too grand" to be alive to bother about mere details. This was her implied attitude.

The group continued to live in smoldering limbo for some time. On occasions, I found myself restless. I was waiting impatiently for the inferno. However, Bob, with his verbal gymnastics, voiced the group's deeper expression. He, in fact, was the group's regulator. I often wondered if the others knew what feelings of frustration I was experiencing as a result of his actions. At night, driving along the parkway after sessions, I would go over the material again and again. Where could I serve more adequately? Was I too inactive? Was I too active? These questions, and a million more, came to my mind.

The solution was like a mist rising. Bob and I had better get matters cleared up between us, I thought. First, reaching within myself, I asked these questions: Why does he annoy you? Is it as simple as it appears? No, came back the response, almost too abruptly. Of course I realized that I was irritated because the group's emotion was held in abeyance by him, but my concern went beyond this. The experience had taught me that there were many things involved.

My meditation continued. In addition to the ever-present personal factors, I recognized that my lack of a wider range of experience with this technique had certainly contributed to my restless state. In spite of such a deficiency, along with my own personal inadequacies, the difficulty still did not seem to be satisfactorily explained.

To approach the problem by retracing my steps seemed to be the way. With this in mind, I asked myself the question: Had I ever had similar difficulties with Bob before? Reviewing my notes of our individual sessions, I found none. Searching my memory, I failed to discover any similar or near similar episodes or feelings. Then, I thought of other cases somewhat like Bob's. Everything resulted in negative findings.

Deeply aroused, I sensed there was something of importance involved. I discussed the problem with several colleagues, who represented a wide diversity of training and thought in our field. Each referred back to the same points, more or less. They stressed that I need either more time with Bob or more experience with the technique, or both. However, this failed either to confirm or dismiss a growing belief that I possessed. I did not refuse their appraisals, but I felt that there was still more involved. Then I took a step. It was, indeed, a calculated risk. I decided to consult the group.

"Bob," I said, "do you notice any difference in me while I'm in the group, as compared with our individual sessions?"

At first there was a constricted gasp, followed by a motionless, dead silence that filled the room. Quizzically, he began, "Well, Doc, putting it to you straight—because if I know you, that's the way you want it—I feel you're more mature when you're in the individual sessions. When you're in the group, you seem almost like a patient."

Startled, but feeling much better, like the dental patient who has just had a painful tooth removed, I relaxed. A meditative moment of silence passed, and I was aglow. Why, of course! He was right, and I agreed. What he had said meant many things to me. Above all, he had accepted my relationship in the group. With this acceptance, I understood the situation clearly. What Bob's words kindled in my mind was that we, the group, were a different configuration from an ordinary group of people. For in his seeing me as a patient, he was revealing that my role was a subjective one. Further, this subjective participation of mine jelled the setting into the most basic of groups—the family.

I could now see a configuration! We were re-creating a family. Bringing the "other people" into the group had been necessary to give us the opportunity to complete the family unit.

I had been competent in the one-to-one relationship only. This one-to-one relationship, when placed in the configuration of a family group, was no longer the same structure. Being a parent to my children all together in the same setting at one time was an entirely different matter from being their parent individually on separate occasions. Obviously, I needed experience with this whole family structure in simultaneous dynamic action, so different from the relatedness to one child (patient) at a time.

In part, my new role had been responsible for Bob's seeing me as a patient as well. Not only had I joined the group as an active subjective participant, but in so doing, I had brought with me my total personality. This accounted for the change in my behavior. It also contributed to his and the others' greater ability to accept me. It was John who made the cogent remark on the subject: "I like the fact that the Doc participates more and more in the group sessions because it makes him so much easier to get along with."

Yes, it was true. I felt closer to the patients and so did they to me. The missing piece of the jigsaw puzzle was now in place. My anxiety and "patientlike" behavior had been my struggle to join this multidimensional structure—our family. It is not an easy thing to become a member of a family, but the reward is great. Bob's words were my reward for they meant that he, as the oldest son, had agreed, as spokesman for the others, to accept an authority greater than themselves—their parent. I had no special need to participate in this role, but rather, it was a matter of necessity to do so. This is what our respective unconscious strivings had been trying to achieve.

At last, the picture was completed. I understood.

Man is born as a member of a group. He is raised in a group. His whole life is a group function. The one-to-one relationship can stand alone, but only for a limited time. The compounded group is society. Society is man.

Previous explanations of my difficulties had lacked this concept, which was to revolutionize my professional career. I felt that a major milestone in the evolution of group clinical psychology had occurred. But it was only emergent; it needed growth and development.

Now that the log jam had been broken, there was an air of acceptance in the group. No longer were there two units present. The members and I were as one. A new-found ease existed in the relationship between Bob and me. We were able to speak with one another most constructively while in the group. With tact and skill, I was able to manage his intellectual "lobbying." In time, my improved management of Bob's strategical maneuvers served in another way. It set an example for the others in coping with the group.

The successful resolution of our conflict created a new phase in our clinical experience. Our group had no completely autocratic leader. Bob had lost his throne. I, quite by my own volition, figuratively moved to the perimeter of the circle. This created something of a void. Each of the patients scrambled to fill the void with an attempt to leader-control the group by his self-concern. Some used direct aggression. Some used passive resistance. Others tried various other manipulative operations. All of it went on unconsciously.

My role became more passive with respect to authority and more active with regard to participation. I gave no interpretations —I had joined the group. Obviously, I was feeling more secure. The patients had unquestioning response to this. It seemed that they were now busily employed gaining personal stature within the group structure. Actually, this was the first significant evidence of encouragement that constructive group function was under way, and I felt that the initial obstacle of the course had been jumped.

3. *Together But Not United*

Despite my feelings that the major resistance to the group as a therapeutic process seemed to have been resolved successfully, I felt that there was less group unity. "Yes," I said to myself, "they have accepted the group as a means of reaching further growth, but the strong, common bond which had been welded together by the emotion of hostility toward the alleged nonaccepting parental figure has, in most part, spent itself." It had been this bondage which had operated to unify them. Now, since the majority were no longer hostile to me, and feeling that I had not rejected them, a confusion had taken its place. For, as long as they had a common target in me, the necessity for each of them to face his or her own mental self-image had been alleviated. The result was that each, to a varying degree, was faced with the problem of developing his own personality structure. In a sense, what had developed might be likened to the change of a person's mode and manner of living without having something clearly defined to take its place.

Quite characteristic of this confusion were the comments heard from Claudia, in the throes of grappling with this new development. "I don't know what it is, but I feel something is missing these days. I feel empty in some way."

"Yeah," chimed in Moe, "it's like the time some of the older boys threw me off a pier into the East River and told me that this would be the best way to learn how to swim."

"Yes, yes, Moe," came back Claudia, "that's it. I feel you've captured it exactly. We seem—or certainly I know that I do—to want to swim, but the old alibis just don't make sense any more. I can't blame it on the fact that someone doesn't want to allow me to swim or has prevented me from having a bathing suit or even said that the weather's against me—it's just that I'm afraid to try to swim. Yet, as I look at Eve, she doesn't strike me as being so upset and I can't understand why she isn't."

Eve turned to Claudia, not fully comprehending her and still very much self-possessed. "Claudia, I do believe you're making too much of all of this," she answered. "It's so simple! You needn't be so lost—make up your mind to what's good for you and do it."

Eve's response instantly conveyed to me that she was denying the whole phenomenon of self-exploration. Not having kept abreast of this current development, she continued to use hostility toward other people as a blind for her own emotional needs.

Yet Eve had spoken thoughtfully to Claudia, and Claudia's response was not in tune with Eve's lack of understanding. In fact, it occurred to me that Claudia might have used Eve's quasi security as demonstrated to fill up the gap that she, like so many of the others, was uncomfortably experiencing.

Bob's response to this new situation was not unlike Eve's. Although I felt his words belied his feelings, he, too, was insistent upon employing hostility to me rather than increasing the scope of his personal capabilities. He, too, had picked up Moe's analogy about learning how to swim and said, "Yes, I've always considered myself a firm believer in rugged individualism. And what is man if he isn't a free and independent being?"

These words evoked a parallel in my mind: the struggle that the thirteen states had had after the Revolutionary War. Like these original thirteen states, we, the group, were united, but each of us had some inordinate fantasies concerning our own "states' rights."

The remainder of this particular session continued to support this concept. They spoke to one another but listened poorly. As they talked, I sensed that they were talking "at" but seldom "with" one another. True enough, each of their contributions had merit and was interesting, but a theme of unity was obviously missing. I felt that their self-exposures really were not designed to produce any inter-personal relationship since most of their conversations would end in the form of a rhetorical question. This evasion of real participation by the use of "why" actually did nothing more than release their tension. It produced no further personality development.

It was quite interesting to observe that, in the main, they were nevertheless tolerant of this series of soliloquies. It was as if each would wait "in line," untouched by either the ones who preceded or those who followed. We heard Tom cry his song of the blues; Bob speak of the stupidity of his professors; Eve of the lack of courtesy demonstrated by people in public places; Moe's bewilderment as to where he was headed; Molly's guilt feelings toward her sister; and John's disappointment in himself for not being able to make himself better liked by his boss. The only one who did not join this "misery-loves-company orgy" was Claudia. She appeared to be listening and made several unsuccessful attempts to address herself to the rhetorical dilemmas that the others had presented.

By the end of the session, I firmly believed that the lack of personal identities and the absence of stronger group bonds had all the makings for an inferno. With nine people meeting twice a week for an hour and one half and engaging in so much repression, there was bound to be an explosion.

The session confirming this expectation came in a rather odd way at that. It had started off within the customary current phase of individual recitals. Betty had arrived late. Tom had the floor and was droning on. He could not understand why his boss would not fire him. He had turned in another poor day's work and had lost the company a valuable account—but still had not been dismissed.

Molly had made her periodic speech. The subject was now a standard. "God damn him anyway! He's not treating me as a person. And if I get my hands on that bastard, I'll kill him. The idea of screwing me without a rubber. What's he take me for, a God-damned fool and a cheap, easy lay? Why I'd like to bite his balls off and spit them in his face."

John, sitting back and studying Molly, could not contain himself. "Molly, how good a piece of ass are you, anyway?"

Not a bit offended, her response revealed an underlying problem. "That's hard to say. All the men I've gone to bed with are always clumsy, or unable to stay hard. I swear, every time I like a guy, he turns out to be half a man. I don't know what the trouble is—whether it's me or them. The occasional guy who's been good in bed has been such a louse otherwise that we've always ended by fighting and hating each other. To myself, I think I'm quite good—but then, I'm always stuck with these puny men—so, I don't know any more."

Bob, with a disdainful look at the group, sent an accepting smile in Eve's direction, as though he were saying, "Kitten, I agree with you, this is absolutely disgusting." Eve, in turn, had found Bob the least intolerable of all, apparently thinking, "Since I'm going to be around awhile, I might as well have *one of them* as a speaking acquaintance."

Claudia, blissful as ever, had been enjoying the repartee. Moe's eyes jumped back and forth as he sat, elbows on knees, cupping his chin in his hands. His attention was fastened on the byplay between Bob and Eve.

Breathlessly, Betty plumped herself in the last remaining seat. A dull silence followed. After a few minutes, which seemed eternal, Betty spoke. She talked and talked, but, actually, little of what she said seemed relevant or interesting. There was, in her chatter, a sense of panic and unrest. Her anxious concern spread insidiously about the room. It was as if she had inoculated all of us with some weird concoction. It made us strangely quiet and pensive. On and on she went.

Gradually, her words became less obscure, more meaningful. Here and there, a phrase or sentence caught attentive ears.

Reaching a hiatus, she approached the internal probing stage. "I know now why I was late. Mother was here, here from Washington, visiting me today. I was afraid, afraid to say goodbye, afraid to say goodbye and come here. I am still afraid, and yet, I could so easily laugh at myself."

Her voice, which had been sad and sunken, rose to a pitch of shrill sharpness. The sounds created were similar to those of a cat walking up the keys of a piano. As her voice went from the bass to high and still higher notes, she neared exhaustion.

41

For a moment, all life in the room ceased. Then, with a renewed surge, Betty again began to speak, looking straight at me. "I want you. I need you. I want you close. I want you very close, oh, so close. I'd like to tear your shirt and love your breasts." Now she had reached the breaking point. "You're my mother, and I do love you so." Gasping for air, she continued to pour forth, "But no, you're my father, and I want to love my father, too."

With this, she went limp and sank deep into the chair. She sobbed, "I am so glad I came tonight, because Doc is so much more my mother." As she spoke these last words, her fantasies faded. The tension in the room was gone, for each member had, breath by breath, gasp by gasp, kept pace with her in superimposement. They felt what she had felt. It was as if there had been but two of us, Betty and me.

Utterly spent, we looked around at one another with knowing gentleness. A glow of compassion permeated the room. Still looking at Betty, I said finally, with a broad smile and quiet voice, "I really feel as if I were your mother." At this, the remaining doubt and insecurity disappeared, with a general sigh of relief.

Moe, after a short restful spell, picked it up. "Say, that was really something, Betty. You're a good kid."

"Yeah, I could even like somebody for a change," chirped Tom.

"By Jesus, she scared the daylights out of me, but she was really giving it out," spoke Molly, with true admiration. This was the first praise she had ever given anyone.

Eve had become confused by the episode. Her feelings were mixed. A response, quite uncharacteristic for her, followed. In the past, whenever unbridled emotions which did not involve her had flown, she had been repulsed. But, strangely enough, this time she had been magnetized. Her involvement, though emotional, was more on the level of a "peeping Tom." "Did you really feel the doctor had breasts, Betty?" Betty nodded. "Why, you poor girl. You're such a darling!" Eve's patronizing attitude had a mixture of sincerity in it. In her confused feelings, I could sense another element—a curiosity about herself. She was saying, in effect, "Why don't I have these feelings?"

Eve's ego-structure was better developed than Betty's, yet there was also confusion concerning her own personal identification. For example, she possessed longings to be a little boy. At one point in our discussions, she had told me of her joy in climbing trees. "I still do; in fact, just last week, when I was alone, I did. My boy friend and I spent a weekend at a dude ranch. I had a visit from my 'aunt from Harvard' [her expression for menses].

"The gang had left me in the cabin, and had gone horseback riding. After an hour I was feeling better, so I went outdoors. There stood some fine beech trees. They were lovely." A warmth crept into her voice as she said "lovely." "With no one around, I did it! Yes, I climbed those lovely beech trees. When I neared the top of one of them, I stopped. It was sheer delight. Now, I know what Antoine de Saint-Exupéry felt when he was up in an airplane."

It was clear. Her message had been a longing for the role of the little son, the one her father had desired. She had worshiped trees more than Joyce Kilmer. To her, they were liberty posts. An opportunity to behave as a little boy was offered to her by them.

Claudia, fully enraptured by all the events, had become verbal. "Betty, I want you to know that I think you're wonderful. I so wish I had a mother, too. The doctor is a man; you've made him into a mother; I can't. This makes you so much better off than I." With this, she became sad and silent again. She just sat, staring at Eve.

At last, with the emotions dying down, Bob was capable of speaking, "You know, it was really nice of the doctor to let Betty castrate him."

Before he could say another word, John broke in. "For Christ's sake, boy, don't you ever leave that God-damned psychology stuff at home? So the doctor did let Betty spill her guts! And you come up with that horseshit of yours again. Man, oh man, someday I wish you'd just come in here as a person, and not as a professor."

Sitting straight up, Bob glared at him. Although he said not a word, his attitude was "Let this ignorant, uncouth misfit feel my disapproval."

John thought he had attacked Bob. Actually, his hostility was directed more toward me. The truth was that John detested the fact that he was a patient. He had fear of human exchanges but was quite unaware of this. On the surface, it was an entirely reversed picture. He appeared warm, friendly and affable. Only with participating did his understructure reveal itself. He, himself, was guilty of the very thing of which he was accusing Bob. It did not reveal itself in the same form but it was identical in substance.

John could not engage in real conversation. He would seem to discuss things with you, but afterwards, you would realize that the air had been filled with words, and he had absorbed none of them.

There was in his resistance to relating (the ability when involved with others to accept each other's emotional feelings) an interesting side light which dealt with a phase of his hostility toward me. It was a natural outcome of such strong fear of human communication. To John, I was like the main switchboard of a telephone company. Destroy me, and his jeopardy would be eliminated. This fear had plagued him wherever he had gone. It did not make any difference whether or not he was directly involved. If he were present where people were relating, he felt threatened. To a degree, the others in their struggles could be likened to autocrats, whereas John was an anarchist. He did not realize it but his distorted pursuit of individuality was a rationalization to free him from human emotional commitments. Unconsciously, he felt that as long as he could be "one" in this world, and there were no "twos" with which to be linked, he could feel safe.

In Bob and me, he saw this threatened. Bob's behavior was frightening because it might stir people to interact, while I was to be feared, since it was my function to foster emotional communications.

With John's attack upon Bob, it was rather obvious to me that he was attempting to kill "two birds with one stone." The first bird was a direct personal attack itself, and the second was upon the subject material, namely, psychology, since it represented the science which dealt with human communications. In the direct attack he was dealing with his own feelings of low self-esteem. That is, he saw Bob as an extension of me, and as such an attack upon Bob was unconsciously one designed for me. His need to attack me was due to the fact that I was "the Doctor." A doctor was "superior" to a patient, in his eyes. Exactly what this superiority was never did turn out to be meaningful to him. Nevertheless, he saw himself as "the patient." This, by his self-induced inference, relegated him to serfdom. And all of this persisted despite the lack of direct, visible evidence to substantiate it.

In fact, the struggle between Bob and myself had failed to alter John's convictions in this area. It had made no emotional difference to him whatsoever that Bob and I had differences without the issue of personal status interfering. Thus, in an effort to shed some light upon the matter, I had said in the course of the session, words to this effect: "To me, the concept of a psychotherapist is that he is the *oldest patient.*" Not only is a psychiatrist human, but in his human mold, he cannot possibly be superior. Knowledge and insight do not elevate a man above his fellow beings; they are merely tools, with the use of which he can only hope to be as good as the best human being. I do not use the word "best" in the sense of being better than, but rather in association with a man's capacity to enjoy life. This ability, and only this ability, looms above the other values.

John listened to my words and they seemed to penetrate his thinking. The need we all had to be a part of a group, to lend meaning to the communication, was slowly being perceived by him. These interactions were arousing his besieged concept of himself. His unfortunately acquired pathway to adaptation which had patterned him into an anarchist was now challenged. This challenge was the effect that our democracy was having upon him.

The facts were clear. I was the president of an embryonic democracy, whose states were in a weak union. Each one demanded federal support and sanction, with resistance to taxation. Each was overly sensitive to his respective boundaries and rights. And as if this were not enough, one state (John) had demanded, in effect, a civil war.

The termination of Betty's now historic session made a lasting impression upon me. It had started with John and Bob having their horn-locking exchange. Then followed a passive period of no conversation. John, I fear, wanted me to rebuff him, but I refused to do so. It was my hope that he would transfer his hostile feelings toward me, instead of toward Bob. This would have been an improvement for him. It would have been progress through the further development of a stronger ego-structure. In addition, he might have discovered that emotional democracy does not injure the individual with its demands to conform.

There was but a minute or two left in the session; I had just about given up hope of any other comment from John, when, to our amazement, he spoke abruptly: "I guess he's my mother, too, but he sure has on an iron *brassière* tonight."

4. *Love Versus Democracy*

"The measure of democracy in a society is its effect upon the heretic." Out of the past, someone, somewhere, spoke these words, and they have never left my thinking. This axiom prevailed when all other understanding in respect to behavior left me. Often, I have been impressed that common sense is the least powerful force in the world. Seldom does it appear to move mountains, while emotional waves, by contrast, sweep forth like powerful oceans.

As the result of these convictions, I had developed an attitude of self-determination concerning the group's behavior. I had thought it wiser not to be "regulatory" concerning the patients' contacts with one another outside the group meetings. When the issue had arisen within the group, I spoke my thoughts. "I do not wish to serve as a policeman. Nor do I believe that you need to serve as policemen to one another. I do think, however, that your outside contacts with one another would be detrimental to your therapy. If you visualize your group experience as a creative enterprise, perhaps you will understand what I mean. This, like any creative enterprise, is charged and highly specialized. The use of it in other settings would cause distortion. It is also medicine. Would you have a surgeon operate in the street unless absolutely necessary? This group therapeutic experience is comparable in psychiatry to major surgery.

"Another important factor is this: the resistance we all have to fuller emoting and relating would unfortunately be misspent in this way. Those tensions and feelings about which we harbor the most embarrassment would be 'carried out' elsewhere, and would not permit us to derive benefit from the 'here and now' principle of group psychotherapy. [This is the process of making sense out of the confusion of our past personal relationships as they repeat themselves with new people in order that we may create the meanings of these struggles which are frequently distorted in our somewhat faded memories.] It would prevent the 'in action' principle [that process of giving expression to unconscious material during a current personal interaction] of the group from occurring. In other words, you would be dissipating your feelings and spoiling the opportunity for growth; and thoughts and feelings without real purpose become not only unwise but dangerous.

"In your discussion this evening, you pointed out that friendly attitudes have arisen. You cannot understand why friendly relationships on the 'outside' could be harmful. Let me illustrate. I am friendly toward you individuals, but still I do not invite you to my home or out to dinner because it would spoil the opportunity to understand our relationship. I believe this would hold true similarly among you as well. You would lose the perspective between your reality sense and those feelings which are out of focus.

"Let me say with equal strength that I do not prohibit this or any other behavior. I merely ask that, if you do engage in this type of resistance, you report it back to us as soon as you are able." With these words, there could be little doubt as to my position. The patients, as far as I could tell, appeared to have understood, and all seemed to agree.

Conditions within the group, by comparison, were rather balanced. They were all speaking to one another, though not yet listening. "You talk about you, and I will talk about me," could best sum it up. Though they spoke to one another, seldom did they actually participate. Despite this, they were headed in the right direction. I reasoned that as long as each of them continued to talk, they were bound to establish a relationship, in time.

Eve had mellowed a bit. She was not as contemptuous as she had been previously. And there was a difference in her attitude toward me. Less of the erotic touch was noticeable in her actions. Her behavior, at times, was distant. No longer would she engage in bubbly, free discourse. Especially strange was her attitude toward Betty. Ever since Betty's "I want to get close to him" episode, Eve had acted as if she were afraid of her. At least, that was Molly's critical estimation of what had happened.

Tom was now both emotionally as well as physically present. He would wait his turn. Then, along with established practice, he would proceed. "Proceed," broadly interpreted, meant that he would enter into a dissertation on his version of life—how life, in reality, did not truly "pay off." His point of view was that trying to live was a mistake; summed up, the odds were against it. Occasionally Claudia, after hearing Tom, would sigh and say, "Why doesn't somebody do something about him?" Then she would shrug her shoulders, in dismay, and be off again in her own fantasies.

Molly's response to Tom's "I-ain't-got-nobody-and-nothing-is-worth-nothing routine" was to try to outdo him by telling more and more depressing stories. Each of these two "gloom twins" had quite a repertoire. Moe's characteristic response to both of them would be, "Say, if you two had my old man for a father, then you'd really have something to gripe about." However, he had never gone beyond this point. He still was not able to forget his memories of Ruth sufficiently to let himself go—to participate fully as a non-preoccupied person.

The Betty-fantasy episode had changed the level of the group. In effect, it had allowed each patient to be permissive with himself and with others in presenting their narcissistic interest. This represented the new tie which had replaced the one of hostility toward me (the first basis upon which the group had been formed.) You realize that this was not a clear break, but an overlapping development.

The two exceptions to this process ("We are united because we can all exhibit ourselves") were Bob and Eve. Eve, as you recall, had lost interest in me. Bob, too, had withdrawn from me. These two smoldered more with hostilities than the others. It was as if they were still insisting upon the need of the first bond—

hostility to me. And by their behavior, they seemed to be saying that they were going to pay back their parents, in kind. Thus, I was again faced with the problem of having two units instead of one. Bob, once more, was the leading male of one unit, and I of the other. He had one other member, I had six. This time Bob's behavior was more cryptic.

It all started off with Molly's comment one evening, "Eve, what's happened to you lately? Did your seduction act fail with the doctor? You sure have been acting like the last rose of summer." Eve sat up, showed her beautiful body to its fullest advantage, and, with her best finishing-school pose, stared, and then slowly turned her back on Molly.

Claudia, trembling openly, inquired whether something was troubling Eve. Her pleading glances begged Eve to speak. Nothing followed but a poisonous silence. As if the larger unit had failed in eliciting a response, it turned to the other half of the smaller unit—Bob. The antagonist was John. "Come to think of it, Bob, old man, you've been behaving rather strangely of late, too. Don't tell me my recent words about your profession are responsible for this. Certainly, a psychologist should be able to defend himself better than you've been doing. And, by the way, what gives between you and glamour-puss, Eve, these days? Don't tell me that she thinks you're a man! That babe wouldn't admit any guy owned a pair of balls. I don't know what cooks between you two, but I'll bet my last subway token that it's you that gets screwed in the end."

Bob, his face alternately white and red with anger, could keep silent no longer. Like a cobra, he struck. "Listen, you wax museum copy of Dracula, get lost! Get off my back, because you give me the creeps. If you want to criticize me, do so, but leave Eve out of this, you son of a bitch."

"Ah, finally got your goat, psychology student," sneered John.

"That's what you think," snapped back Bob.

"Now look, fellows, you're both acting like grammar-school kids, so cut it out," snapped the authoritative voice of Moe.

"Yeah, that's right, Moe, you tell 'em," echoed Tom.

In the midst of this encounter sat Eve, almost unnoticed, weeping uncontrollably. Finally, with what seemed to be almost a super-human effort for her, she said to Bob, "Oh, go ahead, Bob, tell them. Tell them that we've been having an affair."

Bob nodded. He was stricken with guilt. After a pause, he spoke: "Yes, it's the truth."

Eve pulled her head up, slightly defiantly. "And I'm glad of it. It was wonderful—he was so kind and gentle, and not a bit concerned with his own selfish pleasure as so many men are. It's true I didn't reach an orgasm, but I wanted him to have his. Furthermore, I don't care what you girls think of me. If anything, you're all probably jealous."

Molly, still dazed with the news, whispered almost inaudibly, "It's your doing, not mine."

Bob, coming quickly to the rescue, picked up the conversation. "No matter what anyone says, Eve's a wonderful girl. We're going to continue seeing each other because we're good for each other."

Scoffs and doubts, mixed with strong overtones of hostility, rang out in the room. John, highly indignant, said, "You've got the right to do what you damn well please, but you aren't fooling anybody but yourself. What the hell she sees in a puny punk like you, I'll be damned if I know." As he finished these words, he gave Eve a disgusted look.

"Listen, you baboon, you and your damn theories on what people should do and should not do in life infuriate me," screeched Eve. She was losing her composure for the first time. "All you do is sit here like a traffic cop, telling others which way to go. Ooh! I could scratch your eyes out, you make me so mad."

John, with a smug, self-satisfied, ear-to-ear grin, stretched and leaned back in his chair. This, Eve could not stand. She catapulted across the room, grabbed John by his hollow shoulders and pushed him backward. He and his chair crashed to the floor. He rolled out of the chair and got up with a bewildered expression.

"And for two cents, I'd slap your face," she continued. He never had a chance. She walloped the side of his face with her hand, a whacko resounding throughout the room.

Now, not merely astonished, but severely confused, John grabbed her wrists. Have you ever seen a shipwrecked sailor hanging on to a piece of driftwood? This was John. Eve rocked back and forth, attempting to pry herself free. Her lover sat like a ghost, motionless and dead, glued to his chair, the picture of a defenseless child caught by the crosscurrents of an adult world. By this time Moe, all six feet two of him, had stepped into the picture. Like a boxing referee, he separated Eve and John.

"I've never struck a woman in my life, but, by God, I almost did this time," said John.

"There he goes again, with his nobility," said Eve, as Moe led her back to her seat.

Rearranging his clothes, John picked up his chair, but did not sit down. "I've seen some nasty bitches in my day, but she takes the cake," he growled. His eyes never left her.

Quite depleted now, Eve began to sob hysterically, "What have I done?" Waves of guilt washed over her, and tears, and more tears, poured forth. In a few minutes, she regained her composure and after the use of several of our handkerchiefs, again spoke. "John"—in a soft and tender voice—"I'm terribly sorry. John— may I kiss you and ask your forgiveness?"

He was slowly recovering from his confusion. He tried to speak; his lips moved, but words did not come out. Sensing his helplessness, she arose and walked across the room to where he now sat. She knelt before him, and tears returned.

"Oh, John, oh John, you dear boy, what have I done to you? You're so tender and fine." She drew him close and, with a warmth that can be found only in a woman, their lips finally met.

The rest of us reeled back on our heels, stupefied. We could hardly believe the words and actions we had witnessed. Most amazed of all was Claudia. The whole episode had been too reminiscent of her own difficulties with interpersonal destructiveness. Her need to have Eve remain free of such responses and thereby serve as a model for her own development could be understood in her comment, "Eve, I'm so impressed with the way you cleared up this awful mess—and with such gentleness."

My own reaction was as if I had suddenly received the news of peace following a nightmarish war.

The remainder of the session is difficult to remember. We all seemed to be in a state of partial emotional shock. What we said and what emotions we felt must have been close to the primitive.

Now, as I look back upon these events, it seems that the following was the case. Bob and Eve had, simply and severely, rejected the rest of us so completely that it had reawakened those painful memories hidden in our unconscious reservoirs. This had been so "Pearl-Harbor-like" in its effect upon us that we were too dazed to respond appropriately.

I recall, however, saying, without censure in my voice, "Bob and Eve, you have taken matters into your own hands. You are endangering not only the therapeutic lives of yourselves, but of the others, as well. Your membership in this group remains unaltered, but as I have previously explained to you, I consider this behavior resistance to maturity, as well as hostility toward the others and yourselves. I appreciate your being sincere and honest and hope you will continue to be so. It is not sufficient, however, to report or confess; it is necessary to understand." With these words, I drew the session to a close.

When the next session opened three nights later, the air was charged with hostility. There we sat, gazing in all directions, our eyes never meeting. I had started the session with my customary, "Good evening, everyone," but the customary, "Good evening, Doc," did not come back to me. As I settled in my seat, and continued with the usual, "Would someone like to start things rolling?" the silence deepened. I became keenly interested in the seating arrangement. In the left distant corner sat Bob and Eve, next to each other. On my left sat Betty, and on my right, John. Next to Betty came Molly, and then Claudia, with Claudia, naturally, sitting next to Eve. Moe and Tom completed the circle to John's right. Thus, all the males were to the right of me, and all the females to the left. This was the second time a gender-splitting of this type had occurred. The first time had been at our initial session when we all were so frightened. I was not sure as to the meaning this time, but there could be little doubt that it had significance. It is difficult to say where on the perimeter of a circle the starting point lies. Nevertheless, if you started with the point between Bob and Eve or with my seat opposite them, in the configuration, there seemed to be a decided alignment reminiscent of a civil war encampment!

The silence hung determinedly. I'm not sure how long it lasted, but I venture to say it was at least five minutes. From the expressions on their faces, it seemed that the thoughts each one had would have been enough to cause his imprisonment. Claudia, astonishingly enough, broke the silence with something obscure. She reminded me of Tennyson's babbling brook. But her ramblings didn't alter the charged state. The others continued to stare aimlessly at the ceiling or floor as she went on from the weather to books, movies and like subjects. When Claudia's babbling brook finally had run dry, Molly picked up the stream. It was her old familiar song, "I don't like my boss. He rode me so hard that I got angry and he fired me." How many jobs Molly had had during our group experience, I will never know, and I doubt if she can remember. She had usually quit, but always for a "damn good reason."

Unlike Claudia, Molly's routine had succeeded in provoking some comment. Tom, the undisputed, undefeated king of gloom and despair, had been challenged. No mere woman was ever going to wrest the champion's crown from him. His tale of woe would have made an atomic-energy formula look like an ordinary street sign by comparison. This scrambling between Molly and Tom gave us the comic relief we all needed so badly.

Turning to Tom, Moe said, "What happened? Were you afraid Molly might outdistance you in the self-pity race?"

"Listen, Moe," Tom replied in a monotone, "no woman's going to put one over on me with her stories of being mistreated by a man. And they say 'heaven protect the poor working girl.' I'll tell you, Moe, there ain't any woman alive that's worth it."

"Worth what?" questioned Molly.

Tom, with lower lip hanging, grumbled, "Worth listening to. . . ."

Betty, apparently now free enough to speak, came out with, "Doc, do you think I'm an attractive girl?"

"Why do you ask?"

"Well, I was beginning to wonder. I haven't had a date in such a long time, I've almost forgotten what it feels like to be pursued."

"There they go again, those God-damned women, thinking they should be pursued," uttered Tom.

Before Betty could respond, Molly entered into the fray. "A woman feeling any interest in you should have her head examined."

With a curled-up lip, Tom sputtered back. "I'd never call you a woman."

"Doc, Doc," Molly screamed, "when are you going to start protecting us from this weird leech?" Looking straight at her, I gave her a reassuring smile.

All this material that had been exchanged was so much façade. Each one was deathly afraid of his own deeper feelings. What we were seeing, in a highly concentrated form, was a reapplication of the insulation. They were insulating themselves for more self-protectiveness.

Now, the meaning of the seating arrangement became clear. All the women on the left, and all the men on the right, had been sheer necessity. This was their way of exhibiting defense and offense simultaneously. The courtship of Bob and Eve had thrown the group into psychic chaos. They had regressed [returned to an earlier level of growth] to early infancy. Their light skirmish seemed to say that they were against being biologically acquainted. "Let us be sexually undifferentiated children, close to Mother's womb," was their unspoken cry.

Their disdain for Eve and Bob was based on feelings of being expelled from mother's warm, internal protectiveness. The idea of boy-girl relationship was so far above their current wants that it was something like the reaction one has if the lights are turned on during a movie. They had entered therapy with a strong need to return to basic levels. Two of their kind had not only broken the rules, but, far worse, had disrupted their relationship with the parent.

Most resistant to the idea of dependency was Bob. His solution continued to be one of self-medication.

Throughout the session, neither Eve nor Bob made any verbal reference to their relationship, but, on occasion, they glanced admiringly at each other.

A few vaguely structured attempts on the part of the other members to relate to the whole group occurred. All met with the same impervious block. Bob and Eve had simply become one. They participated only in subjects which had no personal connection with them. The roots of their patterns were firmly implanted in this session. Their defensive resistance was to continue for a long time.

5. My Crisis

I was an unhappy man. My thoughts troubled me. The discomfort was not due to a superficial issue. Bob's and Eve's behavior was at the root of my concern. Their lives and the lives of the others were at stake. Questions arose. Were they headed for major blunders? Was this obvious resistance to change and insight an impenetrable barrier? Would I be able to make their behavior clear to them? Were they to remain forever oblivious to their hostilities toward their new parent?

For days, I had tossed and turned during hours of alternate sleep and wakefulness. My wife became worried. She asked, "Are you unhappy, honey?" "Yes," I admitted, but in reassuring her that it had nothing to do with our own personal relationship, I found partial insight. The amount of anxiety I was having was undeniable evidence that this was my problem, and not exclusively a management affair.

After another group session had ended, a clarification came. To my surprise, I had an increased interest in Betty during that particular session. On first reflection, I thought that this was caused by a withdrawal on my part from Bob and Eve. However, with closer scrutiny, some of the mist began to clear. A drive was propelling my interest toward Betty. It was the content of this interest that gave me insight. A renewed concern in her mother's restraints had drawn my attention. The parallel between her mother's anxiety on this subject of sexual behavior, and mine with regard to Bob and Eve, was striking. Thus, what appeared to be less involvement with Bob and Eve, was really the contrary.

These children of mine (Bob and Eve) were attempting to gain my love and approval. Their rebellion ostensibly was a mode of eliciting from me a tenacious love—the love a child clutches who needs the physical presence of the parent for security. As members of a group, this kind of gratification appeared impossible to them. Yet they were unaware of the meaning of this entire communication.

Many things flashed before me with new meaning. Bob's imitation of the therapist could now be seen in a different light. This was his way of attempting to grasp the "tenacious love." Eve's scorn of the group, paired with a few vaguely expressed complaints of rejection by me, similarly acquired deeper significance. The change in attitude at the time she requested me to meet her parents could also be understood now. Her façade of seductiveness, which represented rejection of me, had simultaneously disappeared. This meant that she, too, was anxiously seeking for "tenacious love."

These two desperately hungry people, feeling I had denied them, had the need to unite. Their union was not that of two people closely joined together, but more as if they had become one person [symbiosis].

I had but one course to follow. "Yes," I thought to myself, "you're in this thing, and you'd better learn to *live* with it. . . . No," I continued in my self-consultation, "you won't try to *do* anything. Take it as it comes. So you don't like it, but they do have the right to find themselves." Finally, I gained resolution. "We will all have to face each problem as it arises."

Beyond this, I would somehow have to demonstrate to them that their rejective feelings as they concerned our relationship were untrue. They had misinterpreted my motive. My placing them in the group was not rejective; nor was this a reason for their rebellion in the form of seeking each other out in a misery-loves-company fashion.

In addition, I realized the enormity of the task before us—to show them that what they called love was only a mutual clutching dependency; that what they had created came out of a need when they felt rejected.

I would not coddle them. Instead, I would be more direct and give them the appropriate love they required. I would be careful not to play into their hands and be turned into a pawn. That would only make them suffer more of the same guilt they so copiously possessed—that of being children who had successfully outmaneuvered their confused parents.

What if this behavior were to spread throughout the group? This would be rather unlikely for the others did not appear to have these needs. In anticipation of the problems of the future, I reasoned, by the time the others develop mature sexual interests, the group psychic structure will be more fully in operation. This healthy state will make them choose partners outside of the group.

With renewed confidence, I set out, fully determined. Betty's mother was not going to be my example. To control and over-protect my "children" was not necessary. Where my patients' parents had failed with well-meaningness, I would not. The security within me was expressing itself. My previous lack of confidence and my concern with Bob and Eve were arising from deeper levels. Their sexual behavior had stirred anxiety of the taboo nature that dwells in all human beings. These taboos are incestually rooted and are necessary for all balanced society. My response in seeing this behavior as incestuous was based upon my prior knowledge of these two people. I was thoroughly imbued with Bob's need for a mother, and since in a functional way I had been serving as his mother prior to his entry into the group, it was quite natural, at first, for me to think that his hostility, on feeling that I had rejected him by placing him in the group, had led to his choosing Eve as another mother-figure. On the other hand, Eve, feeling equally rejected for the same reason, and needing to have a father as well as to be hostile to him, appeared at first survey to be involved in the carrying out of these needs. In fact, it was not until I felt more deeply the meaning of Bob's and Eve's behavior that I realized I had been misled by the obvious. I do not mean that they did not have the normal instinctual drives which with growth and maturity are channeled into the socially acceptable area demonstrated by a healthy marriage. Instead, I realized that the precipitating influence was rejection and that the resultant behavior was the desperate struggle to obtain nonsexual love and approval from their parental figure. I could now see that their physical action was like that of frightened children clutching each other for security in the face of panic. The mode of expression had no relationship to its content. The content and meanings were in keeping with the younger psychological levels more closely related to the need for survival.

With this reassurance, my anxiety abated. I returned to my former relaxed self. Thus, the greatest change in the group setting, which had been induced by my behavior, had been altered. With its disappearance, the children of the group could resume their growth.

During the entire episode, I could not help but think how typical my behavior had been of the well-meaning, insecure parent. It proved to me again that what a parent says is not so important as what he does. Though, in a democratic fashion, I had shown them the pitfalls of life, they were not influenced by this behavior. When I was able to set a good example of security, my communications were clear. My words, without security, were mere platitudes, at best.

Human beings learn best by identification. We see better than we hear. Mature guideposts shine as lighthouses in storms. Words are but transitory moments; deeds remain as lasting images.

Parents resist permitting their offspring to attend the school of trial and error. Over and over again, I've heard my patients, in various forms, plead this to their parents, "Won't you please, please let me have the privilege of making mistakes?"

Is it necessary for children to start their lives in adulthood, especially where their parents have left off their own growth? Cannot "intelligent neglect," in this matter, be our guidepost?

The parents' morality should not be projected upon their children before the children are capable of understanding it. Timing is everything in behavior. If we as parents are not able to see beyond ourselves, a map of direction will look most ambiguous to our children. Fools and their opinions, like their money, are easily parted. Participation of parents and children, each as separate individuals, solidifies the participants' egos.

These occurrences with Bob and Eve demonstrated an important issue that is called "Acting-Out." It can best be understood as being the unknowing displacement of a behavioral response from one situation to another. We witnessed it through their love affair which was unconsciously designed to obtain results other than their conscious intentions. However, a further example comes to light. Most men in our culture, like Bob, have moments of doubt concerning their masculinity. This may arise from a whole host of reasons. With Bob, they were due chiefly to the infantilizing effect that his mother had had upon him. He, like most men, preferred not to face this issue. Instead, he too, typically, reassured himself with acts designed to reinforce his masculinity concept of himself. His overindulgence in heterosexual conquests bespoke this struggle. Even his attempt to be the ever-youthful man-about-town related to this. Of equal import, he took an abnormal pride in outdistancing his contemporaries with the use of intellect. This, too, served as a displacement. It is not that all of these activities, per se, are distorted values, but rather that they are not representative of what they were normally designed to accomplish. The examples of sexual insecurity in Bob are rather typical sexual displacements found in the orbit of the mechanism of "acting-out"—that is, almost any area of insecurity can be brought into the realm of denial through "acting-out," but these examples are very common in our culture.

To Bob, his pursuits within such a drive appeared to have one and the same goal. In fact, he rebelled at first upon hearing that his pursuits were not designed for their obvious goal. I pointed out to him in an individual session that his "acting-out" was also a form of recommunication—that his problem was one of long standing. Its origins and ingredients had been repressed and there was a resultant deficiency of the psyche. By this, I attempted to make him realize that what he called love and maturity were only the displacements of insecurity. I had decided to work the problem through with him by doing the ground work in individual sessions. His responses at first were rather intellectualized, but later, as a result, our relationship did strengthen. With the increase of emotional closeness, he finally began to see that the "acting-out" was a recommunication, relentless in its drive to reach security with me. It was certainly fervent in its demands for expression. Feeling rejected by his parent-figure—myself—he behaved as so many children do when stymied—hostilely. In addition, in typical childlike fashion, he was playing one parent against the other—despite the fact that he had found in Eve an ally for his hostility toward me, he at the same time employed Eve as a maternal figure. When I gently reminded him of his parasitic attachment to his real mother, I was finally able to show him that his performance had not led to further growth. Quite the contrary. Although "acting-out" had temporarily dissipated his anxiety, his behavior had left him with insecurity in terms of developing maturity.

These individual sessions returned his anxiety. I told him this was a favorable sign for it showed me that he was now ready to experience the problems that he had been holding in abeyance by using repressive "acting-out." I reassured him that he had my full understanding in his discomfort but that the anxiety was better in the long run for his ultimate growth and security. "I know," he said with a smiling wink, "like when my father used to say this is hurting me more than it is you, but I'm doing it for your benefit." We both laughed, which helped. In any case, the remark broke the previous tendencies for sexual "acting-out" with various women.

I found myself at a crossroad in the early phases of working these problems through with Bob and Eve. They could not help but express all their conflicts in the mechanism of "acting-out." They were like rats caught in a maze and I longed to free them. Usually, my initial efforts were futile. These efforts were seen by them most often as unyielding prohibitions. However, using our group's collective security and support, the opportunity to reach them was enhanced. For the others frequently came to my rescue and pointed out that what I was attempting to demonstrate was not the heavy-handed parent wielding authoritarian unfeeling discipline, but the gentle, knowing hand of experience. The permissiveness of the group at these points was truly a beautiful thing to witness. Their activity aided this problem in another manner. It served as a release and forestalled other expenditures of "acting-out" in Bob's and Eve's outside day-to-day living.

The problem with Eve did not need any extra individual sessions. Her security permitted her to discuss the subject material rather freely within the group. Her insight into the fact that she had fallen in love, in succession, with a series of men, made her suspicious of her motives. She finally understood that her unconscious was destroying her own projected masculinity which she saw in these various men. That is to say, she realized that her own concept of herself embodied a generous segment of masculine identification. This she came to realize, as the weeks wore on, through many discussions of male envy. Her father had been more of a little boy than a parent to her and each time her mother gave love to her husband, she saw this with the eyes of sibling rivalry. On the other hand, this desire to be a little boy was further enforced and complicated whenever she sought her father's love as a father. As you will recall, her father had told me in our interview that "any simp can father a girl child, but it takes a real man to produce a boy." Therefore, she felt it was more advantageous to be a boy. In her relationship to Bob, this revelation took place. She began to realize slowly that she had not really loved Bob as another subject but rather admired and envied him as though she wished to change places with him. This facilitated our goals immeasurably. In fact, from that point on, her "acting-out" with other men ceased. Another gain was that she was less masculinely oriented, that is, she became less seductive in an aggressive manner and developed more gentleness with men. Her relationship with women, after several weeks, improved to the extent that for the first time in her life, women began to enjoy her company. For her, this was like opening new vistas. We saw her enter the female community of our group with almost childlike spontaneity.

The "acting-out" that occurred within our group behavior of course carried some dangers. At times, the others also protested my attempts to bring understanding to them. However, the democratic power of the group always seemed to rally just when it was needed the most. I was indeed grateful at these times for such welcome support. Beyond this, I was finding that, when a psychiatrist sits with eight other people in a give-and-take situation, it is an entirely different matter than being alone with a single patient in an individual session. This is quite an experience as the therapist exposes his blind spots and personality imperfections in the subjective-objective environment of a therapeutic group.

My goal in our group was a delicate balance of emotion and intellect in reaching Bob, Eve and the others. We needed some of each in order for growth to occur. I was guarding against having my patients leave therapy saying, "I understand it all now but can't seem to do anything about it." If possible, I wanted them to be able to be the captains of their ships. I felt that unless a harmonious integration of "acting-out" and meaning came into play, their basic psychic structures would remain unaltered.

Many weeks later, as we neared the critical point in our "acting-out," I called Bob's and Eve's attention to some basic thinking in a group session. My words, as best my memory serves me, carried this message:

"Life is not a common-sense thing. Its charm lies in its inability to be summed up into reason. If reason were possible, its value would be meaningless. Just when we are disgusted with life, something restores our belief. And at that moment we are ready to endorse it as 'absolute,' it fails to measure up. Life is a creative enterprise, which is best developed with the use of imagination. Fantasy is not rooted in reality. Imagination begins and continues with reality as a foundation. Far too often, we see man struggling vigorously and unyieldingly in his pursuit of happiness, and finding only futility. This is not merely haste making waste, but emotional inertia, which yields only to proper perspective. The barriers to the freedom of life disappear slowly when the natural processes are painstakingly dealt with. These apparently are embodied in the ability to accept the self with all of its limitations and frailties, including its ultimate frustration—death."

As I spoke, I was studying, more than casually, the reactions my words were producing. During this pause, Bob and Eve quickly exchanged glances. Of course, I do not know exactly what they were thinking but my impression was that they, in particular, knew and realized that they would be much more comfortable if in the future they would attempt to mold their lives according to such perspective.

It was Claudia who spoke. "Doc, do go on—I feel you've more to say."

"Yes, do," urged Betty.

And now the desires of Claudia and Betty had snowballed, for an eagerness to hear more was unmistakably present on all their faces. They gave me the feeling that at last someone in their lives was giving them a fundamental approach that could serve as a comparatively simple set of dependable values.

My earlier speculations about Bob's and Eve's thoughts were correct. It was Bob who confirmed this. "Doc, Eve and I were speaking exactly along these lines in terms of our mutual needs in this area tonight during dinner. We both have felt such a dearth of a simple, realistic comprehension of this subject."

"Well, then, since all of you wish me to continue and see that I have a few more ideas to convey—I will.

"The willingness to be involved in those experiences that we encounter both with others and with ourselves, at the moment they occur, often determines the degree of the direction our lives take. These two conditions—self-acceptance and the readiness to live— are in direct relationship to our capability to realize the value of life—pleasure. In the final analysis, life is but a short experience and this temporal state with its tragic overtones knows its finest moments as pleasure and enjoyment. And the greatest of these moments is love—which is a temporary if not complete departure from pure reason."

They accepted the message in a manner reminiscent of people who have shared in traveling a tortuous and dangerous terrain—a stronger mutual bond of personal affection was detectable as our crisis passed.

6. *Eve's Dream*

At last my conflict about Bob's and Eve's "acting-out" had been resolved. My understanding of their behavior influenced the others, who gave them tacit approval; not that they were unable to achieve greater approval, but this represented an appropriate response—for they were being actively rejected by Bob and Eve.

Bob and Eve continued to operate as one person and for some time lived in comparative isolation within the structure of the group. They engaged in brief commentary, but never "gave" of themselves. On occasion, they would mildly protest that the others were against them—but this was their projection. The hostile feelings they experienced were due to the continued rejection they were giving the others. In fact, their hostile feelings represented a frustration felt by the remainder of the group. We all truly wanted to accept Bob and Eve, but they would have none of it.

With further understanding, Bob's and Eve's actions became clear. They were compelled to hate the others projectively because they inwardly knew that they had been the aggressors. The facts were evident: they had broken the rules of the game and usurped the authority. The rest of us had been free of such behavior and nothing is so detestable, in the eyes of the guilty, as the innocent.

Their acceptance of our warm feelings for them would have to wait its proper turn. Group growth would materialize, but for a time it would be stationary. Time, and time alone, would heal the wounds. Meanwhile, the power struggle persisted with the same force as ever. Each member, in his own fashion, continued to attempt to control the group. The only exception was that Bob and Eve were a "double entry." Their control operated through rejection.

Circuitously, the behavior of Bob and Eve increased the group's unity. Although they were disturbed by the couple's behavior, they appreciated my understanding of the two. Their appreciation communicated the thought that, "If he has accepted this behavior, then, no matter what we do, he will accept us."

In one of Eve's individual sessions of this period, she entered wearing a shy little-girl smile. "She's like a child about to give its parent a present," I thought to myself. Hardly had the thought occurred to me, when she opened her purse and produced a typewritten note.

"Doctor, last night I had this dream. Would you please read it?"

"Thank you, Eve, but if it's all the same to you, would you read it to me, please?" My reason for choosing this approach was that I felt it would enhance the emotional experience for her.

Slightly startled at this turn of events, but still most affable, she said politely, "Why, of course I will." Her throaty voice had a rich mellow quality as she began to read:

"The dream began in a dirty, dilapidated bar on the left bank of the Seine, in Paris. My companions, especially the women, were angry and disgusted with me, for some reason I couldn't fathom. I wandered over to a circular wooden table in the bar, and began to talk with a stringy-haired disheveled blonde woman, whom I later decided must be a prostitute. I thought it would be exciting to get to know her, and to tell my acquaintances later that I had spent time with a prostitute, so I left the bar with her.

"I did not know our destination, but we walked over what started out to be a bridge, and later resembled the steel catwalks of a building under construction. I recall wearing ballet slippers, and being angry with the prostitute for taking such an uncomfortable route, since the steel railings hurt my feet.

"We walked up and up, and then began to move, with no apparent effort, as if on an escalator. I was afraid that I would fall off into the river below, but somehow I knew that this couldn't happen. When we reached the top of the structure, which then resembled the Eiffel Tower, I felt myself suspended in air, with my hand clutching the steel girders. At this point, something similar to a butterfly net but lacking the netting came out of the atmosphere, scooped me up by my bottom, and transported me through the air to a room. In this room sat three men, and an indeterminate number of women. I sensed immediately that these figures were hostile. The men leered at me.

"I noticed a circular neon tube, which looked to me like a toilet seat, even though it was too thin. I knew that I had been placed on this seat, and that the neon would light up with the words, 'Fuck You,' and a picture would be taken of me in this position, and sent home to my parents. I felt that I had been betrayed by the prostitute, and the word that came into my mind was 'blackmail.' I felt I should have known better than to leave the bar with her."

As she read these last words, she raised her head calculatingly, a quick, pleading glance, a half-smile, on her face. Then she resumed her usual carefree and poised attitude. Despite this, I felt a deeper concern dwelt beneath the surface.

I smiled, as if to say, "I see no need for real concern," and spoke in a casual manner, but in tones indicative of warm interest, "Eve, how did you feel when you awakened?"

"Well, at first I was a little frightened. Then, you came into my thoughts. I could see you—you were where you are right now—and you had a gentle, knowing and accepting smile on your face. I thought, 'Well, "Daddy" thinks it's all right, even if I don't.' However, I was also angry with you, and didn't know why. I knew the people of the dream were those of the group."

Suddenly, with a look of "Eureka," she beamed, "I'll bet that business concerning the sex had something to do with this."

"What do you mean, Eve?"

"Well, it all—my relations with Bob, that is—aroused such earthiness in the others. It was simply awful! The way they became so vulgar and dirty."

Little did she realize that this was her own unconscious attitude. Actually, she was rather prudish and the prudish attitude was a defense for her confused self-imagery as it was associated with her longings to be a little boy.

Without a break in the conversation, I continued, feeling that it would be safer to proceed at the level of the defensive material, rather than to disturb the conflicting roles with which she was so valiantly struggling.

"Eve, which of our group disturbed you particularly with his or her vulgarity?"

"Why—uh—it's difficult to say, but—the men in general."

This, for me, was confirmation of her hostility and confusion toward men and fathers. For in reality, it had been Molly who had been the chief offender.

"I see," I said. "How do you feel toward the girls of the group?"

"Well, as you know, when I first came into the group, I thought they were 'drips.' But lately, I see they're not so bad after all."

Here was my golden opportunity. "Which one, in particular, Eve?"

"Betty. She's so sensitive and thoughtful, and not a bit condescending. Her fantasy in the group that night had such an impact on me. Remember, Doctor, when she saw you first as her mother, and then as her father? Ever since that night, I've felt a bond between her and me. I feel confused and my confusion arises out of an inconsistency. On the one hand, I feel she is closer to you than I am, while on the other hand, I feel more mature than she. I have these parallel feelings with respect to my parents. You see, on some occasions my mother seems to be a little child. At these times I am her mother, rather than she mine. At other times I think of my father as a little boy. It's then I can sense the keen competition between Father and me for Mother's attention. I do resent doing him the slightest favor. For example, I am exasperated at having to give him the easy chair in the living room or having to bring him his slippers.

"That night, when you were so tender with Betty, I had this same confusion. I was feeling warm and close to Betty, and yet I was jealous; in fact, I was embarrassed. When, near the end of the episode, Betty seemed to have gained stature, she appeared to be your wife. I couldn't look at either one of you. It was almost as if I expected you two to enter into intercourse. This made me angry with you, in addition to being embarrassed. I guess I want you to be my own daddy and no one else's. Yet, I want Mother to be mine, and not Father's."

"Well," with a connotation of summary in my inflection, "you've had quite a session, girl," I said and smiled broadly.

With this approval, she broke into a childlike grin, her head dropped slightly forward and her eyes turned away from me. Then gently, with a touch of embarrassment, she met my eyes again, and her quiet laughter spoke her appreciation.

That evening, I reached for the portfolio at my bedside and retrieved Eve's typewritten dream. I read it and reread it. This is what it meant to me:

She was relating to me as though I were, in turn, each of her parents. At times I was her mother, with whom there was an immediate physical bondage—an overly dependent umbilical attachment. She had found this defeating and parasitic. The process originally arose out of a normal psychological need to identify with the female prototype. But the constant association she had had with her mother during her rheumatic-fevered childhood had distorted her concept. This distortion was deepened by the prim overt relationship with her father. It made her feel that the love of a male had to be clandestine. It accounted for the appearance of the prostitute. The prostitute represented her distorted concept of femininity. Thus, when I was seen in the role of her mother, she thought of me as a prostitute. It was not so surprising that she had come to such a conclusion. Her mother actually had, if you recall, advocated seduction as the chief mode of getting along with males. Especially, if one wished to obtain something from them.

Her eagerness to tell her friends and acquaintances that she had spent time with the prostitute illustrated her gratification in being an only child. The entrance into a new family (the group) was symbolized by the wooden table. Her uneasy feelings in this setting designated a challenge to maintain her position as the favor-

70

ite child. Our unknown destination underscored her insecurity as she thought of where therapy would lead her in terms of the unexplored areas.

All this turmoil with her parents had fostered the inversion called self-love or narcissism. The guilt of self-love is known universally—hence the association with society's reference to dirt and dilapidation.

Walking up an escalator together, in apparently effortless fashion, can be interpreted as the mounting pleasure of our relationship. Her slippers, and her anger concerning the uncomfortable route taken by the prostitute over the steel railings, refer to the fact that she blamed her mother in part for her own lack of a better father-daughter relationship. In addition, it spoke of the discomfort of her psychiatric treatment, which was taking her over the untraveled roads to maturity. I felt the Eiffel Tower signified in her mind the pinnacle of a secure love.

Her fear that she would fall off into the river below would be analogous to the fear of isolation. The resultant solitary confinement is an often-seen punitive expectation for desiring forbidden sexuality; this latter represented the fantasied love of father—the other role I also held for her.

The knowledge that incest could not have occurred implied the strength of her inner self, and dealt with her relationship to me. In essence, it said that she had confidence that I would lead her out of the maze. It also implied that I would be an understanding father.

The butterfly net, scooping her up by the bottom and transporting her to a room, told me that, at the height of her panic, she wanted to try a different approach with new people. It was this force which had taken her to therapy.

The three men and the indeterminate number of women were members of the group. She saw only three men as one of the male patients was Bob. In his image, her gratification to be the son her father desired took form. Her incorporation of him made his identity as her own. This explained why she could visualize only three of the male patients. The indeterminate number of women represented her lack of clarity concerning the manner by which she could relate to females. In this she was not alone. People when confused in their roles with others often attempt to neutralize this anxiety. The purpose is to discharge the tension by unconsciously engineering their own rejection. This is done on the basis that then they can believe that the others are the insecure people who cannot cope with the relationship.

The circular neon tube which looked like a toilet seat suggested several points. The light meant vision. Its "too thin" construction referred to the young status of her group existence. Our attitude of democratic representation was revealed by the circular form. Her current dilemma was divulged by the possibility that her picture would be taken on the seat under the vulgar sign. She wanted to trust us with the knowledge of her disturbance but the fear of exposure and retaliation plagued her.

The last sentence, "I should have known better than to leave the bar with her," signified: It doesn't pay to "have" a love object as your "swallowed-up" possession. All this indicated her increased courage to attempt maturity.

Of course, I kept these meanings to myself. To do otherwise would have overwhelmed her. In situations of this nature, the psychiatrist uses associations, new occurrences, memories, fantasies and even other dreams to bring about a desirable understanding. In his relationship with the patient, he attempts to avoid a premature exposure of the latent content of dreams similar to Eve's. The patient is seldom if ever ready for more than a partial meaning of his dream. Complete or unprepared exposures too often prove to be futile. They tend to lead the patient to become either overly occupied or even devastated by his attempts to rectify the difficulties. And as a result discourage him from a more natural adjustment.

The group's next meeting produced further developments for Eve in this area. Betty, in a high state of emotional maturity, participated with the other patients in a to-and-fro camaraderie. There was a charm and attractiveness visible that had never caught our eyes before. We were carried along by her contagious "relatedness." All had engaged with one another, but Eve. There she sat, isolated and bewildered.

At one point, Betty, feeling so accepted by her therapeutic

family, proclaimed, "You people are the nicest family a girl could wish for. You, Doc, are my mother, and you, Bob, are my father."

Hardly had she spoken these words, when Eve came out of her silence. "I can't stand this any longer. Betty, you have no right to do what you are doing. These are the only two men in my life who mean anything to me, and you are taking them away from me."

Betty, flabbergasted, turned to me, with concern in her expression. "Gee, Doc, I wasn't trying to monopolize anyone or anything. Did you think I was?"

"No, Betty, I didn't think you were."

She sighed with relief. "I'm glad of that. I actually like Eve, and wish her the best."

During this entire session, I noticed that Eve was not speaking, and I wanted to reach out to help her. Whenever I looked at her, she disavowed my interest. "What's the trouble, Eve, don't you want to be friendly with me?"

"I don't know," she said, in a monotone, "I just don't know," and shrugged her shoulders, looking at the carpet dejectedly.

Betty apparently needed reassurance when she saw Eve's forlorn state. "Would you think me silly if I came over to you?" she asked me.

Mildly taken by the request, I smiled, and responded slowly. "Why do you wish to come to me, Betty?"

"I don't know, but you are my mother, and I do fear Eve's distress."

"That makes sense to me," I responded gently. "But why is physical closeness necessary? Can't you feel my support?"

"Well, not exactly," came the response. "You see, my mother never permitted us to be afraid, and always scolded us if we were. She said that we weren't little babies any more. Once, when the boy next door frightened me with a snake, and chased me into my house, I yearned to have her take me in her arms. She only laughed at me, and said that I shouldn't behave so childishly. So won't you please help me, Doc, just once?"

As she recounted the story, I carefully surveyed the others in the group. The silent consensus was decidedly in the affirmative. I realized that I had but one course—"Betty, come here." I stretched my arms towards her.

Lightly springing to her feet with joy, like a school girl skipping rope, she came to me. We joined hands, and I placed her on my lap. Our faces greeted and accepted one another with deep feeling.

A collective sigh seemed to rise from all corners of the room. As I glanced over the setting, there were smiles on most of the faces. Eve was noncommittal.

Bob spoke up, "I didn't think you had it in you, Doc."

"Yeah, that Betty is getting better by leaps and bounds," moaned Molly grudgingly, with self-pity.

Claudia, much less in a world of fantasy these days, glowed like a freshly scrubbed child after the Saturday night bath. "This is so wonderful. It's like going to the movies—only it's much better—it's 'for real.'

"It's not only for real but also the feelings I get of belonging while I'm here that last even when I'm away. I've often stopped to think how strange it is that, although my mother and father loved me and had a nice home, this particular feeling of belonging to something or somebody has never happened to me before. I know it sounds funny, but you people aren't just my friends but in some odd way, you're the worthwhileness of my life."

After a meditative moment it was John who spoke without his usual intellectual flavor, and half confessing, "I believe I'm jealous of her."

Moe and Tom, both alert, and with embarrassed grins, just stared at Betty and me. They looked the way six-year-olds do when greeting favorite relatives, known to be bearing presents.

Eve, with gradually mounting anguish, began to speak. "I don't like this. I don't care for it. I can't help it, but it's bothering me. I just wish she'd go back and sit in her chair. It's more than I can take, I know! I realize they have the right to do what they want, but I can't stand it."

Betty, secure at this point, answered her. "And why don't you come over, too? I see no reason why you can't. I feel that this is a family and you belong."

"That's true, but I can't do it," responded Eve, with disappointment in herself. "With me, it's all or nothing at all." This was the inadequacy in Eve speaking. "I'd like to," she said, "but there's the barrier. I know you feel that he's your mother, Betty, and you're his daughter, but to me, you are both parent figures. He's my father, and you, Betty, are my mother."

This monumental step in the therapeutic lives of these two girls was the golden opportunity I had anticipated.

Eve had a feminine identificational subject. In me, her new father figure, there was less of the "little boy," and more of the man.

It was of more than passing interest to me to have participated in these episodes. What was so intriguing was this: The two girls' behavior seemed to indicate that much more than just the surface events had been involved. This appeared to be particularly true in the case of neurotic character disorders. And true, as seen with Betty and Eve, perhaps it was so because these polarities (the relationship between people implying a "to and fro" communication) could overlap and, though seemingly in conflict, yet actively support the resolution of the individual's problem.

The last reaction of that group episode did not occur during the session. Two days later, the day before Father's Day, I received, in the mail, a poem from Eve. It read:

> It's all right with me that you're not my sire,
> I wouldn't have you, not even for hire.
> I'm glad I wasn't created your child,
> I'd want my father to be otherwise styled.
> No, it isn't your baby I'd want to be,
> It's your "Babe," and that's quite different, you see,
> For you, you charming and handsome laddie,
> Would then be my own, my great big "Daddy."

7. *Fatherhood*

Hilarious with the joy of a victorious gladiator, John rose one night within the group to announce, "I'm going to be a father!"

Our astonishment, great as it was, was not limited to the news itself. John, on other occasions, had informed us of Angela's romantic existence in his life, but he had carefully kept us in the dark, not only with respect to the specific developments of the love affair but in failing to give us any glimpse into Angela's personality. There was one important exception to this concealment. This had occurred when he had let us in on their thoughts as the two of them sat on the Palisades watching the Hudson flow under the George Washington Bridge.

Their behavior seemed somewhat out of place in the sense that it appeared to be a substitute for dealing with the realities usually associated with a courtship. Apparently I was not alone in my thinking, for the group had run into a series of frustrations and defeats as it had attempted to bring an increased appreciation of the realities to John.

His response on each occasion was to rechannel the remarks into a defensive maneuver by referring to some obscure Oriental philosophy. It was quite clear in his mind, and he so stated it, that they did not understand him. John's feelings of futility would then arouse him to explain this philosophy which he said was based upon the concept of "the total commitment of one human being to another."

On this particular evening, when he made his startling announcement, he again referred to this philosophical orientation and further explained that this was the avenue that had led the two of them into their mutual physical love. Without waiting for any response on our parts, he continued to explain that Angela and he lived in such a close bond that even when they were physically apart, they remained in constant psychic communication.

Quite frankly, John's psychiatrist felt too ignorant to cope with these concepts and semantics and a cursory look about the group at this moment indicated that the others felt just as futile. However, I could not deny the fact that these two were deeply interlocked and that they were so similar in this metaphysical phenomenon that it even appeared to extend beyond intuition.

Such a complex state is indeed difficult to evaluate. And, as he talked on and on, it was easy to visualize the circumstances that surrounded them. Spring in New York is the most beautiful time of the year, with one of the focal points of this splendor being the Palisades. Of course, no one will ever know which of the two elements—the psychological affinity or the setting—proved to be the stronger influence, but the spermatozoan and the ovum met. We gathered at first from John's account that he considered this as another miraculous conception, but ultimately he acknowledged the truth.

Nevertheless, John continued as if ordained by Nature; as if at long last he had found entity. Not in mere existence but in the most coveted prize of all—fertility. To him, it appeared that within one act of fate, his behavior had converted him from a confused and bewildered boy into someone who fortunately had his magical fantasy materialize.

His façade was that of a man. On and on he talked about their plans for marriage and how beautiful it was to be. He was going to leave college and obtain a job with an engineering firm. "After all, I do have two years of college under my belt now and I can return evenings and finish my education. Anyway, it's time that I put away childish things and entered into the world of grown men."

I knew, as his psychiatrist, that he was not ready to have the bubble burst and I felt it more productive to let him work his way through these rationalizations without registering any doubts.

The group's previous experience was serving as a guide for all of us at this point. Our silent understanding of John was the result of our realization that there was actually nothing to be gained by practical discussions at this time.

He told us that on Saturday he was going to walk the historic streets of lower Greenwich Village, with his beautiful Angela, in search of a nest that would cradle this love-child of the century.

At one point, as he neared the end of this communication, he revealed that in his opinion most people really didn't love one another but that the love that existed between Angela and him would make all other love affairs look pale by comparison. And then, as a symbol of his respect for us, he concluded by telling that no one knew of these events except us, the chosen few.

A considerable pause followed these disclosures. It appeared that some of us were bewildered while others were simply awed by his blissfulness. Each of us, in turn, knowingly but kindly looked at the other. Yet, in no way did I feel that there was even a tacit approval involved. Rather, no one wanted to tarnish the new penny, shining as never before. His white shirt, the crease in his pants, the fresh haircut and the spring in his walk were too much for any of us to wish to disturb.

The one person who seemingly was not so affected was Claudia. She was like a child who had been reading a fairy tale—one that she believed. It was my feeling that she saw herself as the sought after, pregnant one—the loved and admired and cherished one—who had received the gift of love.

Spiritedly, she inquired about Angela. "Is she pretty, John?"

"Well, she isn't what you'd call a glamour girl, but to me, she's a goddess."

"What does she do, John?" Claudia continued.

"She's studying political science at Hunter College."

Betty spoke up. "John, what about Angela's parents? Do they know?"

"Angela is an orphan. She lives with a girl friend in an apartment a few blocks from my home.

"You see," he continued, "I haven't yet asked her if she will marry me. I only found out that I'm going to be a father about an hour before the session began. When I arrived home earlier this evening, there was a letter in which she broke the news; that is her delicate way of doing things. I'm to call her later this evening, as soon as I can."

Tom spoke, with his usual terseness. "I can't understand where you're going to get the money to live on, without some help from your parents, and feeling the way you do about help from them, what is the solution?"

Startled by this stab of reality, "I'll make more, and we're both enterprising. We'll figure it out." He glanced at Tom with mild disapproval.

Molly sat forward in her chair. Now the enchanted spell had been broken. She sighed again, and finally said, with a pause between each word, "Well, John, I wish you would really look at this girl and yourself before you go any further. It seems so strange that you haven't discussed your relationship with her to any degree before tonight. The little you've told us in the past makes me feel that this was nothing more than child's play."

John straightened up in his chair indignantly, and gave me a piercing look, as if to say, "Must I be so abused by this wench?"

My glance was noncommittal.

He decided to ignore her, and spoke to the group as a whole, "I only wish that the child were here now. Nine months is such a long time."

"Were life but as easy as you imply . . ." Bob said with a most condescending attitude. He gave a sigh of dismay, shaking his head from side to side. "If only you knew what you were saying, John, if only you knew."

Pensive silence descended on the room.

John straightened up; he stared glassily in Bob's direction. It

79

was almost as if his eyes, like X-ray machines, had radiated right through Bob's body. Finally, a tense sigh emerged, as his chest synchronously shrank. "You bastard, you! You supercilious, bobby-soxed intellectual. You have never had any feeling for another human being in your life. You fancy yourself a man-about-town, when, actually, you are so glued to your mother's apron strings that they appear as bows in your hair."

Bob sank in his chair, his back rigid, resting on his buttocks. Half snarling, half grinning, he extended his hands toward the ceiling while resting his elbows on the arms of the chair, as if to signify that all was futile; he was misunderstood and unappreciated.

Eve, who had been more than absorbed by John's speech and seemed to have become electrically charged, spoke with biting tones. "He's right, he's right. You are so cold, so glib, so profound, but with such a shell! You speak of love, when ice water flows in your veins, or should I say lemon juice?" Her face tightened; her voice increased with tension, and a scream followed, "Damn it, don't just sit there like a mummy, feel—feel—feel something!"

Bob, with his edges ruffled, moved back in his chair, and cupping his chin in his hands, began to drawl in an oily, thick voice, "You know I love you. You know I care."

Like a flash, John interrupted, "How would she know—by radar? And don't tell me that you're such a great lover that she's supposed to understand by that performance that you love her."

"Listen, you," retorted Bob, "you're trying my patience. I realize you're a sick boy, and I try to be as kind as I possibly can, but you're making it tough. God, Doc, I know you want us to try to get along here, but he sure is difficult."

"Now, don't bring him into it. Always trying to get off the hook, aren't you, Bob? The Doc hasn't got a thing to do with this, so don't cloud the issue."

Eve spoke. "But he's a past master at that. Every time you think you see something clearly, he gives the kaleidoscope a slight twist, and the colors and images take on a new perspective. An out-and-out liar would be easier to cope with."

"You know, I've always thought you liked me a bit, and if it hadn't been for this big stiff of a bookworm, we might have been much more to each other," John said.

"Listen, you four-eyed monster. I've taken enough of your bull crap for one night. Get your own woman. She's mine." Bob was almost shouting.

Eve spoke up. "There you go, taking over and controlling me again, as if I were chattel."

Bob looked at Eve. "Eve, don't you believe that I love you? Don't you believe I care?"

"Yes, I suppose I do, but I get awfully tired of playing mother to you. You're always such a big shot when it never counts, but when the chips are down, it is I who have to smooth things out with the landlady, the taxi driver, and the like. Why, I have even had to intercede with your own friends and repair the damages, after you have alienated them with your Jehovahlike behavior."

Turning toward John, she continued, "You know, John, you really are a sweet boy. I don't know exactly what my feelings are toward you, but they are tender. At times, when you go off on your nonsense and expound theories of Yogaism and existentialism, I could scream, and I even feel embarrassed for you. It's at those times that you destroy all the warm feelings I have for you. It's hard to explain. It isn't that I want you as a boy friend. It isn't that I see you as a little boy who is lost, dirty and hungry. I actually admire your values, your decency, your sense of fair play. You are really a good guy. I guess you call it friendship. I don't feel that way about Bob. Bob is like a column of figures, which never add up to the same total. At the height of my anger and frustration, if he were to ask me nicely to kiss him, I would smother him with my love. He's all the things you say he is, John, but there is a magic about him that compels and drives me to worship him, to idealize him, and, at times, to feel as if I could devour him with my love."

John replied, "Eve, you're precious. That puny little squirt doesn't deserve you, and yet, I appreciate the sincerity and the truth of what you've said, and I feel for him."

"That's what I mean," she answered. "You're always so

willing to see the unvarnished truth and accept it with honesty. That is why you're such a decent sort of chap."

Bob, absorbing every drop of this exchange like a sponge, kept to himself as the tension in the room eased.

At this moment, Moe burst forth, "Yeah, John, you're all right, in spite of those harebrained views of yours that you try to sell us every once in a while. You're all right in my book. I don't know why you're always trying to be so different from the rest of us, because, on you, it's not becoming, so why don't you wise up and join the mob?"

John turned to Moe. "You don't understand, I'm only trying to be truthful with myself. All my life, I've been subjugated. Mother always meant well. 'Eat your food, John. Wear your rubbers, John. Did you get good grades at school today, John? Where are you going, John?' Christ, it drove me wild. Can you imagine how it is never to be permitted to do one wrong thing in your whole life? Now that I have reached adulthood, I've got to keep my promise to myself. I've got to say and think and do all those things that I believe in."

"Yeah, but for Christ's sake," piped up Tom, "do you have to be so crazy about it? Be a person, express your individuality, but how about siding with the human race?"

"Oh, you fellows just don't understand me, any of you," replied John.

"Yes, we do," Moe retorted.

"Well, maybe you do, we'll see," John said resignedly.

At this point, Betty burst forth, "John, you're a lovable boy. I feel so close to you, and I wish you all the happiness in the world. I know I'm not reaching you, but I wish I could. I do want to be a part of all of this. I've been feeling so left out of everything this evening."

Yes, she had been inoculated by the contagious spirit of the evening, and all this talk of wedding, marriage, birth and love apparently had been too much for her immature mind to grasp in an emotional sense. All she yearned for was human contact— she was in love with emotion as some people are in love with love.

John, somewhat confused and embarrassed by Betty's response, grinned sheepishly and glowed in the warmth of her words.

Said Betty, "You're one of my naughty children. We're going to have to do a great deal with you." She sounded like a stern New England mother.

"Get off of it; get off of it!" Molly screeched.

"Well, Doc," Betty appealed to me, "you know what I mean. I didn't want to be caught between the two streams [implying heaven and hell]."

I answered quickly, "Betty, this is for you and Molly to work out between you."

Molly, sensing my neutrality, shrugged her shoulders, and was content to let the matter rest.

"Now then, Doc"—John again took the floor—"you've heard this story of mine. What do you think about my oncoming marriage?"

"What would you have me say, John? I feel it inappropriate for me to offer an opinion at this time. Perhaps it might be wiser for you to continue to discuss it with the rest of the group."

I had sensed that this was not the time for me to inject parental authority. He would have rejected it, regardless of its intent. And of more serious consequence, he might have used it as evidence that I was not looking out for his welfare. Beyond this, I knew that the collective action of the group would be much easier for him to cope with, less disturbing to his self-esteem, even should his disagreement with them deepen. My knowledge of his relationship with his parents had influenced my actions. His memories of their advice had figuratively blinded him to the possibility that parental authority could be wise or just.

I had come to learn, in situations of this sort, the therapeutic value of the group. Whenever I had done otherwise, the individual in conflict used the therapist's position as a target and with martyrdom maintained the distorted viewpoint.

John took my suggestion with ease and turned back to the group. "Well, what else do you think?"

Tom was the first to answer, "Well, I think you're a hard guy to reason with, once you've made up your mind, but whether you like it or not, I think you're trying to capitalize on an unfortunate set of circumstances. You're no more ready for marriage than I am. One day you go out of here sounding like an anarchist, against everything and everybody, preaching the gospel of rights and privileges, and then, just because you've knocked up your girl friend, you're a great family man. You know what I think? I think you're so God-damned glad at having this tailor-made situation arise, and in believing that it's going to solve all your problems of growing up in one automatic step, that you're delirious with happiness, and I do mean delirious."

"Well, I'll be a son of a bitch!" John responded hotly. "Here I am in love with a girl and about to become a father, and as a result you turn into a prophet of doom."

"God damn you! You asked me, so I told you. There's no living with you, John. You say you want everybody to be free and independent, but actually, you just want everybody to agree with you. Even if that were possible, the other person would have to be a genius to try to follow your reasoning."

Breaking in, Moe added, "Yeah, John, as I said before, you're a good guy, but you sure are fucked up. Boy, you've got a lot to learn. Now, don't get me wrong. Look who's talking. I'm not one hell of a success at this, either. I'm so afraid of women that I actually cross to the other side of the street when I see one coming. I'm the biggest lover in the world, except when it comes to saying 'hello' to a babe. You know that movie, 'The Secret Life of Walter Mitty?' Well, he was a real piker compared to me in my daydreams about being a great hero. I was one of those guys who was God-damn mad when the war ended—you know why— because I hadn't yet won the Congressional Medal of Honor. And listen to me, trying to tell you where you are wrong. No, I'm not the voice of experience. Don't call me 'Bob.' I don't know from nothing, but man, you are fucked up."

Eve spoke up, "John, take it slow. How do you know you even love this girl? How do you know she loves you? You are all ready to jump into something, and you haven't even begun to look at any of the practicalities involved."

John crackled back, "I love her and she loves me. I know it."

Tom mocked sarcastically, "He knows it."

Moe turned to Tom, "Lay off the guy. Can't you see . . ."

Eve's soft voice went on, "John, tell us something about Angela. Tell us—oh—the little things about her, as well as the important things. You know, we've heard so little. Please give us the details."

"Well, what do you want to know?"

"Something about her family."

John continued, "As you know, she is an orphan, and was raised in an orphanage. Actually, it's just that her mother has been dead since she was a little girl, but her father is still living. He's an old man, who hasn't worked in twenty years, and hangs around cheap cafeterias in Brooklyn. Occasionally, when he can muster up the two dollars, he puts it on the horses. She tries to see to it that he eats regularly and has someplace to sleep, but often, she doesn't even know his whereabouts. She's pretty; in fact, you might say that she's downright pretty. She's petite and brunette, well-rounded, really bright in school, and her professors are fond of her. They're always assigning her special projects, and that sort of stuff. She's as ambitious as hell. She wants to be a career woman and likes to wear slacks. She's especially interested in social work and is thoroughly convinced that she can accomplish the dual roles of a career woman and mother. Sometimes, I feel fatherly toward her, and sometimes, she seems motherly to me. At least, that's what she says about us. We seldom ever fight—we don't find much point to it. She goes to a psychiatrist, too. I feel as if I'm not as good for her as she is for me, but there are many things I do which seem to please her."

"John," Eve said, "I don't want to play 'the heavy' with you, or be your mother, or act like a psychiatrist, but take it easy. Just take it easy."

And on this note, we all bid each other good night.

The days between the session of John's startling announcement and our next one moved with painful slowness for me, my curiosity rising to fever level. How would it end? What would Angela do? Would they really marry? Would she have the baby? Would John

85

attempt to carry out all that he had said he would? Over and over this absorbing material ran through my mind.

The truth of the matter was that during that particular week-end, John's new problem had sparked many ideas within me about American contemporary life. For example, I thought about the fact that American family life is so frequently spoken of as lacking unity. And as my thoughts continued to flow, I found myself challenging this concept. It occurred to me that perhaps these bonds are stronger than we realize.

Lying about our den, at home, were several magazines dealing with juvenile delinquency. Their contents deepened my thinking. But yet, being somewhat of an amateur student of American history, I found it difficult to reconcile all of the pertinent material. I remembered that in Colonial days, labor was the common enter-prise which bound the various members of the family together. At the end of their day's labors, these family units had to supply their own well-earned recreation. Now that this original struggle no longer kept them physically tied together, the lack of emotional bonds became evident. Apparently the one-roof economy no longer sufficed to bind the branches of the family tree.

However, I did not believe that this change in our way of life was the direct cause of John's difficulties.

Like so many of us, I, too, have been bombarded by the sociologists' evaluation of the broken home, war marriage and housing shortage, as the culprits responsible for such unhappiness. And certainly I had become somewhat irritated by the philan-thropic organizations and political candidates who talked about the city slums as the underlying cause of our widespread emotional illnesses. But seeing John in his awkward but worth-while struggles to reach manhood, I could not help but think of the one hundred seventy million Americans who, despite a living standard never before equaled in the annals of the world's socio-economic strug-gles, had their individual emotional problems. I felt that the rising middle class perhaps stands today as evidence of a strengthening family emotional force.

Of course, I was not unmindful of the underprivileged or the poverty that prevails throughout the country. Yet, far too often these conditions did not seem to be at the roots of problems like John's. If anything, I felt that as America had grown and its cultural freedom increased, these mundane factors seemed to be less accountable. I should certainly hate to believe that man can only maintain his emotional health by giving full exercise to his compulsiveness in a struggle for material survival lest he fall apart emotionally. Indeed, as our work week shortens and our free time increases, those of us who are held together by compulsiveness may find it taxing.

John and his constant reference to philosophy had another effect upon me. It brought to mind that period commonly referred to as the Renaissance—when culture and education were in the hands of an extreme minority. In those days, the multitudes lived within a sphere of emotional and intellectual deprivation. Today, in our Western civilization, we may never transcend the glories of the Renaissance, Rome, Athens or Thebes, but are we not more free to enrich our emotional life with the pleasures hitherto enjoyed only by the privileged class? It would seem to me that the extreme creative ability of the ancients had very little to do with the emotional happiness of those societies as a whole. Thus, the attainment of emotional happiness does not seem contingent upon a golden era, but rather on a diversified participation by the many.

Maybe the garden, verdant with crab grass and all, will never lie enshrined by a museum, nor will father's golf score ever be immortalized, but perhaps the growing possibility of engaging in these activities will be valuable in strengthening family ties.

It was precisely in this area that I felt that John was limited. It was as if he had turned back the pages of time and wanted to live an isolated, richly cultured, esoteric life with Angela. He had resisted modern living on the theoretical grounds that the talented and truly sensitive people shouldn't be burdened with the mediocrity of the masses. It was at these points, in previous individual sessions, and in vain, that I had attempted to make him see that such an arbitrary value had only resulted in a preoccupation over the crisis of good and evil within him, as well as in the course of human history. Surprisingly enough, John had admitted that he had been plagued with the need of approval from others in terms of the good and evil process. At one point in this discussion, I had mentioned how the influence of Freud and more recently, of Benjamin Spock's encyclopedia for the intelligent parent, "Baby and Child Care," was a sign that such rigidities were slowly being replaced. I mentioned PTA meetings and pointed out that here was an organization that unknowingly was replacing the strong arm of the rigid moralists.

At a group session held a few weeks prior to John's announcement concerning his impending fatherhood, I mentioned to John, when he again brought up his great love of the ancient Athenian culture, that in recent years we had made, in our fumbling way, some real gains. I referred to the strong social security act and child labor laws. It was then that I asked him point-blank if he was overlooking these developments and focusing his attention upon the unusual, and thereby carrying an albatross of despair. His reply I found to be quite challenging. "It's strange for me to see you, a man who's involved continuously with broken homes and unhappiness, so optimistic. Sometimes, I feel that someone ought to draft you for a duet with Mary Martin singing that song 'Cockeyed Optimist.'"

"John, I can see that it would be strange to you. Furthermore, I could even strengthen your argument by citing J. Edgar Hoover's statistics on the cost of crime to support your desire for isolationsim. However, let me bring to your attention the fact that within one short generation the care of and the realistic hopes for the mentally ill have improved immeasurably over the old asylum with its criminal implications. You can hardly imagine what optimism I feel when I see the public at large no longer being afraid to make serious attempts to reach adjustment in life, but instead, visiting psychiatrists of their own free will as they would other medical specialists.

"Still, John, before you get a false impression, I do feel there is one danger in our social structure that has not received enough of our attention. This subject is not a simple one, so first let me give you some background. I freely admit the advantages of the vacuum cleaner, the dishwasher and the Laundromat. Their presence has not only freed the homemaker but her family as well. Just think of the convenience of frozen foods and the miracles packed into each box of detergent. These are wonderful products of a free democratic economy—but democracy is not just a slogan to be carved in marble over public buildings. It means better schools, wider roads, more income and most important, time to enjoy leisure.

"Despite these advancements, I feel that silently some drastic changes have come about. Mainly, it is the male that has attracted my attention. Since it is usually he who turns the major portion of his earnings over to his wife and equal partner to spend, she has become the most influential factor in American retailing. His position, either unconsciously or otherwise, is fast fading. This may provide a source of amusement to some, but to me it represents a danger signal."

"How could that be?" asked Eve defensively.

"Perhaps it's that the pendulum has swung a little too far."

"Go on, Doc, what do you mean?" queried Betty.

"Simply this. Women, rightly, put up a fight for their suffrage and freedom but the struggle was so arduous that some distortion, it seems to me, was bound to occur. Personally, I'm glad women are equals in these roles. The fear I have, though, is not that the male will someday rise in wrath and become reactionary, but rather that women, in their quest for alleged democratic equality, will destroy themselves."

"How could they do that?" again asked Betty.

"It's not easy to see, but if the modern homemaker and her side-kick, the career woman, continue to lose their femininity in the process of liberation, their efforts to emulate the male will make them lose the heritage of their species. Woman was designed to be feminine—not masculine. Equality with a man does not mean becoming masculine. Economic independence does not provide for the rejection of her sex and its concomitant life. Supremacy and dominance over the male will lead to her intrinsic unhappiness. Women and men need each other equally in the roles for which they were destined. Perhaps if the present trend continues, she will know only immature little boys—not men. It seems to me that her basic need for equal adult companionship is in jeopardy."

"What the hell are you talking about, Doc?" barked Molly. "You men are all alike."

Claudia, standing up to Molly with vigor, dryly commented, "What's the matter? Does the truth hurt, Molly?"

The pause that followed I took to mean that more clarification was necessary and therefore I resumed.

"Girls, try to understand that what I'm saying has been largely motivated by John's repeated behavior in his strivings for manly independence. I feel that this subject is the background for his difficulty since it's quite a transition for a male to go from his mother to a wife."

Looking first at John and then Molly, I was pleased to see that they were less taut because of this simple explanation. "The concern I have is not about women's activities but their psychological relationship to the family. Perhaps a clearer way of explaining it might be that now that she has greater time for freer expression of her individuality, her psychological incapacity to enjoy this may have contributed to the eruption of what is commonly referred to as 'wearing the pants in the family.' In turn, the effect that this has upon her sons, as seen among the large segments of our male society, is that they emulate mothers more than fathers. Needless to say, this is an unfortunate development and as I look at our society, I'm often struck with the excessive attention paid to mom's apple pie and the glory of the big breast. To me, this attention may be the resultant effect of a society in which the male child is still in the throes of worshiping his mother beyond normal bounds. The shy boy, who engages in intellectualism as a part of his pursuit to be 'the good boy' that his mother wanted him to be, may be the most serious casualty of this trend. It is in this light, and no other, that I have been thinking about John."

John again surprised me in that he did not go into his Oriental philosophy routine and, obviously deeply touched, responded that he could see that, for society as a whole, much of what had been said made sense to him. Also, he was willing to

90

give it some thought in terms of whether or not it applied to him. And so on this note, the session came to a rather unexpectedly peaceful ending.

In the interval that followed John's announcement of his impending fatherhood, which preceded our discussion of "momism" by a couple of weeks, I had the opportunity of seeing the majority of the other group members in individual sessions. Each, without exception, talked about John's situation and all, like myself, felt that his relationship with Angela had elements which might produce a nightmarish result. We all shuddered over the possibility that these two confused people were going to bring an innocent child into the world, born out of a Yogi-like, neurotic fusion. And yet, personally remembering my needless anxiety with Bob and Eve, I was hoping not to play the heavy-handed parent. Up to this point, I felt that I had played my therapeutic role adequately. The group, it seemed to me, had rallied to the occasion, and demonstrated astute understanding.

When we again assembled, there was an air of expectancy in the room. Here at last the pivotal session concerning John's fatherhood had started. "Good evening, everyone," I said, in a rather jovial manner, attempting to conceal my anxiety.

However, John was not present! The rest of us, like parents, gaped, stared and made small talk, when, actually we were deeply concerned with where our esoteric John could be. Wringing her hands, and leaning forward in her seat, Betty gasped with anxiety. Then, in a burst, she said, "Where is he? Where is that boy? I haven't thought of anything else but this situation of his since last session. I feel so apprehensive, and so frightened. I can't explain it, but I just do."

Tom joined in, "If he wanted to punish us, he couldn't have done a better job than by staying away. The damn fool thinks he's a man, and can't even get to therapy on time."

"For goodness' sake, Tom, leave him alone. If you were in a comparable situation, I wonder what you would do," responded Eve.

Moe jumped to her defense. "She's right, Tom. You're always

the greatest authority, so ready to sit in judgment on people, and you're not exactly what I could call an 'on the ball' character. Don't be so eager to criticize."

Tom rejoined, "I suppose you're going to sit there and tell me, Moe, that John's right in getting married to this girl of his."

"That's not the point, stupid."

"Well, what is the point, stupid?"

"Just this—that no matter what happens around here, you're like a vulture, ready to pounce on the dead, and the blind, with your gloomy attitude. And as if that weren't bad enough, you walk around in your own life like a shabby broken-down jerk."

As if Moe's last words had been the bugle charge of a cavalry, the whole group began to speak at once, like neighborhood gang fighters. The air was suddenly filled with brickbats and debris.

"Yeah." The loudest voice of all, which was Molly's, dominated this bedlam. "You're just a bastard, just a stinking bastard. You'll kick a guy when he's down." Slowly the others petered out as her booming voice picked up even more power, "You God-damned hypocrite. You've never been out with a woman in your life. You sit on the sidelines like an old witch and make sarcastic comments about those who have the guts to try and live. Who the hell do you think you are, anyhow?"

Tom, who had started to defend himself in the midst of this sudden outburst, was avalanched. He sat speechless, a caught and trapped animal. His lower jaw moved a few times, but no words came forth. After a moment more of silence, he flopped back in his chair, hitting the back rest with a thud, his hands dangling over the sides of the chair as if the life had been drained out of them. He was the picture of dejected despair. "What have I done to deserve this?"

Sensing the urgency of the moment, I spoke. "Bob, how do you feel about this wave of hostility toward Tom?"

I had detected a slight repugnance on Bob's part toward the assault and had hoped that he would come to Tom's defense, in his typical diplomatic manner. I realized that he would sense I was attempting to bail Tom out, and this would be an opportunity to demonstrate his status as junior analyst.

"Well, Doc," he began, his brow furrowed and serious, his words studied and careful, "I wonder why it was necessary to attack Tom so vociferously. Indeed"—his mood became even more introspective—"perhaps it is their problem. I can't see what they hope to gain, and, furthermore, was what Tom said really so terrible? If I recall correctly, all he said was that John's absence was filling him with anxiety, and to be quite frank about it, it seems to me it's only the truth, for all of you seem to be as edgy and touchy as a collection of prima donnas."

As he spoke, a cautious eye roamed in my direction, testing its effect on me. I gave him all the nonverbal support it was possible to give, without the use of open gestures. Seeing this, he continued, and turned toward Tom.

"Tom"—and as he said the name, Bob rocked his head from one side to the other, rather like the late President Roosevelt saying, 'my friends'—"you're entitled to your opinion." There was a pause. "And don't ever give it up. Not only are you within your rights in voicing an opinion, but the group's attack upon you only represents a projection, a projection filled with shame. They're ashamed of the anxiety which John's absence has created within them. When you attack his vulnerability, they stand like naked children, exposed by their own embarrassment. They can't tolerate the feeling they have. They don't approve of John's behavior; in fact, they don't even approve of John as a person. It's like some bitch, who with a fur coat to cover her sins, acts holier than milady, when in the public view. In other words, they're attacking the person who reminds them of the anxiety, which they are attempting to conceal from themselves. Tom, you're that reminder, and, therefore, an ogre in their eyes."

His voice gained momentum as he went on. With the free jocular expression being replaced by the tone of a didactic lecturer, he continued, "As I think about it, Tom, not only are they ashamed of their hostility toward John, but, what's more important, they're ashamed of the intolerance which John's story has produced in them and the anxiety it has created."

"Jesus! Jesus! Oh Christ! Did you ever, in your entire life, hear a bigger load of horseshit than that?" Moe burst forth. "Of all the God-damn nonsense we've been forced to listen to, from this cold, puny squirt, this takes the cake. Why, even the doctor never gets this technical. Who the hell does he think he is, Freud? I swear if he worked at our plant he wouldn't last two days. The two-bit fourflusher. No wonder people develop a hatred of psychiatry. Boy, if I ever turn out to be a mealy-mouthed crocodile like that, shoot me. Guilt-feeling-projections-abracadabra. Oh, just kiss my ass, Bob." And with this he slumped back in his chair, crossed his legs at the ankle, repeatedly shaking his head in disgust.

A supercilious grin was the best Bob could manage.

Molly, seething, burst out, "That filthy bastard. That lame excuse for a prick. Look at him, with his smug, self-contented attitude, telling us that we hate John. Actually, he himself never speaks to the guy, and the looks of revulsion he gives John when John isn't looking make you think he was gazing into a sewer. Why the hell we have to put up with this God's chosen favorite child I'll be damned if I know. Why the Doc stuck him in with the rest of us won't ever make sense to me. I've only one thing more to say, Bob! You stink; [and as an afterthought] I still can't see what the hell Eve sees in you."

In quizzical and childlike amazement, Betty asked, "Do you really think that's what's the matter with all of us?"

Bob, too insecure to speak to Betty, and yet tempted to do so, for she had acknowledged his erudition in the field of human behavior, resolved the conflict with a slight smile.

Claudia, also somewhat impressed with Bob's speech, and impervious to the hostility it had aroused, joined with Betty. "I don't know much about these things, but I can see what Molly can't when she says she doesn't understand what Eve finds in Bob. I wish I had a boy friend who could explain things to me when I get so mixed up. Maybe he's not the physical specimen that Moe is, but that's not everything, you know. A girl likes to feel that her man knows what the score is, and Bob sure seems to know."

Tom was somewhat recovered by this time. "Yes, I think it helps, too, and I know Bob's right. I know I'm not the only one who feels toward John as I do. It's just as Bob says. I'm the only one who's got the guts to say so, and the rest of you are just too 'chicken.' I bet, if the truth were known, I probably like John better than most of you."

"That's no lie," Bob responded quickly.

"Good for you, honey," murmured Eve, demonstrating for the first time in the group, her loyalty to her lover while he was in conflict with its members. It also represented her first open support of a male.

Hardly had she finished these words when our ears were greeted with the sounds of the opening of the vestibule door. A split second later, like a gust of wind, in pranced John. He came to an abrupt halt. Craning his neck, he looked around the room, spotted the vacant seat, and darted for it. He sat down, attempting to be unobtrusive, but his contact with the leather made the characteristic sound. He straightened up and surveyed the circle. Silence prevailed.

John, searching the face of each member slowly, and with obvious insecurity, broke into a broad smile which spelled confusion. Finally, apparently sensing that the silence was his responsibility, he said softly, "Sorry to be late." Then, he broke into an even wider, almost meaningless, grin.

Silence resumed, but instead of being a hush of suspension, it was one of pain. Each of us exhibited some signs of awkwardness. We squirmed in our seats, crossed and uncrossed our legs, lit cigarettes, stared at the ceiling, studied the carpet, until the pain seemed almost unbearable.

In a low, mumbling voice John spoke again. This time words were as painful as the silence had been. Diabolical as it was, none of us could stand the quiet, and yet words seemed so superficial.

Moe, not being able to stand the irritation any longer, barked at John, "For Christ's sake, man, speak so we can hear you."

"All right, I will—I will." Wringing his hands nervously, he studied each of us as if he stood before his peers, waiting to be judged. "I suppose you want to know what's happening between Angela and me?"

Not a word was spoken.

"Well, it's like this, but I don't know how to tell you—it's all so confusing to me, too. I went to see her, as I told you I would, and she had it all worked out. She told me she loved me, and gave me a big build-up, and then it came. She's going to have an abortion." As he said the word 'abortion,' his head lowered, and his eyes fixed themselves on the floor. It was almost as though he were being guillotined.

Then, slowly, he raised his head, and with tears pouring from his eyes, and in funereal tones, he began, "Yea, though I walk through the valley of the shadow of death, I will fear no evil: for thou art with me . . ."

He tried to go on but the words wouldn't follow. "She can't do this to me," he finally managed to say. "She can't do this to me," he said again and again. The first time he said it, it had been in the same tone as the words of the psalm, but as he repeated it, a low and slowly penetrating anger crept unmistakably into his voice. He stood up. The effect of his standing frightened us. Molly shrank back in her chair. Bob's big black eyes showed all their white. Moe's jaw dropped. Tom was the picture of anticipation. Betty and Claudia looked like frightened rabbits.

Inhaling deeply, and then tossing out his chest, John bellowed forth, "God damn that bitch. God damn her. What right does she have to be a murderess? What right does she have to kill my son?" And like a suddenly deflating balloon, he withered back into his seat with a deadening flop. Again the room was silent.

Eve, least frightened of all the patients, addressed John. "John, boy, John, do you hear me?"

John didn't stir a muscle, and yet conveyed that he heard her and was listening.

"I know what you feel, and it's miserable. This isn't your failure, John, it's hers. If she was half the woman she ought to be, she would never do this. I don't care about the highfalutin, high-minded ideals about murdering the unborn, I think she's rejecting herself as a woman. Not only is she letting you and your child down, but believe me, John, as a woman, I know she is not a woman. I don't believe females are here on earth to be human cows, but my God, when a woman has a child growing in her which she has received from a man she believed she loved—well, that's different. If she were married to another man, or some other practical reason interfered, it would be different. But no, in one impulsive act she is destroying three people. It isn't pity I feel, nor are you my desired spouse, but John, I do love you."

Bob, completely bewildered, was apparently overcome by an avalanche of conflicting emotions. He had some feeling for John and for what had happened to him. But, on the other hand, here was the woman of his life telling another man in public that she loved him. As was typical for him when emotions raged within, he could not be articulate; in fact he couldn't speak at all.

"Jesus Christ! I don't know what to think. On one side I feel John got shafted, and on the other, I feel that perhaps it's best all around when I think of the welfare of the kid involved. God damn it, I don't know," said Moe, as he shook his head from side to side.

Picking up the beat, Tom continued, "Women, women. What the hell can you expect from them anyhow? They want you to love them, feed them and screw them when they want it, but by God, if you meet them on their terms, it turns out they were only playing make-believe games, after all. They don't know what they want, but they want everything, and if you give it to them, they hate you for it. Aah!!!"

This opportunity was too ripe for Tom, with his misogynistic orientation, to let pass without exploitation. Similarly, it was too wonderful an opportunity for Molly to overlook. No little peanut like Tom was going to spit in the face of womankind while she was around to uphold her sex. Of course, the fact that she considered herself a poor representative of the same would inevitably be forgotten at such moments. In fact, the incongruity between reality and unreality in respect to Molly's femininity was as sharp as it could be. If ever there was a body that was of the feminine mold, it was Molly's with her big firm breasts and rounded hips, and legs and arms of Grecian-statuary design.

97

"Listen, you miserable shit," she began, "if you were a man, maybe people would listen to your criticism of women, but you are the weakest excuse for a man in the group. You remind me of a young nanny goat constantly sucking on its mother's teats, and every time mother moves you nah and complain. Sometimes, it seems you are doing mother a favor by nursing. You're just mad at everything and everybody, because first you want the world to recognize you as a man, when actually you don't want to be one, preferring to be taken care of without doing a damn thing for it, and next, you're mad at yourself because the world has taken care of you, and you haven't assumed your own responsibilities."

Moe turned to Molly, "Ah, just go to hell! There's no point in talking to you. You hate men because you think they're going to hurt you."

"They usually do," Molly quickly retorted.

"Why, because they want to go to bed with you?"

"Well, they always do manage to rope me into that deal."

"And, of course, it's all their doing, isn't it?"

"Oh, I realize I have something to do with it, but I don't like it really."

"Ah, see? I was right. The bitches all chase you to sleep with them until you do, and then, they say it's all your fault. What fucking good are they?"

"No, no don't say that!" John admonished softly, as he spoke to Moe, "not all women. Eve's not that way, and I don't think Angela is. It's just that neither of us is ready for it. She's right. I want to be a husband, and father, but I'm not ready. You can't blame a woman for not wishing to raise a child under these circumstances. Don't condemn her."

"Gee," Betty said, "you're so lovable, John. So lovable."

For the first time in the session John smiled, and his face glowed with light, reflecting the result of feminine acceptance of him. Now all that is necessary, it flashed through my mind, is for a masculine figure to accept him. This was my responsibility. The males in the room were not ready for this, as they were still emotionally confused, enmeshed, or lacking in maturity. He needed a father—a kind, masculine person.

"John"—I spoke with kindness—"I'm really proud of you. I feel you have gone through one of the storms of life, and haven't been beaten down by it. You have grown, and are the wiser for it."

I spoke with sincerity, and he felt the impact. They were not empty, idle words, and all present realized it. By the expressions on their faces I could tell they were in silent agreement with what I had said. This is what John had needed: a father who was a man, a father who was kind, a father who was not afraid to express affection in a masculine manner. Some of the residue of the imagery of seeing his father in feminine clothes must have been neutralized, for he spoke up with a voice which was deeper and more resonant.

"I'm really glad you think so, Doc. It means a great deal to me. You know, up to now, I haven't thought much of this group-therapy business, but it sure is the stuff. It's the bread and butter of living. A guy can consider himself lucky to have this experience. Christ, I feel sorry for all the other fellows who need this. You know, when you're mixed up and confused, you don't know what's good for you. I used to think that only nuts went to psychiatrists. Now I believe you have to be nuts not to go when you're as troubled as I am. Really, where else can you go and meet this kind of understanding? What would I have done without this experience? Doc, I don't think you're doing group therapy for a financial motive. It seems to me there's more to people than I had been willing to admit. All my skepticism about dependency seems to have left. At last I've found people whom I can trust. They aren't perfect, but still I trust them."

Our family was now united, as if bound by blood ties. John had a father and a mother, and the family had gone through a crisis, and come out stronger. Optimism permeated our thinking. No one's glasses were completely rose-colored, yet hope prevailed. It was as if the others had felt, and were implying, that if a thing like this can happen to one of us and work out so well, then it can be of help to any of us.

8. *Motherhood*

The session following the one which revealed that John was not to become a father started off unexpectedly. I had been feeling rather pleased with the developments, and thought surely we were in for a spell of relatively smooth sailing. I had reasoned that with the development of family solidarity, our problems would be those of domestic strife, and so was not prepared for what happened. None of us had really appreciated just how upset Bob had become by the healthy relationship that had developed between Eve and John. We were not totally oblivious of his concern, but I know *I* was not thoroughly cognizant of the depth of feeling involved.

As usual, I slipped off my shoes, slid them under the seat, sat back, and gave the signal for the session to begin.

Claudia opened with, "I don't know about the rest of you, but I, for one, have never had such a wonderful experience as I have had here in the last few sessions. You know, I've seen material like this in the movies; I've read about it in novels; but this is better than the movies. It's greater than the novels, and just think, I'm a part of it!" The latter words she spoke like a tenderfoot at camp, seeing a beautiful New England mountain range for the first time.

"I think all you people are so wonderful. It's more than a pleasure to know you. It's like going to college—if you get what I mean. It's not only what you learn in class that makes college what it is, it's that you mature while you are there. The people you grow up with are a part of you, and you're a part of them, and what you learn remains associated with them. Often, in later life, when you remember Sophomore 'Lit,' you don't think of Byron, Keats and Shelley, but you retain the relationship of Keats' 'A thing of beauty is a joy forever,' to the great big stupid fullback who was so adorable when he read the line, fumbling awkwardly. Yes, it isn't the events, but rather, it's the people connected with the events. I almost feel like that song 'Falling in Love with Love.' I just love all of you, and all of this."

I thought to myself, "Well, well, little Claudia. Out of the mouths of babes . . ." She still didn't quite have full identity, but progress was evident.

In this serene setting, little did we expect what was to follow— and least of all, from such a source.

"I'm getting sick of this," a new voice grated out between tightly clenched teeth, "just plain sick of it. Sentimental slop!"

Was this Moe? Was this Tom? No, it was dignified, polished, man-about-town Bob.

Stripping himself of his previous façade, he went on, "Listen, John, I appreciate your having problems. I appreciate what you've been through, but God damn it, get a woman of your own. All I've heard from Eve since last week is John this, and John that. I'm so fed up—so God-damn fed up with John and more John that I could vomit."

"So vomit," rang out from the opposite end of the room, from the ever-earthy Molly.

"Oh, shut up, you fishwife," he went on, not losing a step. "I come here, and what do I get—a bunch of screaming infants. The Doc tells me this is a place where I can benefit myself. All I can see is a bunch of half-assed, not even diapered, infants."

"You son of a bitch," came forth Moe. "The Doc told us that it wasn't good for us to have outside contacts, and what do you do? You take off with Eve, and go to bed with her. You have no reason to bitch and gripe. You haven't played the game, so you've no right to squawk."

"Right," echoed Tom, "not only didn't play the game but positively fouled it up."

Unruffled by the remarks of Tom and Moe, Bob addressed Eve. "Who do you love here anyhow—that bewildered child or me? I can't understand you. You tell both of us you love us. You tell me I'm wonderful, and all that, but here, you treat me as if I have leprosy. Here, you treat John as if he's the only man on earth."

John looked at him, "Did it ever occur to you she thinks I'm more of a man than you are?"

"Now, John, that's uncalled for," spoke a critical Eve. John shrank back, like the dutiful son who had been admonished. After all, one could push a good thing too far, and he knew it.

Eve now looked at Bob, "As for you, for once in your life listen to somebody else, and I don't mean listen with your ears only. Don't just hear my words, with a lawyer's attitude. You know what I mean, so that you can argue back with logic and common sense, but without feeling the impact of the ideas with your heart. Bob, I love you. In fact, I love you very much. There are many things wrong with you, many things which I wish were different, but that's why you and I are here. Since I've come here, I've begun to appreciate love. I had been to bed with a few men, had rolls in the hay, fast cars, fast talk and fast action. When I first saw you, you were like any of the other smooth talkers and flashy dressers. But then something happened. I can't say what it was, but as therapy went on, I began to feel different. No, I didn't begin to feel different. I began to feel. I liked what the Doc stood for. I liked these people, these very same people whom I had thought were vermin in the first session. I can't explain it, but that's the way it was. Bob, you're like me in many ways. You've been kidding yourself so long, you believe it's the real McCoy. It's not fair for you to try to restrain me from having a life with other people. You simply have to get this through that stubborn head of yours. If I see another man who can be a little happier because I'm nice to him, you've just got to let me. In this you must let me alone. There is more in life that's good than you and me."

"Well, all right, all right. I get you. I hear you, but do you get me?" Bob asked.

"I don't understand," Eve said; "what makes you think I don't get you?"

Bob was struggling against what he knew was the truth. He knew he had been exposed, without malice, yet he felt betrayed and hurt. Leaning forward in his chair, his hands turned up and out as though he were pleading for understanding, he said, "You know, I simply don't seem to be able to make myself clear. I find the girl in my life who means more to me than anyone ever did before. She tells me she loves me, and then this shmoe"—pointing to John—"gets into the act. I stand up and try to claim what I believe is mine, and, by God, nobody understands me."

With this, there was a collective gasp of exasperation from the group. It was as if they had said, "What does it take to get it through this guy's skull?"

John picked up the issue, having fully recovered from his previously overextended position. "Bob, I'm not trying to take your girl away from you. I just want to have a relationship with her, too. I'm not trying to be cute, or funny, or pull anything, believe me. I really can't understand why you're so upset about it."

Bob said, "You don't, huh? Well, maybe that's because you're not in my position. Suppose you were—would your stand be the same?"

"Sure it would," John responded without a moment's hesitation.

"You just don't understand," answered Bob.

"While all this was going on between Angela and me, during these past couple of weeks, and with Eve helping the way she did, something struck me. I wasn't going to tell anyone, but now I will. I'm a little bit ashamed of it, but perhaps it will make you see."

He paused, looked around, and seemed to be rallying some last minute courage. Taking another deep breath and sitting up straight, he said, "Eve is the mother I've always wanted."

With these words, his eyes dropped to the ground and then quickly darted up toward Eve to detect her response. He couldn't hold the gaze long enough, however, and with embarrassment, glanced again at the floor.

The momentary silence that followed came to an end with

Bob's now somewhat less hostile voice saying, "Well, we'll see. O.K., we'll see."

Claudia was proud of Eve. "Yes, she's John's mother, and on her, it's beautiful. She sure is going to make a good one. If only mine had been as nice."

Eve was silent. This was all new for her. Slowly, she was being transformed into a woman. There was now a dignity that hovered over her and encompassed the beaming Claudia.

Claudia had attached her wish to a star—a star called Eve. As Eve went, so went Claudia. Now, however, Claudia could speak whereas before she couldn't. A richness was becoming evident in her. Her recent conversation had showed deeper attributes. The others were treating her with more and more deserved respect. No longer was she looked upon as a pathetically lost little girl hiding in Eve's shadow. The group often encouraged her not to identify with Eve. Molly would say again and again, "Claudia, just be Claudia, and you'll be all right."

By this time, Eve had recovered from the shock of being called John's mother, and was able to reassume, to some degree, her sophisticated exterior. "See," she quipped, "Bob, I'm just your rival's mother, not his sweetheart."

With this comment, she had taken the pressure off herself, and repressed the anxiety connected with being a mother. This particular role of mother was too explosive and unknown for her to accept openly.

Bob replied, "All right, so you're his mother, but I still don't like it."

"Man, this takes the cake," Moe chimed in. "The guy just doesn't want to have a gal. He wants to own her. If I were Eve, I'd give him the gate so fast he wouldn't know what hit him. That possessive son of a bitch."

"Now Moe, it's not quite so bad as all that," Eve said.

Bob barked at Eve, "Leave him alone. He doesn't know what he's talking about."

"Are you ashamed of being a mother, Eve?" Claudia said quietly.

"Why do you ask?"

Claudia shrugged her shoulders, "Oh, I don't know. Just one of my stupid questions, I guess."

"Don't back down, Claudia," Tom advised. "You're on the ball. I had the same feeling. I think she's afraid of being a mother."

Smiling, Betty turned to Eve, "Come on, Eve. You know you're not afraid of being a mother. You're too good a person to be afraid of motherhood."

Molly turned her attention to Betty. "What are you doing? Turning this society babe into the modern version of Whistler's Mother? The only resemblance of this girl to Whistler's Mother might be the chair they both use, if you get what I mean. And in case you don't—Whistler's Mother stayed in her chair, but this girl is off her rocker." There could be no doubt that Molly was bitterly envious of all the admiration and attention that Eve was receiving.

Eve, now a battle veteran, merely gave Molly a cold, condescending glare.

Claudia sprang to her heroine's defense. "Maybe it's just because it's all new to her, and for that matter, it's all new to all of us —but I still maintain Eve would make a good mother."

John was ignited. "Oh, all this fuss over names and labels. Christ, just let it go. I'm happy to be here and glad we're together— let's forget all this business of playing psychiatry. I like Eve, she likes me, and I wish you'd just drop the whole thing."

"I'm for that," spoke up Moe.

"All right," Bob added quickly, and the session came to an end with Bob and John staring at each other as if a cease-fire had been declared.

The next session came just before a weekend. We had all settled down comfortably into our now permanent seating arrangement. Bob chose that chair which was farthest from the entrance, but facing it. This way, he could majestically survey all that threatened him, and set up the necessary controls. Eve sat dutifully on his left. Tom and Moe, like a couplet, followed on Eve's left. On Moe's left sat Molly, followed by John. John, therefore, faced Bob and Eve.

On the three-seated sofa, Betty and Claudia sat on either end, tenaciously occupying what they believed to be positions of favor, on either side of the therapist.

Claudia was on my left, between Bob and myself. She then had not only the support of her father-figure, in the form of the therapist, but also of her older brother, Bob. Next to her older brother, of course, was her mother, Eve. No one told us to take these places, but it would have been sheer bedlam at this juncture of our development for anyone to take the wrong seat.

It had been customary that sessions preceding a weekend would find one or more of our young adults slightly dressed up. Sometimes this was for a date, sometimes a trip home, but usually some special occasion. Claudia had never been much for feminine adornment. In fact, her appearance often gave me the feeling, especially at the beginning of her therapy, of mild neglect. It was probably her concern with her problems that had on these occasions prevented her having the well-put-together look that more secure women have. Yet, there was nothing unkempt about her. Whereas many women are less attractive without their garments and foundations, Claudia, without her unbecoming clothes, would probably have reversed this. Her clothes were in marked contrast to the beauty of her youthful figure. Slightly hunched posture increased the effect. How unfortunate, I thought, that this girl's emotional illness was capable of thwarting nature and hiding her natural beauty. This evening, however, there was a new Claudia. She was dressed in a brown tweed suit tinged with orange. It had been beautifully tailored, accentuating the rich contour of her bosom. Her soft, gentle hips filled the straight lines of the skirt, and the little turned up edges of the jacket at the waist gave her just the right air of sophistication. For the first time in her life, probably, she was wearing tasteful eye make-up, and as I turned to the left, a whispered fragrance reached me. Her filtered cigarette, in a hand drooping gently at the wrist, completed a picture of stressed femininity. No longer would she hold her cigarettes between the ends of two fingers, flicking the ashes with a firm tap of the index finger in a masculine fashion. Now the cigarette was like a delicate fan of one of the ladies of the "Mikado." The other girls stared in wonder.

What was this metamorphosis? Betty, peering around me, was the first to speak. "My, Claudia, I think you look elegant."

Claudia took the comment in stride and nodded pleasantly.

Betty went on. "It's such a beautiful suit you're wearing, and you look so attractive in it, I am really happy for you. You make me happy by all you've done."

"Yes," said Eve excitedly, "it's wonderful. You're so pretty, you make us all feel aglow. I can't express it exactly, but it just feels good."

Molly, no longer capable of remaining quiet, said, "I'm jealous." This was the highest praise that Molly could offer.

Eve spoke, "Molly, really—I don't know . . ." and her voice faded as if to imply that there was no point in continuing.

Molly sputtered back, "All right already. So she's dolled up. What do you want me to do, split a gut?"

In mellow tones, Betty addressed Molly. "Molly, can't you ever be nice to anybody?"

Molly growled, with rising anger, "What do you mean? I said she looked well. What more do you want?"

"It's not that," replied Betty, "it's that you get so angry, no matter what happens."

There was a sudden pause. This obviously had struck home with Molly, and with the group as well. However, after a moment or two, Molly was again in command of her defenses, and said, "You know, Betty, you may have said a mouthful, but I'll be damned if I know what the hell it's all about."

"I'll tell you what it's all about," John interposed. "It's simply this. Whenever anyone here amounts to anything, does something, or can be the object of approval, it reminds you of what a failure you feel you are. If you were half the person you thought you could be, you wouldn't be such an angry bitch."

"Listen to who's talking," snarled back Molly. "Why, you four-eyed baboon! You idol-worshiping jerk! You—you—you—"

The words just couldn't come fast enough for her ideas. It was as if a trip hammer had jammed. Of course, this was a cue for the old master, Bob. "Now, Molly," he said in his best paternal voice, "don't let John get your goat again. Remember you're only rising to his bait when you do so."

"Yeah, you're right, but he's still a miserable bastard." The latter was spoken with much more freedom.

As if the last exchanges had not even occurred, Moe picked up the loose thread. "Claudia," he said, his voice sparkling, "you're getting to be quite a dish." With this, a pride came forth, and she was aglow.

"Thank you," she said, and batted her long false eyelashes for all they were worth.

"Scarlett O'Hara could do no better, I'm sure," mumbled Molly.

"Not at all, not at all," came back a gallant Moe.

"Yeah! Be his guest, Claudia," Tom sneered. "Yeah! Be his guest." He was experiencing jealousy of Moe. He couldn't bear to see his "brother" deserting the comfortable niche he had carved out for them in an exclusively masculine society. He saw his relationship with Moe as the ideal brother-to-brother relationship. By his own appraisal, he felt himself and his therapy brother were at an adolescent age level. In fact, this particular level of adolescence was an early stage of that growth period—a phase where boys are decidedly not interested in girls. It is during this stage of early adolescence that the healthy boy is deeply immersed in athletics, collects cards with baseball players' pictures on them, bears scraped knees like banners, and respects the gym teacher far and above all adults, including his parents. Roughly it would approximate the age of eleven or twelve years.

Claudia's accentuated femininity was a threat to Tom's adolescent state. It was as if his slightly older brother had suddenly discovered girls. He, a year behind his brother, wasn't ready for this. What would he do if his brother became interested in advancing from this comfortable state? Who would be his companion, who would be his confidant? All his life he had been lonely, and now at last he had met Moe. Moe was kind, manly, extremely honest, and he had trusted him. If Moe became involved with girls, he could only see himself slipping back to his former isolation.

At this point, however, despite the heightened insecurity he felt and his annoyance with his "brother," he was also obviously embarrassed and ashamed, for hardly had he uttered his sarcastic quip when he shrank sullenly into a droop-shouldered, chin-on-chest picture of despair.

The group, although noting this physical response on Tom's part, did not have the temperament to coddle or cajole him. Their attitude said, in effect, this is your problem, boy, and you had better stop such immature behavior. Girls are not to be feared.

Claudia needed very little encouragement, and having received it from Moe's remark, she was actually radiant.

"Yes," she said, with the spring of a robin walking across a lawn, "I have some news for you people. I don't know exactly how to begin, and I suppose it's all just plain foolishness—and further-more, I'm afraid somebody will laugh at me—but"—and she looked around the circle to see how her words were being received—"you see—well—I have a boy friend." As this message spread through the room, she again studied each of us, with double-takes that denoted her insecurity. As might have been predicted, Eve spoke first.

"Claudia," and her voice held comfort in its tones, "this is wonderful."

"You really think so?" asked Claudia. "Eve, do you really think so?"

"Yes, I do," responded Eve. Never could a mother demonstrate more pride in her daughter than that which Eve was giving Claudia. For a moment there was silence, the silence which bespeaks action to follow—and it came. Claudia got up out of her chair, slowly at first and then with increased speed, and finally she threw herself around Eve's neck. Tears joined tears. First Claudia's, then Eve's. Lipstick stained Eve's soft accepting cheek. She held her child firmly to her bosom, while patting her at the same time. Eve rhyth-mically rocked her maturing daughter.

The rest of us sat frozen, but slowly we began to thaw out. Tom couldn't look. Moe just sat there with his eyes fixed in amaze-ment. Molly, a mixture of divergent tendencies, leaned forward, and gazed at the floor. Bob, imitating an "old grad" in an overstuffed leather chair of the Harvard Club smoking room, was nonetheless deeply stirred. Betty was thrilled, and looked it. She had identified completely with Claudia.

I was happy, with an inner joy that makes you feel as if there is a potbellied stove glowing inside you. So stirred was I that when at last Claudia turned her head slightly and found me in her view, I said, "Yes, Claudia, it's wonderful, it's all wonderful." At this, she grinned broadly.

My remarks had apparently been not only pleasant, but conductive. Bob was thoroughly affected by this turn of events.

"I know now that this group therapy is for me. I know I used to hold it in contempt, as if it were less then the real McCoy, but, brother, this *is* the McCoy. I feel a sense of belonging now, and that's some feeling. Eve, honey, you're a real darling, and I'm glad that you're my baby!"

Moe followed him. "You know, in our family, life was pretty rough. My mother could never show us any love, because our father said it would make sissies of us, but when Claudia took Eve into her arms, like a small child who runs to embrace its mother—Doc, that's what I needed, that's what I have wanted all my life. Doc, do you really know what it is not to have your mother kiss and hug you and love you?" As he finished these words, his eyes filled up with tears. They never flowed, for he quickly blew his nose, as if he were protecting himself.

"Yeah, this is all wonderful," said Tom in a low monotone, "but I don't see where it is going to help me," and stopped just short of incurring the group's wrath with his self-pity.

John, rather excited and overjoyed by the experience, turned to Bob. "It was a treat to see what went on between Eve and Claudia, but for me there was a greater joy."

"What was that?" Bob queried.

"Well, simply this," John went on, "you—the way you've finally come around. You know what I mean, not simply because you've decided you're one of us, but somehow or other, you've become more 'regular.' You might even say I think you are a 'good Joe.' There's even a more masculine way about you. I don't picture you parading your male prowess any more, as if you weren't so sure

110

you'd always have it—or even worse, acting as if you might lose it, desperately trying to reassure yourself that you hadn't."

For the first time in the group, Bob didn't fight back defensively at John. Instead, although startled, he accepted John's constructive intent.

"John," he spoke in moderate tones, "I really appreciate your helpful attitude. And furthermore, I have some similar feeling toward you. I think you're turning out to be a hell of a nice guy. I guess I was in the wrong. I was wrong in thinking you were attempting to steal my girl. After seeing this exchange between Claudia and Eve, I understand: A lot of us here, including myself, have been cheated out of a very valuable commodity in the human equation—mother. . . . Isn't it funny"—after a moment of pause —"that we need so many different things? As a child I thought about mothers as being someone we needed to feed, clothe, and take care of us, but now I see more and in a different light. By Christ, you can't ever be a man, marry and become a father if your mother doesn't love you. I don't get the exact connection, mind you, but it's there, and I'm sure of it. I also know that the Doc, even though he's been rather silent, has been very forceful throughout this exchange. Maybe it's just because he is silent, and allows us to do all these pent-up things, that makes the difference, or maybe it's more, but don't ask me what that more is. I just feel there is more to it than that. I don't know what his feeling is toward me, but he's something damn important, even when he just sits there, and doesn't say a word, but just allows me to live."

These words caused a tremendous impact upon the group. There was an immediate recoiling. Bob had spoken the truth, but it was more than we could sample, let alone assimilate. It reminded me of the cliché, of how hard most of us work at making a living, but work so little at living.

John was the first to recover. "Well—uh—well—uh—Bob you—uh—have really said quite a bit there, and I agree with it, but there's an awful lot that I'd like to think about. In fact, I even wonder if you fully appreciate yourself what you have said. The more I think about what you've said the more I feel that you had a moment of clear vision, but that really you aren't as 'with it' as it sounded. Mind you now, I'm not deriding you or underselling you, it's just that I feel it's so new for you and me, and for that matter all of us."

I whispered quietly to myself, "My how these two boys have grown. They're going to be all right."

While all this had been going on, Claudia remained seated in Eve's lap, and Eve still held her, her arms circling her waist, as both sat facing the group.

Molly had recovered now. She turned toward me, and her voice conveyed her confusion. As she spoke, she wanted something. She was anxious, and yet for this moment she was willing to be slightly accepting. "Doc, what is it—what is it with me?— When I see Eve and Claudia there, I'm deeply embarrassed; and yet I admire them. I tried to make fun of it, I try to think it's nothing, but I know that isn't so. I guess what I really am saying is that I would like it for myself. The only difference being that I'd want it with you. I don't need a mother as much as I need a father, and I think you'd make a good one."

I smiled at Molly. This was her highest point of emotional contact so far. "Molly, I'm pleased and complimented that you would choose me as a father. Do you realize that it's quite an honor for someone to say to another that they'd love to have him for a father? I can't imagine anyone giving greater respect to another than that which you are giving me at this moment."

Deeply moved, she smiled as never before. She was radiant with happiness. It was an aliveness that painters frequently strive for as they portray this emotion. To us it was a moment that each held in cherished esteem. Finally she spoke.

"I suppose I've been happier in life, but I can't remember when. If this therapy never does another thing, it's done this, which is quite a lot."

Her hostility was absent for the first time. Her primitive mode of expression had disappeared.

Sensing that Molly and I had reached the saturation point, and that words from another would not be interfering, Eve broke in. "Oh, Molly, I knew you had it in you. I knew that you weren't what you pretended to be. No one could really be as tough and hard as you were, and still have stuck at this group therapy as you have. You've confirmed what I had secretly held, and even told Bob, that you were not the virago you pretended to be."

"You're right about that, Eve," Molly answered, "you're absolutely right. I don't even like it myself. In fact when I am that way, which is the majority of the time, I actually hate myself. I try to be different. I try to be nice. I get good advice to be otherwise, but all the common sense, all the good advice doesn't seem to change me. This is the first time that anything has changed me, and there's nothing common sense about it."

"Yes, I know what you mean," Claudia said finally, "because I'm a new person, and it's all directly traceable to knowing and being with you people. My mother always tried to make me into an image that I would have loved to have fulfilled. You know what I mean, girls. Charming, well-groomed, polite, easy with small talk, and all the rest of the social routine, but somehow the harder I tried, the worse it became. Mother meant well, but it just seemed I couldn't do what she wanted. I don't know whether I unconsciously didn't want to, or whether her goals were always a little too advanced at the moment for me. Whatever it was, it came off wrong. When other girls were dressed in their party desses, and I was in mine, you could always be sure I'd be the one with the crooked ribbons. And no matter how hard I would try, at the last minute, the seams of my stockings would inevitably be slightly awry. At school, my hard work would rate only a B on an assignment for which other girls would get an A with far less effort. I'll never forget the time at college when I loaned my spring formal to my roommate for the Junior prom. Naturally, I couldn't go. I had the measles, of course. That night, just before going out, she sneaked into the infirmary to see me. There she stood in the blue and white taffeta, which was my favorite gown, and one in which I looked my best, but I was sure that she looked prettier than I ever could in the same dress. She looked as if she had stepped out of a bandbox. I always looked as though I'd gotten dressed in a hurry. Maybe it was that my cosmetics were just off focus, or that a slight wrinkle was pressed into the gown, but there was always some slight imperfection to spoil what might otherwise have been a fine, smooth picture. It wasn't as if I cared that it wasn't quite perfect, but what hurt was that this slight imperfection always made me feel as if I couldn't be loved by my mother. It wasn't as if I felt rejected, but rather as if I wasn't fully loved. It made me feel that my mother loved me because, as my mother, she had to, not because she really approved or wanted to. I never felt that she admired me."

As she finished these words she turned toward her new mother, Eve. "Eve, you are my mother come true."

Eve followed right in stride with, "I suppose Bob is going to say later on that on me it looks good," and she said these words with tongue in cheek, most affectionately.

Taking a deep breath, and slowly letting it out as she spoke, Eve then said to Claudia, "There's one thing I suppose is kind of Victorian, but let me say it anyway. You know what difficulty John has just gone through with his girl. Please, Claudia, do be careful."

9. *Growth*

Just before my departure for summer vacation, Bob came and asked if we might have a few words alone, in my inner office. I agreed as I sensed no neurotic reason for this request.

His story concerned an uncle and an aunt, who lived in Brooklyn. They had an only child, a girl, about twelve years old. She unfortunately had suffered a complete loss of her hair, head and body alike. This child had been to one of our well-known diagnostic centers, and even though she had received the very best that the medical minds of the big city had to offer, she was still without improvement. In desperation and confusion, someone had suggested a visit to a psychiatrist. And, as such, I was being approached in the case.

Thus, my initial appraisal had been correct. Bob was not attempting to improve his own status with me. Rather, he was revealing genuine human interest in one of his relatives. I advised him to have his aunt call to arrange an appointment, which she did the next day.

About a week later, the plump, aggressive, domineering woman, of approximately fifty-five, brought her unfortunate child to my office. Together we spent about forty-five minutes reviewing the long-drawn-out history, not only of the child, but of both sides of the family, in great detail. We went over the voluminous medical history once lightly, and certain features stuck in my mind. As she spoke, I had the opportunity to survey the family's emotional climate and its intricacies to some degree.

Arriving at this point in the consultation, I found myself leaning toward a completely physical diagnosis, seeing very little need for psychiatry on a causative basis. If this were my child, I, too, would feel more than reasonably concerned and bewildered, but I certainly did not feel that the treatment was primarily a psychosomatic problem. It then occurred to me to wonder why this woman had been advised to seek psychiatry for her child. I leaned a bit forward in my chair and without changing the mood or pace said, "One more question. Why were you told to seek the services of a psychiatrist in this matter?"

Startled, and apparently stunned into openmouthed silence, she rocked her head back, before darting it quickly forward again. "Are you a psychiatrist?"

I nodded gently.

Almost indignantly, she answered, "Well, I didn't know that. I had wanted to try a chiropractor. . . ."

Several days later, when Bob came in for his next individual session, we had an entertaining time of it. We laughed about our respective naïveté, and "the things that happen to good Samaritans."

The whole mood of this private session was one of conviviality and warm acceptance. After we had finished laughing at the backfire of our good intentions, we began to focus upon Bob's more immediate problems.

"Well, Doc, you'll never believe it, but I have turned poet."

"Really, Bob? Tell me about it."

"Okay, it's like this. I've been doing some thinking about where I'm headed—and what my relationship to Eve is all about. It seems to me that despite therapy I've been doing very little 'stocktaking' of myself. So the idea of facing myself with myself occurred to me this past weekend. I went to my desk and drew out pen and paper. At first, foolishly, I made up a list of personal assets and liabilities, but this, as you probably could have told me, didn't help a bit. Then, while I sat there, it hit me—the whole idea could best be expressed by a poem. After all, as you and I once said, while evaluating the forms of art as media of communication, poems really represent the highest mode of exchange of feelings and ideas—so I began to compose one. I didn't know what I was going to say nor did I care. I merely let the pen 'loose' and let it speak. At times, I didn't even know what I was saying but I'll tell you this—when it was all over, I felt great. I never felt so free and yet united about my feelings."

"Say, Bob, that's wonderful! I'm curious—did you by chance bring it with you?"

A broad smile crossed his face. "Well, as a matter of fact, I just happen to have it with me," and he winked. "I've called the poem *Ma Femme*. Would you care to have me read it to you, Doc?"

"Yes, I would, Bob, very much so."

"Okay, here it is," and he proceeded to take a large billfold out of his inner jacket pocket, open it, and pull out a paper which was folded in thirds. He began to read. His voice was firm, strong, but betrayed a slight embarrassment.

"Sometimes, she says I'm a little boy.
This, I would not ever care to deny.
But on other occasions, a wise perceptive
Old man do I appear in her eye.

What is this wondrous dichotomy,
Which seemingly belies the anatomy?
Where does the labyrinth of the psyche
Hide the clue to this obscurity?

Soft and erotic, graceful in form,
This lovely lady is not forlorn.
Her "innards" are known to this boy and man,
For reflections bring images without plan.

The mother, who childhood never knew,
A virginal mother ever must be.
Sons are her loves, whose father she
Could never know in such complexity.

A mother's small girl responds to Dad's
Silent call with pleasureless joy.
For in this state, where loneliness lies,
A perceptive man is as a little boy."

"I like that, Bob. I'm pleased that you've been wrestling with
your problem. And I'm truly surprised that you could be quite that
emotionally honest with yourself. What did Eve say when you read
it to her?"

"I haven't read it to her yet. When I see her tonight, I will.
She's been visiting her family for the weekend, and it was during
her absence that I wrote the poem. I've picked a quiet little French
restaurant in the Village, and while we're sipping our wine, and the
candle burns low, I'll read it to her."

"Bob, I see you're really starting to take your romance with
Eve seriously. Fundamentally, up to now, Bob, I've been disappointed in what you and Eve have done."

"I can appreciate what you mean, Doc. I know you feel we're
acting-out, and I know Eve and I have caused you great anguish
and concern."

"Yes, Bob, there's no use hiding it; I've been troubled by the
behavior of you both. But note I said 'have been.' I no longer feel
that this is pure acting-out, Bob. I don't feel it's wise to become
clinical about why I've had a change of opinion. Let me say merely
that I have confidence that you and Eve will work out the neurotic
entanglement with each other. I still feel it was unfortunate in its
beginning—that it was an act of aggression, in defiance against the
democratic authority of both the group and me. I have no doubt
that you have suffered enough anxiety so that, by your own unconscious actions, you have reached the place where you are at last
ready for the much needed broader perspective.

"I feel that it was inevitable and necessary for you to do what
you did. You probably would have done this elsewhere if you
hadn't done it here. Therefore, in a way, I'm happy that you did it
here where meaningfulness can be brought into your awareness. It
seems that this was your way of finding yourself. If you had been
prevented from doing this, you would have been denied your right

to pursue a clarification of your own realistic self-image. It must be obvious that it had to be done. No one can give you experience. Each of us must gain it for himself. Words of wisdom are empty without our own experiences to change them into meaningfulness. This, Bob, is why I no longer feel that your behavior was a simple act of defiance against the democracy of the group. Of course, I'm not unmindful of the fact that you had a partner, and that she shared with you the burden of your mutual doings and needs. My hope is that you derive meaningfulness from your behavior. By this, I mean that you both will grow and mature to where you can experience self-acceptance and have the ability to enjoy the enjoyable. I have no definite conclusion in mind as to the inevitable outcome. This, I feel, lies in the hands of the future."

Bob seemed to accept this with pleasure and relief. He spoke appreciatively and after a few minutes said questioningly, "Doc, remember when John said I spoke the truth, but didn't fully understand what I was saying? Remember?"

"Yes, I do," I answered.

"Well, Doc, that's how I also feel about my poem. I feel I said more than I understand myself."

"I see."

And he quickly moved in for what he hoped to be a successful conclusion. "Would you explain it to me?"

"Now Bob," I said in a fatherly manner, implying that he should know better, "in all honesty, you couldn't really expect me to do that—could you?—in terms of good therapy?"

"Guess I was just trying, and I really do know better."

"Then why don't you try to tell me what it means, or rather, what you feel about your poem?"

"Well, that's not easy. That's not easy," he repeated. "Of course, I know that I'm talking about Eve and myself, but the parts about mother and father which just flowed from my pen as I wrote I swear are very mysterious to me."

"Bob, why not quietly reread the fourth and fifth stanzas of your poem to yourself, and when you finish, tell me how you feel— not what they mean to you, but what they bring back to you?"

He followed my suggestion and upon finishing his review, he

raised his head, rubbed his chin thoughtfully, then spoke. "First off," he began, "it seems to me that I have accepted the idea that I'm somewhat less than mature. By this, I mean I sense a willingness to accept myself without panic as a little boy at times. I no longer need to be a wise, perceptive man. As we sit here and talk, you have crystallized into a father to me—not my own father, but the kind of father I've always wanted. And perhaps of even greater importance, as we've been talking about Eve, I'm not willing to be her father, or her little boy. The truth of it is, I'm quite fed up with both roles in our relationship. No more Eros with Aphrodite, but man with woman. I want her to see me as her equal because I feel such a sense of equality with her. This is quite new for me as you can probably gather, Doc. I've either placed women on pedestals or lorded it over them, but lately, since things have gone so well between you and me, it all seems much easier. It's easier to love Eve. It's easier to love her as a contemporary. I suppose it's like saying she has her parents, I have my parents, and now Eve and I can be the same younger generation."

He quickly added as an afterthought of more than just passing value, "Our talk today has brought it into focus for me. I trust—I trust myself. Yes," he repeated reflectively, "I really can trust myself now." As he spoke these words, a small sigh of relief was audible. "I trust myself in this way, Doc"—his lucidity increased—"I am no longer afraid of my emotions. Sometimes they lead to constructive ends, and sometimes not, but I feel secure, especially with Eve. I believe as long as we maintain our emotional relationship that a worth-while end inevitably will result. You cannot imagine, Doc, what a relief that is, what a relief to say what you feel without constantly worrying about whether or not you are going to pull a 'boo-boo,' whether or not you are going to make an enemy, lose a job, a friend, or in general make life miserable for yourself. Yes, I trust myself. I'm no longer afraid of doing the stupid thing. Making mistakes doesn't plague me any more, and, Doc"—looking me straight in the eye—"I have you to thank for this."

"Thank you, but that's not quite true. You have yourself and all of us in the group to thank. No one of us could do this alone—that's the beauty of it all. The healthier we become, the more we trust not only ourselves as individuals, but the easier it becomes to trust the others."

"Doc," he said, after a meditative pause, "you know I've heard you say things like that before, but now I not only hear you, I understand you. It's the first time I haven't taken down your words like a recording. My mind has heard you instead. It's as if I had permitted you and your ideas to enter, where previously just a vacuum existed. Isn't it strange that some of the more fundamental truths we know and repeat are just empty words to us?"

"Yes, Bob, I agree. It's only when personal experience with someone else occurs that the words are no longer just words, but become concepts by which we can then live." We looked at each other with deepening communication. What had happened had served to give substance to the thing that all human beings knowingly or otherwise live by—their own philosophy of life.

In our next session, it was evident that Bob and Eve had reached a fruition. Gone was Bob's usual scowl and furrowed brow. His smile revealed more than pleasure—security. This security was echoed in Eve, who was wearing a simply tailored beige dress, trimmed with a soft green, and, to round out her autumnal appearance, a matching green silk scarf around her lovely neck. The scarf was held in position with a riding pin of old silver. Her clothes indeed represented a departure. Previously her favorite colors had been red and blue. I did not know whether she was aware of it, but the change from the red and bright blue colors that both she and Claudia had worn signified improvement. The love these girls felt for these two colors was closely tied to their disturbance. As they had attained more emotional security, the growing fondness for the softer shades of green, brown and yellow represented a projection of their new tranquillity.

The session had been running ten minutes or so, and the exchanges had been of no great importance. The spirit of the occasion had been slightly festive. At this point, however, Eve, who had participated in the friendly exchanges, spoke.

"I'd like to tell all of you about the wonderful time that Bob and I had the other evening. I had visited my parents, and had come

121

back feeling depressed. As I look at it right now, I begin to see why. It seems to me that therapy does this to all of us sooner or later. By this I mean that during therapy we renew our hopes that our parents will be as loving and understanding as the members of this family right here. I suppose we reason, consciously or not, that if strangers can come to mean so much to us—have come to love and understand us and to assume the same roles that the members of our family were designed to do—it's quite natural to expect our real families to behave in the same improved manner next time we see them. Of course, it never works out that way, but hope always beats in the hearts of love-hungry children. On leaving my parents' home I felt these words coming to me: 'Eve, you little fool. You should have known better. You walked into the intimacies of your family again, with your guard down, expecting this time to find them different. You little fool you—when will you ever learn? Bob and the group with Doc are your family, they love you, they want you, they won't let you down. They may be uncouth at times, but they're dependable, and reliable, and never fail in their attempts to be constructive and understanding—the most precious feelings you have ever known. And what did you do? You forgot that your family hasn't changed a bit.' It's not that I walked away feeling hostile to my father and mother, but I was disappointed. Now, at last I'm ready to accept reality. They are what they are, and they won't ever change. I've made up my mind not to try to change them any more, but to try to accept them and their limitations, with tolerance. True, I don't expect this will happen overnight, but I can see it developing in the future."

As she spoke the climate of the group had changed. It was still friendly, but now serious. These fundamental truths were not evident to Eve alone. They were germane to all of us. There were silent gestures of affirmation. This time, as Eve spoke, she raised her shoulders and slid back in her chair as if her body were saying, "Now that that's over with, on to the pleasant part." I was about to tell you, before I got sidetracked with my own story, that Bob and I had had a pleasant evening after I returned. I'm sure you girls know what a date means in a spot like that. I suppose it could be labeled a morale booster, but just between us girls"—and she winked as she spoke—"I could have smothered him with kisses when he phoned me and invited me to dinner. Well," she continued, "he chose a simply wonderful little French restaurant in the Village. It was sort of an off-beat place: a dozen tables at most, checkered table cloths held down by candle-dripped wine bottles. The high point of the evening occurred after liqueurs. The darling had written a poem. He read it, and in the flickering candlelight, I realized that I was, and am, really in love."

She continued. "Since that night, Bob and I have talked things over, and have decided to live together."

A collective sigh of mixed content filled the room.

Bob was the first to speak. "The other day, in an individual session with the Doc, several things were ironed out. I understand now that Eve and I had been behaving like two infants. I refer to infants in the sense that I've studied them while a psychology student, and was impressed that infancy is the most powerful state of existence, psychologically speaking. The infant has the family at its beck and call. It contributes little if anything to the family's welfare, but requires complete subservience. It demands love, but doesn't return it. Its slightest irritation becomes a command for those responsible for its care. I now see that Eve and I have been behaving like that. I'm not sure what this new phase of growth represents. However, I love that girl and feel she loves me. I realize further that we have quite a lot of therapy ahead of us still. Our living together will no doubt bring about problems—nonetheless, I'm tired of running away from problems, and so with love as our motivation, and courage as our direction, we're going to launch this new adventure."

With this, Molly spoke—irritably. "Listen, if you love each other, and I'm not saying you don't, then why in the hell don't you get married?"

"I'll tell you why," John burst forth, "because they're not really in love." The tone of his voice revealed more than his words. He was angry and upset.

Back came Molly, "Well now, come to think of it, maybe this is just more play-acting on their parts."

"I'm not trying to be moralistic," came the high tones of

Betty, "but don't you think, Eve, you're going a bit far? And since you feel that you both still have a lot of therapy to go through, what's the rush?"

"Yeah," Molly rejoined, "what's the rush anyway? What about this business that you said you and the Doc had talked over, Bob?"

Bob resorted to his defensive professional guise. At first he stared coldly at Molly, and then as if coming out of a conference with fellow intellectuals he said, "It's like this. The Doc reassured me that although Eve and I had behaved like acting-out children, he felt there was some merit and realism to our relationship."

"Did he give his permission or approval to this new development?" broke in John.

"Why, no, he didn't," rejoined Bob. "You know the Doc; he just wouldn't give permission or approval in such a matter."

"Yeah, I guess he wouldn't," said Moe in a casual manner, "but I often wish he would."

"Why," Bob bellowed, "why?"

"Well," drawled Moe, "it seems that if he doesn't, you two will forever take the bit in your mouths and run away with it."

"But that's precisely the point," was Eve's comment. "He trusts us. He believes in us. He is willing to let us discover ourselves, right or wrong, and work out our destinies as individuals. That's what I realized in my disappointment when I returned from visiting my parents. I noticed then how unlike my parents the Doc is. They never had faith in me. They always felt I would do the wrong thing. They never gave me the luxury of trying things out. They never permitted me an even greater luxury: the right to make a mistake, and discover for myself that it was a mistake I needed to make and work out. How are we ever going to grow unless someone of worldly experience relates with us and gives us the confidence to try life out?"

"Hurrah for the do-it-yourself kid," said Moe. "Now I know what psychiatry is, it's a do-it-yourself package," he said satirically, and repeated the phrase again, with even more sarcasm.

"Not so fast there, smart guy," Bob retorted, "there's a great deal of difference between do-it-yourself and a relationship in which another person says, in effect, 'Try it and I will help you explore the unknown and yourself.' There's a lot of difference between those two," he concluded.

"Maybe there is," said John, "but still and all I think you're taking unfair advantage of Doc's liberality."

"That's it," snapped Molly, "that's it exactly. It isn't the Doc's system that's screwy here, Bob, it's you and Eve."

Her voice now revealed a very deep hostility. And as she spoke, my memory evoked the story of Molly's childhood, the time when she had seen her mother and father having intercourse. "No wonder Molly is so deeply upset by this," I said to myself. "She must be reliving this unconsciously, with Bob and Eve representing her parental figures. That entire primal scene must have been reawakened in her mind by these recent events."

I spoke, carefully weighing my words, "Molly, these are pretty harsh words you're using toward Bob and Eve—it's not that you haven't the right to use them, but what interests me is your necessity to be so adamant. In other words, how does this concern you?"

"Gee, Doc," she said, startled, "I don't know. I'll be damned if I know, but now that you mention it, I do seem concerned. You'd think that I was directly involved. Maybe it's because I'm jealous" —and after slight hesitation—"maybe it's because I feel that Eve is getting better. Honestly, Doc, I think I would die if anyone here got better and was discharged before me. You know I think I'm the smartest and most talented person in the room."

My only response was a quiet "Oh." To myself, I was thinking, "Yes, she is in competition with Eve and Bob, but that's good. At least her imagery of herself as a woman is solidifying. She certainly doesn't need to know that her sexual desire in the matter is incestuous in nature—to 'beat' Eve with Bob as the object. It will serve no real purpose."

"You know, Molly," Betty said, "maybe it would be better if you and I would just let Bob and Eve work it out between themselves. They've been through other crises up to now, and without our expert help seem to be better off than they were before, so how about giving them a chance—O.K.?"

"Yeah," replied Molly with a sigh, "it's their funeral, not mine."

Claudia, who had been a spectator at this tennis tournament, bobbing her head from side to side with the exchanges, and rooting for both sides of the argument alternately, slowly came out of her confusion. Her loyalty to her ideal mother—Eve—had been shaken at times by the rediscovery that her parents were doing the thing she unconsciously thought of as "dirty"—having sexual intercourse.

This is a common outgrowth of children who have not been able to adjust to their parents as natural people—and thus they fantasy their parents as angelic figures who do not engage in the animalistic ventures of sex. Also, I felt that had Claudia not been so dependent upon her mother's approval, she would have joined the ranks of those who disapproved. Since her very existence still depended upon her relationship to Eve, a quasi-tolerance held sway. This little girl, so typical of many other little girls in a similar position, chose only to talk around the situation, and not truly about it. She began, "Bob and Eve do make such an ideal couple, and really there is much to be said on both sides of the question. I can see both points of view, and I'm sure the Doc knows what he's doing." This position revealed her misuse of her religious training. She was employing me as a godlike authority in order to rescue herself from the premature exposure to the nakedness of sex.

"Well," I said to Claudia, "that may be, but really it isn't quite the issue at hand. The issue is simply that, when humans need to find their way, kindness and tolerance are more helpful than rules and regulations or references to good and evil."

"I see what you mean, Doc," she said, rubbing her chin between her thumb and index finger.

"By the way," I added, "how are you getting on with your boy friend?"

"Fine," she responded, almost without thinking. "We have been seeing each other rather regularly. You know, Saturday night stuff. We go to the theatre, museums, listen to recordings at my place, and all that sort of thing."

"What does he do for a living?" asked Eve with gentleness and concern.

"He's in a training program at one of the Madison Avenue ad agencies."

"Well, that's nice," Eve responded.

"Oh, not that nice," Claudia answered, with a little flipness in her voice.

"Don't tell me," Betty said, "don't tell me—you——"

"Yes, I do sleep with him," rejoined Claudia. "What of it?"

Visibly disturbed but silent, Eve lowered her head and stared at her shoes. To me it spoke of the embarrassment a mother feels when she learns her daughter has lost her virginity before marriage.

"Well, well," spoke Molly with an air of knowing resignation. "Our little Claudia has fallen again. Just another deflowered maiden running out her course."

"You make it sound so sordid, Molly," Betty said irritably.

"I must agree," said Eve in a passively aggressive manner.

"Well, who the hell do you think she is?" bristled Molly. "She's no better than the rest of us."

"Oh, that's not the point at all," said Betty.

"Well, what is?" Molly asked.

"Well—it's—oh, you know very well," said Betty. "She's so —well—I can't find the right word or expression, but you know."

What she was really trying to say, but was afraid to express for fear of embarrassing Claudia, was that Claudia was too fragile and delicate a person to be treated so harshly. And furthermore, now that she had made some real progress in therapy, this was hardly the time to attack her. To the contrary, encouragement was indicated. Nonetheless, bloodthirsty Molly was not to be distracted from her compulsive need to see herself superior to all others. "It seems to me that there's a double standard around here. If some of us engage in sex, it's dealt with at the same level as if we had had an argument with the boss or a battle with our parents, but when dear Claudia strays from the straight and narrow, she's treated as a carefully nurtured hothouse flower. So what gives?"

"Listen, you bitch," snarled Eve, a lioness in ferocious protection of her cub, "mind your own business. You don't give a damn about anyone else, you only care about your own selfish hide. Your destructive desire is very clear to me."

Her piercing defense made its mark upon Molly. But once aroused, Molly had never been known to quit a fight in the middle, so she went on. "Drop dead, you sophisticated, poetry-loving whore."

"I can take care of myself," said Claudia defensively. "I'm not afraid of her or her foul mouth. She can't smash me. As far as I'm concerned, she doesn't exist."

So our little girl Claudia had learned to flick the ashes.

"Good for you," said Betty.

"You see," Claudia continued, "now I know who I am in this world. I am a person, and a pretty nice one, too. I feel that I've found myself. I have friends, a good job, a nice boy friend, and people like Molly just don't seem to be able to batter me around any more."

"Say, say," Moe said, "I really think you've got something there. You really do seem to have found yourself."

"Yes, and if I might quote myself," spoke Bob with admiration, "on you it looks good. On you it looks very good."

"I never thought it possible, but here it is right in front of my eyes, a little girl growing up," commented John deftly. "You know, Claudia, I thought you'd be the last one to show improvement around here, and now you've done this."

By this time, Molly realized that the group had decidedly rallied behind Claudia, so she could no longer sustain her attack without losing face, and she wisely dropped the matter with a shrug of the shoulder, as if to say, "Let the fools believe in foolishness."

Eve was even more pleased than Claudia. No mother hen could possibly have displayed her approval more affirmatively than she did at this moment. "Claudia, there are so many words inside me, that I just feel that I'd better keep the majority of them where they are, and say simply, 'Claudia, you're so precious.' "

"Yes, Claudia, you're certainly a long way from where you started," said Bob.

"I feel I've come quite a way," she responded quietly, then turned to me. "Doc, we've talked so very much about love during this session. Could I ask you a question?"

"Of course," I responded, "what is it?"

"Well—what is love?"

"I assume you mean 'mate love,' Claudia, is that right?"

"Yes, Doc, that's what I mean."

"Claudia, I think your question is most timely since we've been discussing this so extensively all evening. Furthermore, as we're practically at the end of the session, permit me to give a rather extended answer. This is what love means to me: Love is an emotion. Mate love is the highest form of maturity. There are other forms of love, but they never take as much from us, nor are we expected to give as greatly in these other forms.

"The expressions of love run the gamut from tenderness to extreme anger. Within the state of love, some of the properties are recognizable. However, one may have the properties and still not be 'in love.' The properties are best understood as follows: Loyalty, emotional integrity, and the ability to subjugate the self and its needs for the benefit of the other's needs and wishes in order to produce a greater opportunity for happiness with that loved one. In fact, this latter encompasses the entire concept of freedom for the love object. The love object is endowed by the lover with great latitude and permissiveness, even to the point where the boundaries become slightly unrealistic. The love object is seen in the eyes of the lover as transcending many shortcomings and personal inadequacies, with a slight touch of enchantment replacing what would otherwise be annoyance. Although all this be true, as good food needs proper seasoning, so love needs to be seasoned with the test of time.

"Love is usually associated only with tenderness, but what it really requires for survival is an aggressive pursuit of the individual's expression for adjustment. Each party requires personal assertiveness. When passiveness exists in the love relationship, it lacks that which brings substance to the love. An ardent individuality is an integral ingredient. If a person, active in his love, reaches his personal happiness, he has created happiness for his mate."

When I had finished, Molly's ruffled feelings and the group's previous distress over the decision Bob and Eve had made seemed allayed. The silent communication carried by our expressions revealed that we had all understood at least one fundamental—love was closely involved with tolerance. And, as a result of the interaction, permission had been granted for all of us to continue in our struggle out of loneliness.

That we had profited from this, our mutual experience, was shown in the events which took place in the following weeks. It had never been my custom to have any real rules or regulations about the conduct of our group behavior. This applied both collectively and individually. In my mind, to do so would merely have defeated the aims. The freedom permitted in the absence of censure or judgment had proven itself the best method for liberating otherwise suppressed and self-exposing material. This release, although bringing forth an array of problems, served as the soil for repair and growth.

A rather specific problem of long standing had been irritating to me on recent occasions, but I had become rather accustomed to it and said nothing. However, this was not the case with the rest of the group. On the contrary, their annoyance was rising, with the passage of time, from a level of apparent nonconcern to the height of open battle. Arriving late at the group sessions had become quite the topic of discussion.

Molly and John were the two chief offenders—Molly in particular. Tom, after his initial tardiness, which had added to his usual harassment, had seemed to shed this burden. The others were seldom, if ever, late.

Most 'put upon' by the lateness of the others, was Bob, although he seldom demonstrated his concern. Instead, it was Betty who displayed her emotions most clearly on the subject. But her attempts to rectify the situation, like so many of her crusading attempts, had only come to an abortive end. She had apparently given up hope some time ago of any change in the distressing lateness of the others.

The issue again became current shortly after the episode dealing with mate love, and was led off by Moe. Apparently stimulated by the discussion, and particularly by my words dealing with extending permission to those for whom we care, he asked the latecomers, "What are your feelings toward us when you're late?"

Molly's instant guilty reaction was "What business is it of yours?" This immediately embroiled the entire group in a long discussion of whether or not it was their business, with the 'pro' faction finally coming out on top. The door was then wide open for lengthy discussions of lateness and its meanings.

The widest imaginable ranges of interpretation erupted. They ranged from Molly's, "It can't be helped, things always seem to happen to me" to Bob's "I feel they're plain acts of hostility." I refrained from entering the discussion, despite some furtive attempts to commit me to some position.

When the session closed, we were little further than we had been at its beginning. However, there was one slight sign of progress—they did agree to re-open the discussion of the subject at the next session.

And, for the first time in weeks, they were all on time for the next session. I did not know whether the promptness was caused by the discussion, for curiously, they never broached the subject at all. I did not call this to their attention. To do so would have revealed a position which could have destroyed the growth potential. I kept my neutral silence.

My patience was soon rewarded. Both John and Molly reverted to their usual lateness at the following session.

"This is getting downright disgusting!" bellowed Moe.

His furious reaction represented the greatest anger we had ever seen him display. He was supported first by Bob, and then by Betty. Even Eve registered a complaint against John. A touch of comedy was provided by Tom who said, "Boy, John, if I can get here on time, I don't see why you can't."

At first Molly remained still. It was typical of her in this kind of situation. We had become accustomed to her building up 'steam' for sudden explosiveness. Like clockwork it came, "You can all go to hell. I'm doing the best I can, and that's all anyone can ask!"

It was Bob who came to the rescue. His experience in his work with children had taken him into domestic court. Here he had seen, as the result of the teamwork between psychiatrists, psychologists and social workers within the framework of the court, how they managed some of the delinquency problems, especially training and similar characteristic difficulties. The vitalness of this experience he felt was that he had learned the difference between restrictive and punitive actions as opposed to firm discipline given with kindness. He explained that at first it was hard to see this difference but that later he realized that these children needed a dependable, consistent and reliable authority to serve as a model in becoming human beings capable of getting along with others. He cited the case of a boy in which the only way to reach him and have him understand this value was to remove him from his home environment and give him what amounted to a new family as found in an institution. In this new setting the child was finally able to see his rebellion.

And as Bob talked about this boy he came to realize that it was essential for a child to have the courage to engage in verbal exchange with whomever he felt in conflict. Otherwise, the child would, in frustration, rebel, without realizing what was causing his rebellion. Bob concluded the telling of his experience by citing the fact that the removal from the original family produced in such cases a hitherto unappreciated value in the child's mind. This value appeared to be a renewed attempt to belong to a group structure, as this boy had demonstrated by his behavior in the institution. The verification of this he saw in the boy's new pattern of engaging in discussions rather than in physically destructive behavior. Some time after the boy had improved, he told Bob that it was easier to fight through his differences with others than it was to hold in anger. Such feelings had made him secretly go off by himself and break things belonging to others, which later led him to feel ashamed of himself.

Strongly impressed by what Bob was saying, I joined him in agreement, and said, "It is an important realization for all human beings to discover that they have less anxiety once they accept the idea that not running away from difficulties with others contributes to their basic security."

Then the group began a long discussion dealing with the clarification between corrective discipline and punitive retaliation on the part of the group. The consensus reached, with one exception—John, of course—was that there was a marked difference between these two items. It was then that Moe suggested that the group adopt a practice illustrated by Bob's experience with the boy. He proposed that, when lateness occurred, the matter be first investigated by the doctor as to its realistic unavoidable nature. Then, if the opinion of the majority of the group was that the lateness was not unavoidable but was an act of defiance, the group, instead of engaging in discussion, would request the late-comer to leave that session. In this way, the nonverbal aggression would be encouraged to take verbal and direct expression in the next session.

Again, John protested quite vehemently.

Personally, I was very pleased to hear Molly say, "Even though I've been one of the most frequent offenders, I'm for this method. I do see the merit of it."

Moe asked me if I would conduct a poll to see whether or not the group would accept such collective authority. All voted "yes" except John, and I abstained so as not to discourage John from further objections.

At that point, it was Molly who said to John, "Well, it's the majority's opinion and I want to know if you're willing to accept it."

John shrugged his shoulders to indicate that he didn't have much choice in the matter and that he would make his decision when and if such an occasion arose.

Claudia asked if anyone besides herself needed clarification as to what the majority had agreed to pertaining to such behavior. There was a chorus of "yeses" to this and so she proceeded, "I understand that the Doc is to be the judge of this domestic court. And that, as the judge, he is to interview all late-comers in the presence of the others, i.e., the jury. And then it's up to us to decide whether the lateness was unavoidable or an act of rebellion against one or several members of the group. If two thirds of us consider that the late-comer had come late because he or she didn't want to face these people, the person in question would be asked to leave for that session, to underscore that it's easier to fight and solve one's problems than to stay away or come late, since the value of 'belonging' is so vital to people in general and especially to people who use such means of defiance."

Again, a wave of "yeses" followed, with the now customary exception of John's approval.

With this turn of events, it became obvious that I should sum things up. "Very well, I understand your decision, but I would like you to consider a few additional points. Since you have appointed me the judge and interviewer, it might be better if I did not join in the voting. Also, would you agree that by my remaining neutral in these deliberations, it might be more possible for both the late-comer and the others to experience the maturing value of accepting the responsibilities involved, without depending upon my judgment?

"This way, you, the group as a whole, will have to engage in a real thought process and rely upon your own inner resources. I admit that there is some inherent danger that the group may make a mistake, but mistakes are often the soil in which things grow and therefore, despite the momentary blunder, the over-all effect of growth can be enhanced."

"I like what you just said, Doc. It gives us the necessary stimulus to take what we do more seriously than would have been the case if we'd relied on your judgment," spoke up Tom.

"That goes for me, too," quickly followed Moe.

It was Betty who said, "The Doc sure does want us to have the experience of growing. It's just the opposite of the attitude that was present in my home."

"It puts a big burden on all of us," broke in Molly. "I'm not so sure that I feel comfortable with this amount of authority but I feel that the Doc is right."

"Well, is there anyone against this last part that the Doc has added to our original agreement?" questioned Eve.

Slowly, in a guarded way, everyone responded to her in the affirmative, with John saying, "That's the only part of this whole damn thing that I *do* agree with."

134

As you might have guessed, it was John who presented the court with its first case. The circumstances, as you also might gather, were bound to be complicated. My questioning revealed that he had left work and gone home instead of coming directly to the session. He realized that this was cutting it rather close, but he alibied that he had done this successfully in the past and that if his subway train had not stalled for fifteen minutes between Grand Central and my office, he would have made it in ample time. I asked him to retire and wait for our decision. He obeyed promptly. The discussion was a lively one. In all truth, I thought the group conducted themselves well. They discharged their responsibility with zeal and keen awareness of the issues at stake. Molly was most revealing in the matter. Although the one having the greatest difficulty in being on time, she was the most erudite in her discussion. Her canny ability to decipher the rationalization aided the jury's decision immeasurably. In my role as judge, I remained silent throughout the jury's deliberations.

After approximately twenty minutes, Moe, as the foreman of the jury, reported the decision. It was unanimous. As judge, I was to tell John that despite his lack of healthy respect for his group, he was not to be expelled from the session this time, but if his lateness occurred again on the same grounds, he could no longer participate in that session or in any other in which he flouted the group's authority.

John received the recommendation of the court with dignity. In fact, he was amazed at the justness exhibited. He had fully expected to be expelled. The 'fair shake' he received went a long way in persuading him to accept an authority outside of and greater than himself.

Acting as jurors in a court also had its beneficial effects. A discussion in the following session showed evidence of this most clearly. The interval between sessions had given the group an opportunity to reflect upon their decision and action. They entered the session with pride. It was Moe who praised Molly. He told her that the value of "belonging" that she was demonstrating had reacted favorably on him and perhaps this was true for all of the group. This set off a whole round of appreciation for her guidance.

And before the discussion had ended, some other realizations were reached. Namely, that they had collectively formed an authority greater than a single individual—and that this authority had aided their own self-respect.

Perhaps most surprised of all was Betty, who said, "It actually was a thrill to think in unison with other people." It helped Tom in appreciating how it felt to be on the other side of the fence when authority had to hand out discipline. His comment was, "and I used to think it was easy to give orders!" The discussion ended on a happy note, with the judge congratulating the jury and acknowledging their maturity. The jury, in turn, complimented the defendant upon his dignified acceptance of their decision.

10. *And All Through the House*

In mid-December, Claudia came in for a special individual session. Her affair had been going rather well—in fact, it was quite remarkable how closely it approximated the characteristics and properties of the romance of Eve and Bob. The latter's relationship had developed as they had planned earlier in the fall. They had taken an apartment. Their sharing a common abode brought about none of the unwarranted problems feared by their fellow group members. Quite the contrary; proximity had brought about an emotional intensity not previously reached. The warmth and respect the two felt for each other had not completely allayed the skepticism of the group. Nonetheless, Bob and Eve went on blithely enjoying these arrangements. There was, however, a trace of hostility in their efforts: I frequently felt that this determination of theirs to get along was in some small way a manifest of "We'll show them." This was mostly a matter of omissions—that is to say, by comparison with other couples they refrained abnormally from ordinary disputes and quarrels. This special characteristic is a "tattle tale gray" sign which exists quite frequently when couples are not legally wed.

The feeling I received from Claudia's enchantment in terms of the parallelism brought a picture to my mind: That of a little girl playing house—a little girl dressed up in high-heeled shoes and her mother's clothing, playing house with the boy next door. This game that children so frequently indulge in has much to be said for it. Its healthy aspects are seen in the fact that the children so closely imitate their parents' marital structure. Similarly, it was almost as if Claudia were riding in the wake of her mother—as Eve, the mother ship, plowed through the seas.

The degree of Claudia's romance was somewhat less in scope than that of Eve's. No doubt the never-to-be-forgotten memory of her frightful marriage served to curtail the depth of the relationship. On this subject, as far as one could tell, Claudia had been demonstrating very little conscious self-recrimination of late. Instead, the nightmare of her marriage was influencing her very behavior in this affair without conscious design. Her increased concern with discretion and contraception, for example, demonstrated this clearly.

New-found courage was evident. In her disastrously fated marriage, her energy seemed to have been that derived from hostility and running away from loneliness, while in the present relationship, her energy bespoke a resourcefulness kindled by her group experience.

On this particular day, shortly before Christmas, Claudia looked the picture of a fresh young cover girl. She was at her loveliest in a rust-brown cashmere sweater set and matching plaid skirt. Her chestnut hair was brushed in a tasteful page-boy arrangement. The week before, she had stopped after a group session to request this appointment with me. The request was a departure from her usual behavior and so showed its importance. She had arrived on schedule and this too reminded me of her increased sense of responsibility. As we sat down, I opened the conversation with, "Well, it's nice to have the opportunity to talk alone, Claudia."

"Yes, it is," she replied. "It's been some time since we have, hasn't it?"

I could not help noticing that she had learned so much, so well, from Eve. It was as if she had gone to finishing school. She was the image of poise and sophistication as she sat before me. Deftly, she smoked her cigarette. She moved her head with feminine aplomb in emphasizing various points.

"I've been having some physical distress," she went on, "and my distress is not confined to my physical symptoms. That is, I can't seem to make up my mind whether what's troubling me physically is what you might term psychosomatic."

"Well," I said gently, "why don't you tell me what your symptoms are and let me relieve you of the burden of attempting to make that decision."

"Fine," she responded. "But first I must say how happy I am that I'm able to discuss this at all, and especially with a man with whom I'm emotionally involved."

I moved my head in simple approval in order not to break her trend of thought.

"It all began two months ago—or was it three? Well, anyway, at that time, I had a menstrual period which was unusually heavy. At the time, I didn't pay too much attention to it. During the next month, I noticed that at times, during relations, I would have sharp pains, despite the fact that I was having more sexual pleasure than I had ever experienced. At first, I felt that these were due to the physical activity, but later, when the same pains occurred even without physical relationship, I realized that was not the cause. In addition, I have felt somewhat logy and heavy in this area. I notice that my ankles are swollen at the end of the day. At times there seems to be a return of my listlessness and lack of interest—you remember, the way I was at the very beginning of therapy? So you can see why I'm confused. I don't know whether it's my guilt feelings about sex, and I'm starting to slip back, or if there is something really physically wrong with me."

"Claudia," I said, and I'm sure she sensed my acceptance, "you've made me happy by placing this confidence in me. It's a pleasure to see you use the sound judgment that you have by seeking medical advice." She smiled with appreciation. "May I point out to you, Claudia, that you, yourself, have mentioned that you have an emotional involvement with me as a 'man.' This is as it needs to be for successful psychotherapy. However, it precludes my giving you a physical examination." Hardly had these words left my lips when she heaved an audible sigh of relief.

"That makes me feel better. It would be too confusing for me if you examined me."

I smiled and nodded silent agreement. Changing the subject without being obtrusive, I moved quickly into the next phase of her problem. "Are you emotionally prepared to be examined by a colleague of mine?"

"I believe I am," she said.

"Well, then, that's fine," I said in a deliberately paternal manner. "I have great respect for Dr. Green, with whom I share hospital affiliations. In addition to being an excellent gynecologist, he has a background of psychiatric experience and more than a passing acquaintance with psychosomatic problems of the female pelvis. I feel sure that you will find him pleasant and just what you need in this situation."

"Doctor," she responded, "anyone you recommend would be perfectly all right, I'm sure."

I thanked her, and we left it that I would call Dr. Green, and that she was to stop in after the group session that evening to confirm the arrangements.

Before Claudia left, we spent a few minutes reviewing her current psychiatric status. This amounted primarily to my letting her know how pleased I was with her obvious improvement. Further evidence of her improvement was the acceptance of this praise without affectation or denial.

That evening the group seemed inoculated with holiday spirit. There was an increased, joyous friendliness which found expression in constant reference to the holiday and its influence upon the various people.

However, Eve sounded one element of discord in this otherwise harmonious atmosphere. She was unfriendly to the point of silence. I had never seen Eve like this before. True, she had been passive and silent at other times, but now her expression and mannerisms suggested a state of being which was alien to us. As I look back upon it, a trace of fear seemed mixed with a sense of not belonging to the event.

Here she sat, very much a member, very much a vital part of the group—and yet detached. For the longest while, this single discordant note wasn't commented upon. Bob, apparently not wishing to embarrass Eve, kept taking side glances at her when he felt that she wasn't noticing him.

In the presence of his silence, I could not be sure as to why he did not speak to her but I felt that as a part of his loyalty to her, he did not want to be upsetting. He was not unlike the person who is very close to someone ill at ease and does not make open reference to the distress because of fear that speaking would hinder rather than help matters.

Eve's painful silence continued, nevertheless, without disturbing the prevailing harmony. Even Claudia, her favorite child, refused to become enmeshed in Eve's distress.

Betty had the floor. "I have an idea. I hope you won't consider it silly or childish, but I think it would be fun if we could have a little party here at our next session since it will be the last meeting before Christmas. Maybe we could exchange gifts from a grab bag or something of the sort."

Immediately, there arose two factions. The responses were firm indeed, with no middle ground.

Bob more or less led the "con" group. He was the first to answer Betty's proposal. "Such nonsense—such childishness. You'll never get me to go along with this," he said with the disgust that an urbanite might easily display for the naïveté of a rural unsophisticate.

"I don't believe Betty meant that you had to, Bob," said Claudia in slight protestation.

"Yeah," Moe said, "what's all the hullabaloo about? She only came up with a suggestion which is at least appropriate for the season of the year. So what if it is a bit childish?"

As dependable as a seventeen-jewel watch, Tom gave his almost predictable response. "Nah, I don't like this idea. It's too much work. I've got enough problems of my own without starting this kind of stuff."

"Now I'm not saying I'm in favor of this, mind you, or for that matter against it," John spoke up in a courageous voice, "it just sounds to me as if Betty is trying to please the doctor."

With this, I looked directly at John in openmouthed astonishment, but said nothing.

Betty darted back at him. "Are you kidding? Why, he's as innocent of what you accuse him as possible."

"That's not my point," rallied John. "It's just this. I didn't mean that the doctor had put you up to it, Betty, but merely that you think that the doctor might feel this is a good idea to make the group work better together."

"You know, sometimes I think you're completely 'bats,' John," said Betty. "I don't believe you ever give me credit for a single shred of originality."

"You're wrong again," said John. "I believe you have a lot of originality. After all, look at your occupation—dress designer—you've got to have it. It's just that you're always trying to think up things that will bring you closer to your dear doctor."

"Oh, John, you make me sick," she replied. "Of course I think the doctor is a perfect dear but that has nothing to do with it. I was simply thinking of the fun we could have. I can honestly say that I was only thinking of us, the patients, for a change. It was almost as if the doctor wasn't the doctor. I mean, if you understand me, that we were all just equals for a change."

"You mean like an office party, Betty?" Molly asked.

"Well, in a way, but not exactly. It's hard to say what it reminds me of, and I suppose, now that I think of it, Bob is right to a degree. It reminds me of some of the parties we had when we were in school, just before Christmas."

"As far as I'm concerned," Molly said, surprisingly, "although it sounds childish and I'm not really much for it, I'll string along with what the majority decides."

"By the way, we haven't even asked the Doc his opinion on the matter," said Bob.

There was an air of hope in his voice—hope that I would somehow disperse and nullify this distasteful scene for him.

"Bob," I said, "I feel that it is not my place to give an opinion in this matter."

"Well, if that's the case," he went on, "perhaps it's best that we do continue to discuss it." Like a ward politician at election-time, he turned to Moe and said, "Moe, can you see yourself as a former college basketball star and Korean veteran standing in the center of this room fishing a gift out of a Christmas grab bag for yourself? Really, can you?"

"Look, Bob," said Moe with low-grade annoyance, "I think you're giving me a selling job."

"Not at all, Moe, not at all," said Bob. "I'm merely appealing to your manliness."

"Who're you kidding?" returned Moe. "That's not the issue at all. The point is simply this. You don't seem to sense that there is therapy involved in playing this make-believe, kid game, Bob. The reason you don't see it is, that it's *your* manliness you're attempting to rally and protect. And what's going on while you're doing this? You're missing the boat. I mean while you're protecting yourself from participating in a kid's game, you fail to realize that a kid's game might produce some valuable material. I know that every time we do do something here and play it out in some kind of re-enactment, it always jogs my memory, and then I begin to feel differently and usually better about these very same memories.

"It's sort of like this: the thing that I can't remember any longer needs to be forgotten because of the painfulness. I'll give you an example of what I mean, Bob. The time we were talking about baseball here and the Doc joined in the conversation. You see, my old man was a real bastard. I had forgotten just how bad and low down he made me feel. I was feeling so low down and worthless, I didn't even remember how I got to that opinion of myself. Then this past October when the Series was on and we were talking about it at the beginning of one of our group sessions here, the Doc's interest in baseball amazed me. Not just because a psychiatrist knew so much about baseball, but because he was so friendly about it at the same time. When he accepted my opinions concerning players and the game, it suddenly made me recall an incident of my childhood. Do you all remember it now? I told some of you about it the last time we met, just before the session began. But in case you've forgotten or didn't hear about it, I'll repeat it.

"That son-of-a-so-and-so old man of mine beat the living daylights out of me once because I went to the Yankee Stadium to see a ball game out of the money I received from a nice old lady as a tip. He thought I had stolen the money from the cash register. Well, when the Doc was so friendly, it lifted a mist that had been hanging over me for years—a mist that used to say to me, 'Moe, you're not much of anything.' It never made such a difference that I was a good athlete and popular in college or for that matter in the Navy, and now I know why. I couldn't accept myself because my old man wouldn't accept me. But ever since we had that talk with the Doc about baseball, I can stand myself. So Bob, I hope you can understand me and why I feel you don't realize the importance of playing or living through a child's game."

Bob, like the rest of the group, was visibly moved by the sincerity and clarity of Moe's communication. After several moments of appreciative, respectful silence, he said, "The only thing I can say after that is, I'm for it."

"And you?" inquired Betty, turning toward Tom.

In his usual flat tone, he responded, "Oh, I guess I'll go along."

Suddenly it struck each of them. Eve had not spoken during the entire session. Again the author of the idea spoke, but this time benevolently. "Eve, you haven't said a word all evening. Is anything wrong? Are you upset?"

Eve dropped her gaze to the floor and her shoulders sagged. A moment or two passed before she spoke, with a sigh. "I know I haven't spoken all evening and I can't remember when I've been more melancholy than I am now. It would be foolish to say I know why, because I don't. All I know is that ever since I arrived this mood has been with me. I wasn't this way before the session started; it's all a mystery to me. If you don't mind—it's not that I don't appreciate your idea, Betty, or your concern for me, but would you mind terribly if you just went on without me?"

"I understand," said Betty, more puzzled than truly understanding.

With this, Eve said a polite, but short, "Thank you."

Bob reached over and took her hand. She looked a little startled, gave an appreciative smile, but resumed her previous mood.

As one might expect, Eve's behavior bothered Claudia. She waited no longer. Obviously distressed she said to Eve, "It pains me to see you so."

Eve replied, "Claudia, I'm sorry—but I can't help it. You'll just have to let it go for the time being."

"Very well," Betty said in a somewhat more cheerful tone, "let's do what she asks. Let's leave her alone."

A low acknowledgment of Betty's suggestion followed. All of us were able to divert our attention from Eve, except Claudia. We went on to the remaining business at hand.

Ignoring his previous position on the subject, Bob suddenly concentrated his attention upon the matter. "Let's see," he began, "how should we do this?"

"I suppose the best way," broke in Molly, "would be to put the names in a hat, and then we can all draw and give a gift to the person whose name we have."

"Not so fast," John interrupted, "I'm still not convinced that I, myself, want to participate in this event."

"Here he goes into outer space again," snapped Tom sarcastically.

"Oh, go to hell, Tom," John burst out. "I've got a right to do what I want here. I don't have to sacrifice my individuality for the good of the group."

"Man, you're really gone," said Bob mockingly. "You're real gone. Nobody's giving up any of his individuality when he engages in group interaction. The truth of the matter is, you can't give up what you haven't got."

"Okay, have it your way, Einstein," John barked at Bob.

In swept the peacemaker, Moe. "Look, John, nobody's forcing anything down your throat. Look at Eve, for example. The group has respected her request to be left out of these arrangements, hasn't it?"

"Uh—ah—I guess so," he answered; "I guess so."

At this point, I broke my silence. "John, do you have trouble receiving gifts or compliments from people?"

"Well, as a matter of fact, I do, Doc," he said, slightly recovered from his deflation.

"Well, John, you're not alone in this. Several of us here, I feel, in our protests tonight have revealed this particular inadequacy. In fact, I don't quite agree with the attitude that says 'It's better to give than to receive.' I have found that many people have had more difficulty in receiving than in giving. This, I believe, is due to the issue of humility. Grandiose people can dispense gifts to others so magnanimously that they feel the act proves their superiority. Thus, when the tables are turned, receiving becomes equivalent to inferiority. Humility is not inferiority, but rather dignity with self-respect. In terms of receiving and giving, humility is a free and accessible two-way street."

With these words, for the first time in the history of our association, I was able to catch John's eyes without his turning away. The moment that followed was gratifying for both of us, though brief. He said but two words—"Thank you."

Betty, who obviously had picked up considerable self-confidence throughout the session, continued to develop her project. "I agree with you, Molly, let's put names in a hat. Also, what do you say about doing it this way—let's limit ourselves to a dollar and let's say that everyone has to create something; not merely buy it."

"Sounds okay to me," said Moe.

"Me too," added Claudia.

"Okay," said Tom.

"I agree," came in Bob.

"And me," followed John.

"I'll make it unanimous," concluded Molly.

With this accomplished, I spoke again. "As the host, I will serve the food and remain outside of the exchange as I feel this will ensure the highest degree of equitable therapy."

With silent acknowledgment they apparently accepted the necessity of my position. Had I entered into the exchange, obviously there would have been seven people to whom I could not have given a gift. Conversely, one patient would be in the favorable position of expressing himself to me without the others having an equal opportunity. It would have reduced the group psychology to individual psychology. They were immediately able to perceive the idea and they accepted my decision.

By offering the food, I symbolized my desire to maintain the group function and equality between all of the patients and myself. In addition, it fostered my position as the parent figure.

"Well," I continued, "would someone volunteer the use of a hat?"

Bob sprang to his feet and walked to the closet, typifying the role of the oldest son. In so doing, he said, "It's a pleasure to offer my lid."

Betty turned to me and said, "May I write the names on separate pieces of paper, Doc?"

"By all means, Betty."

She opened her feed bag purse and produced a small notebook. Quickly, she tore out seven pages and jotted down the names. As she finished, Bob walked over and extended his grey felt hat, and she dropped the folded pieces of paper into it.

I then turned to Bob, "Would you please do the honors?" He looked at me with some hesitance but quickly recovered himself. Beginning with Betty, he went from left to right, stopping in front of each patient to be sure that none had drawn his own name.

Eve, although improved, was still under the weather. I gave her a quick smile, turned to the group and bade them good night.

I called Claudia into my inner office to give her instructions about her gynecological consultation. She was to go to Dr. Green's office on Saturday at noon. I assured her that I had given him what I considered the germane history.

She showed her newly found courage and also gave herself some reassurance by saying, "I've begun to understand something about the need of being a person in one's own eyes. As I look back, I realize that I was unable to accept myself; and that furthermore, I may have even been in love with myself. I now realize that loving oneself leads inevitably to hating oneself. I suppose self-love and self-hate are nothing more than opposite sides of the same coin. I know I couldn't grow to like myself until I stopped this vicious circle of self-love and self-hate. I believe I loved myself by getting into one unfortunate situation after another, then soothing my wounds with self-pity, which is just another guise of self-love. When I hated myself, it was as if I were indulging in self-punishment for two reasons: One, because in loving myself I became guilty of not loving anyone else. The second reason was that when I failed to live up to the image created by the self-love, I naturally, of course, would have to hate myself for such failures. Sometimes, when the self-hatred got too intense, I couldn't stand it any longer and I began to hate others as if they were me. Do you know, Doc, that I've written in a little notebook which I carry in my purse the saying 'People who can't be people, can't stand people.' I realize now why they can't; because self-pitying people simply aren't people to themselves."

"Well, well, my dear Claudia," I responded with deep admiration for her lucidity and maturity, "you certainly have come a long way, and I'm very proud of you."

"But, Doctor," she protested, "it was your being a person to me that started it. It made me think—if the doctor can treat me as a person and expects me to be one to him, it certainly must be possible. It made it so much easier to be nicer to myself. So you see, Doctor, although I appreciate your being proud of me, this wouldn't have been, were it not for the 'you-and-me' spirit that exists in our wonderful group."

After Claudia left the office, I remained for a while longer in meditation. My reflections produced an array of possibilities. Perhaps her rapid strides of emotional progress did have a connection with her physical illness after all. It was possible that they were not related in the usual psychosomatic sense, but maybe the physical state had brought on a greater rate of insight. I had seen this process occur in others before. Whenever these people became physically ill, they seemed to pay more attention to themselves and the world about them. This increased their sense of reality. In fact it reinforced their relationship to reality. With this speculation, I concluded my brief, intensive sojourn and headed for home.

11. *The Party*

The day of the party was a busy one. During free moments, the various members of the group came to my office with odd-sized packages wrapped in brown paper which concealed a gift wrapping and the identity of the giver. The purpose of this extra trip was to insure the anonymity of the giver. The gifts were left in the spare closet. By nightfall, the closet was jammed full and the spirit of Christmas was undeniably coloring the simplest thoughts and actions. I even detected a note of envy in my secretary. She half jokingly sighed, "Ah, to be a patient!"

I had purchased some apple cider and an assortment of German Christmas cookies. In so doing, I had discovered a pleasant excitation within myself, even though I understood, in a general way, what had been set up. The festive mood, with all its surprises and newness, had captivated me unmistakably.

In looking back upon it now, it wasn't so strange after all— I guess we all desire to be pleasantly surprised. I certainly did not have any detailed premonitions about what was going to happen, but merely knew that something of promise was in the offing. Certainly there was no way of knowing what the event was going to mean to each individual, yet undeniably I felt that we were all going to engage in something different from what we had ever done before, as individuals or as a group.

Along with this air of the unexpected, came a lucid perspective. It was like being able to see the whole area of our journey. In seeing this imagery, the about-to-occur session seemed to represent the halfway mark of our travels. There was a comfort in this. And though there had not been any verbal verification by the others, the manner in which they had finally got together in spirit for this occasion removed from my mind any doubt that we were a functioning group. The painful days of early growth were behind us. No longer did anyone raise questions concerning the validity of the therapy in our group. We were looking ahead in our lives to the immediate future with an attitude of hoped-for enjoyment rather than bemoaning our painful pasts.

When eight o'clock at last arrived, the group-therapy room was a picture of gaiety. Nearly everyone had arrived a half hour earlier. Some pretended the reason for this was holiday office closings, but their joyous anxiety was very much like that of children standing on the staircase Christmas Eve, waiting for Santa.

Each had gone out of his way to dress for the occasion—Betty in particular. She wore a red wool sheath dress in keeping with the season, and her long dark hair was tied in a pony tail by a matching ribbon. With her face wreathed in smiles, her beautiful teeth and carefully lipsticked mouth completed this red and white picture.

Even Molly had taken pains with her appearance. She wore a green silk dress of simple design, obviously fitted and properly tailored. As a result, her firm-bosomed figure looked quite appealing.

Tom, shoes polished and all, wore his best navy blue suit. Although he had made every attempt to look well for the party, he still lacked that "finishing touch."

Moe, however, did make the grade. He had on a medium grey flannel suit with a red-plaid tie. In general, he gave the impression of being a type he certainly was not—one of the well-groomed Madison Avenue boys.

Bob, in a beautiful Brooks Brothers brown tweed suit with a blending tan Italian silk tie, radiated an air of luxury. The aroma of his handsome, long-stemmed pipe scented the room pleasantly.

His posture—one leg extended nonchalantly over the arm of his chair—completed the picture of gentry at home. He told a series of humorous anecdotes which helped put the group at ease.

Eve, who sat beside him, was still depressed. She looked pretty but was much too conservative in her appearance. Her Dior blue gown, with its high neckline, trimmed with black jet, was the one incongruous note in the room. Still following the cautious route in relationship to Eve's distress, Bob went right along with the most comfortable thing for her. That is, he did not force her into small talk or participation. It would have been wrong for any of us to assume that this was an indifference toward Eve on his part; actually, it was an appreciation of her desires.

John, perhaps the happiest of all, had on a dark brown worsted suit with a matching bow tie and surprisingly was the most attentive to Bob's stories.

Claudia was pretty. She looked like a debutante in a ruffled gown of pale pink taffeta trimmed with light blue. As she sat listening to Bob's narrative, she folded her legs and clasped her hands about her knees. She was the last one to catch my eye; it was difficult to draw my gaze away.

"Merry Christmas, everyone," I greeted them, instead of with the usual "Good evening," as I sat down.

In my own enthusiasm, I completely forgot my duties as the host. Recovering quickly from that faux pas, I arose, excused myself and explained that I would bring in the refreshments. All the girls asked if they could be of help and I accepted their offer. We went into the adjacent kitchenette and everything was ready to serve in a jiffy.

During the last stages of these preparations, I went to the closet containing the gifts. I removed the brown paper wrappings, returned and, with assistance from the boys, placed the gifts in the center of the group.

Now the spirit of the occasion has reached its gayest peak. Furtively, to release his own inner tension, Bob said, pointing to me, "There he is, our great big Santa Claus."

As the object of the remark, I responded, "Believe it or not,

151

people, I'm enjoying this." This brief exchange released the extreme tension which was bringing us precariously near to the kindling point.

Without further ado, I picked up the nearest gift. Its card read: "To Betty." It was the largest package of all. Betty rose, and came over to unwrap it. The present was in a three-by-five-foot corrugated cardboard box, and after some awkwardness, she finally had it unwrapped. Her reaction was delighted. Betty, as the instigator of this special evening, had appeared to be radiantly happy, and upon seeing her gift every vestige of restraint was cast aside.

"Oh, oh," she bubbled, "isn't it wonderful? Look everyone! Why, it even lights up. It's so clever. It must have taken whoever gave this to me days to make."

We all gazed at her gift. It was a giant-sized doll, but one made out of varying sizes of tin cans. It had a battery and light arrangement so that the eyes lit up. A mop, dyed brown, served as its hair, complemented by a bright yellow dress. The legs were made up of several cans of graduating sizes. With the doll went a mounting stand attached to the wooden skeletonlike supporting internal structure. Betty cuddled the doll's head close to her.

"Is this supposed to be me?" she asked, with a tongue-in-cheek laugh. She turned the doll's head slightly, and behold, it began to speak! In low metallic tones it rumbled, "Come, let's do something. Come, let's do something," repeating this mechanically over and over again.

A small recording apparatus had been linked up to a battery, and the creator had so constructed the system that when the head moved it released the recording.

Betty was so moved by this final touch that spontaneous tears flowed over her cheeks—the tears of a human being suddenly overwhelmed by an abrupt introduction to a hitherto unknown area of herself.

"Of course," she cried, "it's me—it's me! I'm happy but ashamed. It's wonderful to know that others know me this well. And yet, I can't help but feel embarrassed. I know there's no need to apologize for my actions in therapy, but I do feel a sense of responsibility for my outbursts from time to time and I'm sorry. I will always keep this wonderful doll. Whenever I need reassurance that others have loved me despite myself, I'll turn on the lights in the doll, and listen to its litany. It's the gift of a lifetime."

At this point, I broke in, "Betty, it's fine that you appreciate the creativity of the gift-giver as well as the obvious understanding the gift shows. However, may I point out to you that no inanimate object should serve in such a fashion for an emotionally healthy person. I hope that as the years roll by and you look at this doll you will smile and say, 'This is the way I used to be—now I am more fully related to people.' In the final analysis, Betty, the manner in which you treat yourself will determine whether or not you have friends, and will also determine what kind of friends you have, and the nature of your happiness. No artificial prop such as this doll or any other ritualistic symbol can ever replace the warmth of a human relationship. And so, Betty, whenever you feel unsure of yourself, don't turn to something idolatrous or for that matter away from yourself. As you have seen from others' experiences here, we never are so inadequate as we believe ourselves to be. Work yourself back into self-acceptance by 'living it through' with another human being."

The air of the room had changed from enchanted amazement over the mechanical genius exemplified in the gift to a more sober tone. This connoted the depth of the passive participation they had felt while listening to the exchange between Betty and me.

"Betty, who do you think gave you your gift?" I asked.

"Gee, Doc, that's not too hard to guess. Tom, of course. First, his job makes him gifted with materials of this kind. Second, I have always felt that, despite his gruff exterior and passive participation, he understood the various crises I had gone through. I say this because whenever he looks at me there is a gentler understanding in his eyes."

"It's true, Betty," Tom said with extreme embarrassment, "I do feel I understand what you have been going through. And what the Doc said about being warm and friendly is what I meant.

You see, both of us are sort of like tin cans. We are stiff and unbending instead of being warm, especially when it comes to boy/girl friends."

Haltingly, her hands pressed together in front of her, and with her head tilted to the side, Betty spoke directly to him. "I—I—guess you're—uh—right." And then, in a more composed manner, "Thank you, Tom, very much. Thank you very, very much." These words brought a round of approval from the group, showing their admiration for Tom's fine contribution.

"Well, shall we go on? But before we do—how about some more cake, cookies and cider?" I interjected.

Claudia came to me, "May I do the serving, Doc?"

"Of course, Claudia, that would be fine."

While the refreshments were being passed, I reached for the next gift. Marked "To John," it was a rather small box, unlike its predecessor. As I gave him the gift, John smiled and said, "Thank you." His hands revealed a slight, understandable tremor as he removed the wrappings. It was a necktie, obviously not purchased in a store. Hand-knitted, it was scarlet and slightly longer than usual. He stared at the tie for some time before speaking. Then, in a voice revealing confusion, he stuttered, "It's got me puzzled. I don't know what the message is. Obviously the one who gave me this has put considerable effort into the project. I guess I'm afraid to speculate. This reveals my usual fear—I don't want to be unappreciative or offending. For all I know the person may have felt kindly toward me, and yet somehow there's a disturbing quality about it all."

"Go on, John," I said encouragingly. "This is therapy. You must have courage to explore."

"Okay, I will. I feel that one of the women gave this to me, and I feel that she must be confused in her feelings toward me. That is because the gift represents two extremes. Anyone expending so much energy must care quite a bit about me. On the other hand, the other extreme is revealed by the angry overtones present. The color is so furious, and the stitches are spaced so differently, which suggests that, though this is a person who knows how to knit, she was switching back and forth in her emotions while work-

154

ing on the tie. It's as though she didn't know whether or not to continue her kindly feelings. The impression it gives me is that the girl involved likes me, but is also hostile to me. I don't know whether she is hostile because she likes me, or if she is hostile and likes me, but whichever it is, I must represent a dilemma for her." As he uttered these last words he seemed to have picked up a sense of self-confidence. He surveyed the room with an air of "Well, I've solved that one."

The expectant silence was pierced by Molly's voice. "Yes, yes, all you say is true, John. It was I who gave you the gift, and I am quite confused about my feelings toward you. One minute I think you are terrific and the next minute I could bash your head in. I'm both driven toward you and repelled by you, and the more I think about it, the more I begin to realize what I'm doing. As long as I see you giving people hell and standing up for your rights I think, 'What a guy, what a guy. He's such an individual.' But just as soon as I feel that you accept me and want to get closer to me, I feel like hurting you."

"Sounds like love by proxy," quipped John.

"You're right, but go to hell," she retorted with a mixture of emotions both hostile and friendly.

"All I know is this," John continued. "I like you—I think you have the makings of a person. But I swear I never know how to take you. You're so inconsistent. In fact, the more I think about it, the more I realize that the only consistent thing about you is your inconsistency. When I come here nights, I always say to myself, 'Now, John, old boy, old fellow, wait and see what kind of a position Molly takes on something before you try to get involved with her.' I've found, from having my toes trampled once too often, that this is the best approach with you. I never sail right in until I know just how the land lies with you."

"I don't blame you, John," she quickly answered, at the same time seeming to sink within herself with remorse.

Sensing this distress, John ventured once more, "Molly, there is no need for self-incrimination. You're only feeling sorry for yourself now. You haven't injured me. In fact, this whole thing has brought us more understanding. Granted our relationship leaves much to be desired—we'll never get anywhere with ourselves and others if, every time we try and the thing doesn't come up to our expectations, we return to our shells. So look, girl, don't die on me, stay with it. I'm your friend, and you are mine."

She raised her head, looked around the room, then turned to him with a childish smile. "Okay, you win. I'm with it."

"Well, let's see who gets the next gift," I said to keep the session moving. This one, for Bob, was a two-by-three-and-one-half-foot flat package. He unwrapped it rather uneasily. Upon its exposure there was a collective "Ah" from the entire group. It was a water-color original, showing a man standing on a high windy hill, surveying the landscape. It was done in a primitive style but the work was obviously that of a professional. At the foot of the hill there flowed a river. The over-all impression of the picture was that of a lonely young man seeking communication.

At first Bob went through a long dissertation upon the beauty of the gift and its fine professional quality, associating it with well-known works of modern art. He continued in this vein almost as if he were a guide in a museum giving an unusually friendly talk about one of the exhibits. Not once did he stray from this seemingly calculated approach to reveal what his personal feelings were.

Finally, Tom interrupted him impatiently. "Yeah, but what do *you* feel, Bob—what do you feel about it? What does it do to you?"

A sombre silence fell upon Bob. He made several attempts to speak, but only parts of words came out. At last he said, "Well, I like it. It's very beautiful, and I guess the man in the picture is actually supposed to be me."

"If that's the case," I said, "what is the man in the picture feeling, Bob?"

"Well, Doc, he's obviously lonely and feeling it. Furthermore, it gives me the impression that he's had trouble and has gone to this spot to hold council with himself."

"What do you believe his story to be?" I interjected.

"Perhaps he's been disappointed at home, and has gone out on this walk in a state of dejection. Perhaps he hopes to find himself while communicating with his own thoughts."

156

"Do you think he will, Bob?" I asked.

"Well, maybe he will, but I rather believe he'd be better off finding a friend."

"Exactly, and isn't that just you?" I responded.

"Yes, it is, and it's funny how a picture like this can get *you* to see what is the most obvious thing to others," he went on, almost in soliloquy. "Yes, it's true—I need friends, and yet I'm afraid of having them. It's almost as if I believe only weaklings need people. I now realize I really owe you people a great debt. You've had to fight, argue and almost literally hammer me down to get me to be one of you." Releasing much of his inner tension, he came forth with a rhetorical question. "Why do we so frequently fight that which we need so badly, and which is so good for us?"

After a moment of thoughtful silence, Moe spoke. "Bob, I feel at long last that you're really one of us. Now maybe you can appreciate why I took the position I did concerning this party. Maybe it's silly and childish, but I know that this kind of thing does recapture and clarify things for me. There is nothing like reliving, re-enacting some childish nonsense to remind us of the material we have never been able to handle. More than that, it doesn't only remind us, but it makes it easier for us to live with it from then on. It's like having a second chance at something that needs a second chance. Whenever one of these chances comes up, it makes me feel like I'm going to take a re-exam in a course that I flunked. This whole group experience is like having the opportunity to take re-exams in life over and over again until you pass and master the experience. And when finally I do pass, at least I get that feeling that I can make an effort to stop justifying myself. I realize that a great part of my defensiveness has been exactly on this basis—justifying my failures to live in past situations."

Bob, truly humble, said to Moe, "Lately, Moe, you certainly are as helpful around here as the Doc himself. Twice in a row now you've straightened me out when I needed it. It shows what can happen to a fellow here if he does stop fighting the interaction, and just goes ahead and accepts the people around him. Yes, I do feel you're all my friends, and at the moment I feel especially grateful to Betty, for it's obvious that no one else but Betty painted the picture. It's her talent; it's her medium of expression. I feel she has caught my feelings and problems very well. What is so truly surprising is how well all of us have grasped and understood each other. I guess I've been living in a vacuum with respect to so many of you here. I'm so prone to overestimate myself, and underestimate others, especially when it comes to understanding someone psychologically. Yes, I see it very clearly now. It isn't formal education that qualifies an individual for understanding, but a much more penetrating force—interest. We people are certainly exhibiting and have exhibited an interest in one another, and this outdistances an academic approach by far. Just the other day I received an efficiency rating for work where this lack on my part had been noted. I didn't understand it then, but I do now. The report said that I, as a bright student who knew the literature and understood the mechanisms of human behavior, frequently failed to come up with a corresponding picture of my clients in the clinical setting. You people have made this clear to me. The answer is my lack of interest—emotional interest, that is. What you do surpasses all my efforts, despite my education, because what one lacks in knowledge is never as important as what one lacks in emotional investment."

"It seems wonderful, Bob, to have you really feel one of us," said Betty. "I know I'm using superlatives again, and I use the word 'wonderful' a great deal, but I really do mean it."

"It's nice of you to say that, Betty."

"The feeling I got while painting the picture was: here stands Bob, quite a guy, all alone up on the hill, with the world drifting by as a river. If he would only come down off the hill to the river, he might find what he expected to find on top of the hill. You're such a fine guy, Bob, and now that you've finally joined us I hope you will stay with us. There's no need for you to have a relationship just with Eve, and not with the rest of us. We, or at least I, like both of you equally, and see no reason why the two of you need to isolate yourselves from us."

"Betty, you're so right," he said without a trace of his previous condescension. He continued, "My anxiety in relating to the rest of you has never been aroused quite so much by the girls as by the other fellows. But I'm beginning to appreciate that perhaps that, too, is more my problem than theirs."

"What say, Bob, shall we continue?" I injected.

"Okay, Doc," he replied.

With this I picked up the next gift. The card read "To Tom." It was a small round package neatly adorned with Christmas wrapping paper. I walked over and handed it to him. Clumsily he began to unwrap it. In the middle of the procedure it fell to the floor, and he looked up, embarrassed, as if to say "You know me, I'm the awkward one." With tolerance and slight humor in the air, no one said a word and all waited patiently for him to get to the present. At last it was unwrapped. He held up for inspection a beautiful hand-woven leather belt. Attached to the buckle was a card on a string. Someone said, "Read the card, Tom," and he did. It read: "Pull up your pants, you're a man."

The pause that followed was broken by the giggling of the girls. Tom became obviously mortified. As might be expected, Moe rode to the rescue in brotherly fashion. "Don't take it so hard," he said; "it's not said to hurt you, and after all, it's not such bad advice at that."

"Did you give it to me?" he cried out.

"No, I didn't," he said, somewhat surprised, "but that's not the point."

"Well, what is the point?" Tom demanded.

"Isn't it obvious?" said Moe.

"What is it—what is it really?"

Moe began, "Tom, I didn't make this belt for you, but first off it's a damn nice piece of work, and something you ought to wear with pride. Furthermore, the message points out in a friendly manner, I think, that it wouldn't hurt you a bit if you developed a similar dignity and pride about yourself."

"Is that right, Doc?" Tom questioned me.

"Well, like Moe, I didn't make this belt, of course, but I do feel that the one who did has caught the idea rather well."

Resigned and dejected, Tom sat with his forearms on his knees, taking stock of himself. A moment later he turned to me again. "I

159

guess all of you are right. It's because I feel so unworthy that I go around looking like I do so much of the time. It seems that every time I try something or attempt to be on the ball, I fail. Other people always seem to get things done so much easier than I. If it costs somebody one dollar to go somewhere, it will always cost me two. If I go to a party and like a girl there, she always goes home with some other fellow. At work it's the same thing. I only get a raise if everybody else does, never one for myself—and if I put in a good day's work, the boss acts like he's got it coming to him. When I went to school and brought home good marks, my parents would say that's what I should be getting, and I was expected to do that well.

"In other words it always seemed to me that if I did something well I was expected to do it well, and if I did something badly I got hell, so it just seemed to me, no matter what happened, good or bad, it never turned out to be worth while."

"That's exactly the point," Bob thrust in. "You are standing around in life waiting for it to compliment you, because you know how to breathe properly. You give me the feeling that no matter what you do, it isn't what you do that counts, it's the praise that you crave. And, brother, take it from one who knows, seek praise and you'll never be satisfied. You'll always be a failure until you can learn to appreciate and enjoy the fun of doing things rather than walking around in life with the attitude of 'What's in it for me?'"

We all looked at Bob with pride. This time he had not guarded his feelings when giving his opinion.

"I guess you're right, Bob," said Tom.

"Well it's time you knew," Bob retorted. "It was I who made that belt for you, Tom. When I took the last remaining scrap of paper with your name on it, I was really happy. Happy because it was you, and happy because it was one of the men of the group. I've always been able to get along so much better with women than men, and in the case of my own brother, we got along particularly badly.

"I reasoned with myself," Bob went on, "that since the group has turned into a family affair, perhaps this difficulty of mine, getting along with my brother, might have a chance to be resolved.

You, Tom, do not exactly resemble my brother in many ways, but there is this major factor. I was always closer to Mother, and beat him out in most of our competition. This—my always winning—I now realize, increased my guilt no end. Therefore, Tom, when I say to you 'Be a man and pull up your pants,' what I'm really saying is, 'Don't let me be so successful in beating you. Also, take better care of yourself. It really will reassure me that my own progress is not made at someone else's expense.' "

"I see what you mean," said Tom with a little more self-confidence. Bob's acceptance of him had had a desirable effect.

Tom went on. "It's really true, for in my own family I had an older brother. He was Mother's darling—and I hated his guts. As I was saying before, when I did something right, my mother would merely have that attitude of 'It's what you're supposed to do,' but when my brother did something well, he would keep on pestering her until she finally broke down and admitted he had accomplished something worth while. I have never gotten over hating both of them for it—maybe this will be a turning point for me."

These words, assisted by another round of cider and cookies, seemed to cause a release of tension in the room.

The next present was wrapped in bright red paper with a green ribbon, and was addressed to Moe. With a broad grin on his face, he rather forcibly opened his package. Out came a pair of black hand-knitted gloves. His initials were embroidered in red across the cuffs, at a diagonal. He put them on quickly and beamed with pleasure. "Thanks a lot," he said with an enthusiasm that seemed to carry beyond the importance of the occasion. He admired the gloves on his hands over and over. "I don't know who gave these to me, but I'm really happy with them. I can just see the fellows when I drive to work on Monday morning wearing them. They'll be asking me if I got them for Christmas, and, of course, I'll say that I did, but little will they realize the circumstances." As he said this, the smile already present on his face broadened, and he winked airily.

Taking this as a cue, I stepped in. "I guess now is as appropriate a time as any for the knitter to reveal her identity. I assume it is a she—or does one of the fellows knit?" My feeble attempt at humor produced a short and abrupt chuckle, out of which came the lighthearted voice of Claudia.

"Well, if you must know, it was little 'ol' me. And I did it with my own lily-white hands. Furthermore, it does please me to see you so appreciative."

With this the group really burst into uproarious laughter. If ever the group had a pet, it had turned out to be Claudia. There wasn't a soul in the room who didn't like her. Others could do stupid things, or say the inappropriate and arouse intolerance and hostility, but not Claudia. She was anointed with a special immunity. It wan't as if she were the parent's favorite child, but rather that she was everyone's pet. Therefore, you can imagine how exhilarated Moe felt when he realized that his wonderful present had been made by none other than the group's darling, Claudia.

At that moment, I could not help but reflect upon Moe's life—his short-lived marriage and the tragedy that had been his. "Now look at him," I thought to myself, "see how he has grown." His melancholic days were behind him. There was a *Kaffeeklatsch* quality about him. A taste for life was back. Daily events were enjoyable and laughter had replaced sullenness.

While the hilarity continued, I turned my attention to Claudia. I was equally proud of her. Gone was the fragile, unrealistic, wistful girl I had first known. Here sat a fun-loving, pleasant young woman, truly at ease. Her guilt was ebbing away. She no longer engaged in the tortuous pursuits of all punishment. A passive resilience now characterized her approach to life. Like Moe, she, too, relished the party. Her pride over her handmade gloves imparted a quiet comfort to the rest of us. I believed she knew our feelings and they served to enhance the occasion for her.

When the laughter subsided a little, I reached for the next to last gift. It was a flat box about a foot square wrapped plainly in white paper with a white ribbon. On it was a card of instructions saying, "This side up—for Molly." I carefully placed it on Molly's lap. She demonstrated equal care in removing the paper, and in raising the lid from the box. Her first audible reaction was in the nature of a groan. We all gathered around to see what she had re-

162

ceived. A plate lay in the box, and on it was a face made out of chopped liver. It had olives for eyes and raisins to outline the features. The lips were made of beets. In general, the expression, especially as revealed by the mouth, sagging at one of the corners, was one of a snarl. "This is some present," she moaned, "some present!" Then her anger fully mobilized, she began to sputter, "Who in the hell gave me this—what son of a bitch had the nerve . . ." She was livid.

Slowly, we all returned to our seats in deathlike silence. The hurricane warnings were up. I believe it was Tom who muttered "To the hills." On she ranted, lambasting everyone and no one at the same time. Only after the first wave of hostility had subsided did she begin to attempt to analyze who the culprit could be. Carefully and calculatingly, she narrowed down her tantalizer, by process of elimination, to the only remaining individuals who had not yet been identified as gift-givers: John and Moe.

"Now, let's see"—building up steam—"which one of you two bastards could have done this?" She looked first at John. "I wonder if it could be you. You're hostile enough at times, and lecherous enough, but somehow or other you just haven't enough guts to pull a trick like this, so that leaves Moe. Well, that dirty son of a bitch has been in the Navy, and in a place like that they think up all kinds of wormy, screwy things. I never would have suspected that he hated me that much, for somehow or other I always thought he was a square shooter, but I should have known better. What can you expect from men? Yet the more I think about it, the more I realize, even though he is a man, we never fought or had that much trouble between us—as a matter of fact, it seems to me the bastard's always making peace around here—so maybe it was not him after all. Well, that brings me back to John—yes, I guess he did it. Maybe I underrated this son-of-a-bitch's hostility. I've known men like him before: no guts until they get a chance to protect themselves. You know what I mean, Doc"—she turned to me in an effort to elicit sympathy—"safety in numbers. He wouldn't have the nerve to do that except in a group. You know, like a kid in a gang. He feels he has his gang with him, so he can get away with murder. But I'll tell you what I'm going to do. I'm not going to push it in his face. I'll be a lady. Yes, sir, I'll restrain myself. In fact, I'll take it home, and give it to my cat."

She seemed quite pleased with herself in apparently ferreting out the guilty party, and in remaining a lady according to her own value system by not pushing the plate in his face. The group breathed a collective sigh of relief, but everyone was still very much on his toes, aware that any moment could bring on another eruption. For they all realized that the actual identity of the so-called culprit had not been definitely revealed.

"Molly, I'm glad to see that you responded with feelings concerning the gift," I said. "It's valuable for all of you to be outspoken while here in the therapy setting. Such a course fosters growth and a greater comprehension of reality. I'm sure if you stop and think about it, Molly, you will realize that, regardless of which of these two gave you your gift, he was expressing his involvement with you. Do you agree, Molly?"

"I do, Doc, but God damn it, why do people always have to be so hostile toward me?"

"All I can say, Molly, is that it cannot be answered in the form of a static *why*. It's much more involved than a simple 'why.' Human behavior seldom, if ever, can be placed on as simple a basis as—why. Now, Molly, are you ready to have the person who gave you the gift reveal his identity?"

"I guess so."

"Well, then, who gave Molly her gift?"

There was a short, poignant silence, quickly relieved by the manly voice of Moe—"I did."

"You made it?" Molly said to him quickly.

"Simply because that's how I see you," he responded unflinchingly. "Molly," he went on, "I looked at it this way. I wasn't trying to be mean or nasty. I was hoping that if I could get you to see how you appear to others, perhaps you would change. Your snarling, biting ways are really unnecessary, Molly. They make people turn away from you, and at times against you. . . . I may be all wrong about this, Doc, but I'd like to try to answer that 'why' question. I think the reason that people turn on Molly is—she asks for it.

There's something about her—she won't rest until she has succeeded in baiting you to hate her. Sometimes I feel that she isn't happy until she's unhappy. It's as if she couldn't be satisfied until she's dissatisfied—with everything and everybody. I know that she's had a tough life, but who the hell hasn't? She can't say that she's had it any tougher than I have had, but I'll be God damned if I can see any justification for doing what she does. Believe me, I don't hate her guts—even though she tries like hell to get everyone to do so. Actually, I feel sorry for her. No pity, just sorry for her."

Completely overwhelmed by the course of events, Molly, with furrowed brow, sat in meditation, silently absorbing what had been said to her. The silence grew. A short while later, with everyone obviously determined not to speak until Molly did, she said, "I've been thinking over what Moe said. It's a tough dose of medicine to swallow, but I guess he's not a bastard for having prescribed it. It's true and at times I've gotten a glimpse of this myself. I've never seemed to be able to do a damn thing about it, but I do feel a little bit encouraged. As long as there are people like all of you in this group, people who aren't afraid of me and who will keep putting me back on the track when I get off it—I guess there's hope for me."

"Yes, Molly, that's true, but with one condition—that you also keep trying to help yourself," I added.

"That's right, too," she responded anticlimactically.

In an effort to recapture the festive mood, I picked up the tray of cider and cookies, and passed it around again, starting with Molly. Then I picked up the last gift. It was an oblong box about a yard long, wrapped in green paper, and tied with a fancy white ribbon. The card on it read "To Claudia."

With a cavalier's sweeping gesture, I presented it to Claudia, who was sitting at my right. She smiled, going along with the playacting. When she had the box open, her first response was a joyous scream. "It's roses. It's roses," she cried, "and they're red. It means that someone cares." She spoke as though the last doubts of her acceptability had melted away. The long-stemmed red roses, twelve of them, had been handmade out of various types of paper. Their stems were wired, covered with green paper. They were truly splendid. After lingering over them a while longer, she turned toward John. "John, you know I couldn't have dreamt of anything lovelier."

"Oh, think nothing of it," he said, imitating a Kentucky hillbilly.

"But, I do think something of it; I think it was so sweet of you."

"Well, what do you expect?" he said in matter-of-fact tone. "If you don't know by now, you ought to—you're one of our favorite people here, and I do believe I speak for more than myself."

"I'm all a-fluttter, as the saying goes," she responded. "There's nothing more to say. This has been the pleasantest Christmas party I've ever known—and I would rather spend time with you people than with any other group I've ever known. There's only one thing that's spoiling the whole picture—and that's Eve. She's so troubled and sad, and it almost seems as if—unless she's happy, I can't be. So, Eve—why can't you? Please say something, won't you?"

At first Eve's speech was slow and precise, but gradually it built up in feeling and intensity as she spoke to the group. "As you know, I asked not to join in this gift exchange. I appreciate your accepting my request without rancor. You must have understood that it was not because of a personal rejection of the group or any of its specific members. Nor was my action based on an inability to give or receive from you people specifically. The truth is quite the opposite. I'd have enjoyed immensely having the fun and the anxiety you all experienced this evening. When this subject came up last session, the harder I tried to be with you, the harder it became. Had you asked me why then, or even right up until the middle of this session, I wouldn't have been able to give you an answer. I simply didn't know why.

"But sometime during the middle of this evening the association came back to my mind. I was at college, living in a sorority house. Every year, about a week or two before Christmas, they held an affair which was called 'Good Fairy Week.' In similar fashion, we drew names out of a hat and anonymously gave little gifts to the person whose name we had drawn. Little things, not more than a dollar, just as we did here. I didn't like the girls in my sorority, and I felt unloved by them. The whole sorority life to me was phony, stupid and hypocritical. Petty gossip and competition. Little digs and cryptic innuendoes behind your back. It made it all ridiculous to me.

"The whole idea of sororities and sorority sisters was so disturbing that when that season of the year came around, I actually became nauseated. We had to go around and plant these little presents in our fellow sisters' rooms with labels attached: 'From your good little fairy.' It was impossible. I felt like a fool.

"Knowing no way out, I tried to save face with myself, and still carry out my part in these stupid dealings. There was a shop, a little gift shop, just off campus. The proprietor was self-possessed and domineering. In addition, he had an obsession for cats. The place was actually alive with these fiendish creatures. Several times during the years I lived in the sorority, I went to this particular shop and pilfered gifts for the 'Good Fairy Week.' In this way I kidded myself into thinking that I wasn't giving to the inane affair after all. At first I was frightened and embarrassed about my behavior. Later, however, I gained bravado. One day when I had gone to the shop with a boy friend, I slipped three small items into my bag, and proudly displayed them to him after we had gone out of the shop. He was thoroughly disgusted with me, and shortly thereafter ended our friendship. You'll never know the anguish and torment I've suffered because of this whole affair, over these past years. I've never been able to enjoy a Christmas since." With a big sigh she continued, "And so now you know why I couldn't take my place with you tonight." As the last words left Eve's lips, Claudia sprang to her feet. She darted over to her, and knelt at her feet, grasping Eve's hands in her own. "Oh, Eve, Eve," she said—and then, after a prolonged pause—"you're so sensitive—you give so much of yourself to others. You're the finest girl I've ever known."

Still depressed but trying to be jocular, Eve said, "Oh, Claudia, how you exaggerate."

"No, no, I mean that," Claudia replied. "You're absolutely as beautiful inside as you are outside. I mean, you've always presented yourself as being one who was so insincere. But we know you aren't. Your claim to insincerity is nothing more than a delicately balanced sense of super loyalty. If anything, your sense of integrity is too great. Isn't it so, group?" and she turned her head around to see their response. Universal affirmative support was her answer. It appeared to me that the group understood that Eve was caught in the meshwork of the problem of "phobic stealing." In other words, the sorority sisters and the cats in the shop had precipitated such a degree of anxiety that the only resolution for her was to reject the intimacy of these close feminine associations.

"See, I told you so," said Claudia, looking up into Eve's eyes.

Eve smiled back, and then looked over at me. "Doctor, do you agree, too?" she asked with searching tenderness in her voice.

"Yes, of course, Eve," I replied, "I agree with every word. I'm afraid you are misusing your old-fashioned Boston morality." She accepted my observation with appreciation and returned a knowing smile.

Then another pause followed. We all seemed to sense how close we were while silently looking at one another. It had grown quite late. At length, I turned quietly to the group and said, "A Merry Christmas to all, and to all a good night."

12. *A Decision Is Reached*

Christmas had come and gone. Since it fell on a Saturday, the following day gave me time to reflect. Such a time lends itself quite naturally to meditation. And the bleakness of that typical late December day was a fitting background for my feelings. In my own way, I, too, had gone through the ups and downs of the season. When the cuckoo clock called four P.M., my mood, influenced decidedly by some leftover Christmas eggnog, was not in keeping with the clock's sprightly tones.

It was not difficult for me to understand why so many people have acute distress at this time of the year. To begin with, the five weeks or so of activity between Thanksgiving and Christmas led up to this one day—no one day could possibly ever hope to reach the expectations placed upon it. It is the day when the family spirit is supposed to be revealed in its fullest splendor. But the truth of the matter is that no holiday can make a man more of a human being than he actually is. Each of us, thoroughly possessed with unconscious childish fervor, in an air of semihysterical confusion, somehow expects things to be different. The Christmas tree with its associated ornaments, the gaily wrapped gifts, the bustle of the kitchen with its appetizing odors, tease us into feeling that in some miraculous manner, unqualified happiness or bliss will be ours. The whole affair cannot possibly end in anything but anticlimax, or at least a letdown. And, in the events of this forty-eight- to seventy-two-hour span, we see men and women alike unknowingly repeating a cycle. The cycle reminds me of a condensed version of one's lifetime experience. It is as if the human being going through the Christmas occasion expected his adult life to be now the sugar-coated affair it was supposed to be in his childhood days. And when it fails, as it must, to live up to this unrealistic expectation, depression ensues. It is not merely that anticipation is greater than fulfillment, but rather reality can never hope to compare favorably with our imagined unrealities. The mature know this discrepancy. Their healthy response to it is known as adjustment.

Thus speculating, my comfort in the Barcalounger was disturbed by the annoying ring of the phone. Wishing it would stop, but not having the strength to ignore it, I answered.

"Hello," came back a strong masculine voice. "Is that you, Case?" (Case is my nickname. It is the Anglo-Saxon version of Kees, the accepted shortening of Cornelius in my native Holland.)

"Yes," I replied. "Is that you, Bernie?"

"Right the first time. I thought you would like a preliminary report on that young lady scheduled for me to see."

"Fine, go right ahead, Bernie."

"I'm afraid it isn't a happy story. On physical examination, I found an enlarged area in the left adnexa [tissues of the ovaries and tubes]. My estimation is that it would approximate the size of a large tangerine. I feel that it is in the body of the ovary itself. It's very hard and irregular, and I doubt if it's an ordinary enlarged 'chocolate' cyst. Furthermore, she shows evidence of venous congestion in her lower extremities. What in the devil this has to do with it, I can't be sure, but I have scheduled her for Tuesday, and will do an exploratory laporotomy."

I had been standing by the telephone desk in the hall, but with an automatic movement I pulled the chair out and sat down with a thud. "You can't imagine, Bernie, how sad I am to hear that news. You see, she's such a nice girl, and I've grown so fond of her—in fact we all have—she's the pet of the group therapy unit I've been telling you about from time to time.

"The poor girl has had so much misfortune and especially in

recent years. It has only been of late that she has truly begun to live and have her rightful share of happiness. It would be so unfair if anything should go wrong now."

"I understand, Case—I do understand," he replied. "Chances are she'll come through O.K. Tell you what, just as soon as I'm finished, I'll call you and give you what probably will be good news."

"Bernie, if ever anyone deserved a break, she does—and that's why I'm so glad she's in your hands."

Putting down the receiver, I returned to the den. In spite of Bernie's reassurance, I went over the disappointing news again and again in my mind, and it was some time before I finally came to terms with the unpleasant reality of it all. In the case of the group, I decided that the proper approach would be to "play it by ear," reasoning that until I knew the postoperative course, there was no other way of determining what further path to pursue.

Tuesday night's session opened in a cloud of recall—a rehashing of the party, and its effects upon us. Molly was the most vociferous. She again went through her series of complaints concerning the gift she had received—the face made out of chopped liver. She told us about the weekend, and how she had stared at this face repeatedly with alternating waves of hostility and resignation. The group more or less let her have the reins, and as a result she finally played herself out. By these responses, they best conveyed that they felt her hostility was a sign that she could not accept the truth concerning herself. By now the group had learned to deal with this type of behavior. Whenever a patient went off on a tangent of hostility because he or she could not accept a reality, they permitted the energy to expend itself. Thus, the hostile individual, not finding a recipient, would soon discover that his attitude was based upon his own shortcomings. The refusal of the group to become enmeshed in Molly's attempt to seek a scapegoat produced silent approval within me. Vainly she attempted to defame Moe. Every emasculating maneuver ever practiced by any man-hating female was employed by her. Throughout this attack Moe sat calmly and listened to her, like a parent determined not to be influenced by a child's temper tantrum. Finally, when Molly had really exhausted herself and a lull fell over the room, I spoke to the group.

"I didn't have the opportunity to tell you earlier—our Claudia is in the hospital." There was a collective "No!"

"Yes," I replied. "It's not an accident or anything of that sort. She merely went in as a result of a physical examination. She came to me with an ailment, and I referred her to a surgeon. The physician has kept in touch with me, and scheduled her operation for today. As yet, I have not received his postoperative report. I have great confidence in this man and I feel she stands in no unusual danger." These words struck their target, and there was noticeable relief.

"Will she be out very long?" Eve asked tensely.

"I shouldn't imagine so, Eve."

"What is the nature of her ailment, Doc?" inquired Bob.

"Well, the physical examination suggested an enlargement of one of her ovaries."

"Is that serious?" Betty inquired.

"That's most difficult to say without exploration, Betty. As a matter of fact, that's why the operation was performed."

"Oh," she said, further relieved.

"When do you think you might hear from the surgeon?" asked Moe.

"I expect to hear from him before the day is out. These men frequently are in the operating room for many hours. Therefore, I imagine that after he gets squared away, I'll be hearing from him."

"I see," said Moe.

At this moment Tom joined the conversation. "It will be kind of funny working around here without her for a while."

"It sure will," said John. "She's certainly been the star pupil," he added.

In came the booming voice of Molly. "Yeah, the apple of the Doc's eye."

"Christ," Tom barked at Molly. "Here is a girl sick and in the hospital for an operation, and that's all you can say."

"Look, I came here to get well, and not to go around wiping the noses of sheeplike girls. I have no illusions about this group therapy. To me it's business—the business of getting well. I have no time for stray and bewildered sheep. I admit," she continued in flat tones, "I'm sorry to hear that this has happened, but brother, I'm here to get what I need, and I'll be damned if anybody is going to stop me, and furthermore," she added, glaring at Tom, "that goes for you or anybody else around here."

"Yes," said Eve in a most condescending manner, "we know—we know—you're the rugged individualist, but what you don't realize is how much you are paraphrasing what the Doctor says."

"That's right," she snarled. "He's told us we're here for our own benefit, and no one else's."

"Yes, dear," said Eve sarcastically, more upset by the news than by this exchange. Apparently she was fighting with Molly as a diversionary tactic to quell her own anxiety concerning Claudia. "But he never meant it in the manner that you exploited. When he said it, he was giving us a creed to follow in respect to group function. He was giving us a sense of proportion, with kindness and humanity at its core. You," and she said the "you" with an indictment in her voice, "are cruel."

"Oh, go to hell, you snob. You spout about cruelty. What do you know about kindness? After the way you've misled so many men, your talking about kindness is ridiculous."

"Listen here," spoke up the authoritative voice of Bob. "Eve's not that way any more. She has been quite the accepting and understanding woman with me." As he spoke these words, each of us appreciated the sincerity and truth of them. Of even more importance, however, was the increase in masculinity to be noted in Bob. In similar situations in the past, he had served weakly as the compromiser and soother. In fact, previously, whenever two women fought in his presence, he would serve as a tranquilizer, usually in a patronizing manner; but never with decision and definitiveness. Nothing was ever truly resolved by his efforts. But now there seemed to be an absence of hostility toward womankind in his behavior. His intervention was constructive, not only because he was supporting the woman he loved—but, of greater revelation, he was standing for principles rather than hostile cryptic platitudes.

Before Molly could retrench her defenseless position again, John spoke with directness. "I'm proud of you, Bob. And that's all I can say about it. I'm just proud to see you do the right thing."

"That's right," Moe chimed in. "You're a changed guy. I wouldn't say that Eve is making a man out of you exactly, but she sure is helping in the right direction."

"To tell you the truth, fellows," Bob said smiling, "I owe a great deal to her, and to all of you. I no longer care to be the Seventh Avenue sharpy I used to be. I see it for what it was worth, and it wasn't much. No more playing around with chicks for me. I'll get my dolls in the five and dime from now on, but they won't be animate—and they'll be for my kids, I hope."

By this time Molly had borne up under the dissension as long as she could, and she let go with, "I think you're all crazy, but I'm just going to do what's good for me anyway."

Betty turned to Eve. "Gee, I envy you, Eve."

"Why?"

"Because you have such a nice guy in Bob."

"You're right; he is a nice fellow," the very accepting voice of Eve answered.

"I've been thinking lately," continued Betty, "that Bob is getting more and more to be the guy I felt he was the night he read his poem to you in a Village restaurant. He has a lot of quality, and it's only just beginning to shine through."

"It's funny your saying that," said Eve. "Just the other day I was thinking that way, too. I had said to Bob over the Christmas weekend that he was becoming more the man that I thought he was when I first met him. It seems to me that as he improves the more interesting he becomes. It's amazing how his thinking is crytallizing. He's so socially nonprejudiced, and more liberal politically. Why, he even seems to get more enjoyment in doing the same things he's always done."

"What do you mean?" inquired Betty.

"Oh, it's hard to say, but—well—historical novels, opera and modern art. He always liked these things, but it's the way he talks about them now. His critical values have more substance. For example, I noticed it recently when he discussed the Brancusi sculpture that was exhibited at the Guggenheim Museum."

Taking a second breath, she continued. "Of course, it's all of this, but there's even more to it than I've said. There's that man-to-man quality which is now becoming more clearly defined in Bob. When I first began going out with him, he had male friends, but there was something shallow about these relationships. Nowadays, there's less backslapping when he and his friends get together and warmer feelings. The supersalesman routine is gone. Instead, there's a quiet exchange of ideas in an atmosphere of respect. Even his relationship with his brother has changed notably. Those two were always sparring in a competitive way. Today, they met each other for lunch as friends do. You know, like buddies whose friendship was fused under fire."

Her next sentence was interrupted by the shrill ringing of the telephone in the other room, giving the emergency signal. I excused myself and went in, closing the door behind me.

"Hello, is that you, Case?" Bernie's voice inquired.

"Yes, Bernie. How is she?"

"Well, it's like this. We went in, and there, almost completely obliterating the broad ligament, was a huge solid teratomatous mass [a tumor containing embryonic remains congenitally derived]. It had destroyed her entire left ovary. Fortunately for her, the capsule was intact, and I don't think any spill-over occurred. We removed the mass, and its adjacent parts, including the tube. After the operation I sectioned the mass, and found everything in it but the kitchen sink. However, it contained, among other things, thyroid tissue, and this might have caused her a hormonal disbalance. The mass alone may have been sufficient to cause some of her collateral venous drainage to be impaired, as it filled her cul-de-sac [a blind pouch between the front wall of the rectum and the uterus]. Her previously inflamed leg veins made it essential that I place her on anti-coagulant therapy. I will have to give her time in bed for the trouble to subside."

"What do you think of her chances, Bernie?"

"Roughly speaking, I'd say that since the capsule was unbroken, and there wasn't any gross evidence of other tissues being involved, she's got a pretty good chance. You know, Case, you can never say for sure in these cases. We'll have to see what the microscopic report says. What's amazing to me is how this girl could have had such a large mass, and not have known it for such a long period of time."

"That's not hard to understand from my viewpoint, Bernie. You see, she was a girl who was so sick and disturbed that any physical malady was merely accepted as a part of her mental status. She couldn't discriminate between depression and a logy state due to a heavy mass in the pelvis. Apparently it was only when she got well enough emotionally that she could make this differentiation."

"That makes sense to me. It certainly points out the danger that these cases run. She's lucky that she got it out before it was too late, isn't she?"

"Yes. I certainly feel much better about her chances now than when you first told me of your findings. How is her morale, Bernie?"

"Excellent, I would say. She certainly thinks the world of that group—you know, I believe she's more anxious to see them than her father and mother, who were here with her today."

"It doesn't surprise me to hear that at all—the group feels the same toward her and I gather by now that you know my own feelings."

"Yes, they're rather clear. I still can't quite figure out how it all came about, but I see it and realize that it's a great thing you people have among yourselves."

"That's true; it's a good thing to see people caring for one another, as you say—but I must get back to them now as we're actually in the middle of a session. Thanks again, Bernie."

"Not at all. I'll keep you informed, Case. Good night."

"Good night."

For a moment, I hesitated. A chill came over me. I did not move. I suddenly realized that a rather important decision had to be made and it had to be made before I walked out of the room to join the group. What should I tell them? How much of the truth should they know? These and other implications ricocheted through my head. If I tell them, they would need to discuss it with Claudia. If I don't tell them, would I not be crediting them with being less than responsible? What does good therapy dictate? I slowly sank into my chair. I could hear the faint sounds of the group as they continued on without me. Elbows on the desk, and the fingers of both hands running through my hair, I pondered these questions again. Then it came to me. I would tell them the truth, at the level that they could understand—minus the technical language; to do otherwise would fail to recognize the status they had richly earned. Basically, there wasn't anything to hide. Claudia was out of the woods. True—there was that inevitable possibility of something going wrong. Fortified with clarity, I returned to the group. Though this decision took only brief minutes, its demands caused me to reach back and call upon the inner resource that all of us carry, labeled "Use Only When Necessary."

"I'm sorry I had to leave the group, people," I began, "but I'm sure you heard the emergency ring on the phone—though it wasn't such an emergency after all. The call was from Claudia's surgeon."

My words made only a slight dent in their anxiety, but reassured the group to a degree, at least.

"The surgeon said that she had come through the operation in excellent shape. Furthermore," I implied, "considering the condition she had, her chances of full and adequate recovery are good. It seems that one of her ovaries had a growth on it, which was removed. Naturally, she'll be in the hospital for a week or so, and will then rejoin us to resume her regular routine."

The relief was evident. Several of the members who had been sitting motionless felt free to stir again. Some slid back their chairs. Others reached for cigarettes, and one or two even smiled faintly.

Then, after Betty had come up with remarks signifying her relief, Eve spoke. "Doctor, may we go and visit her at the hospital? I know how you feel about patients having outside contact with one another, but I thought, under the circumstances, this might be an exception."

"Yes, it would be wonderful if we could," Betty said.

"Yeah, maybe we ought to go see her," Tom echoed.

"Why not, Doc, why not let the bars down for once?" Moe urged.

And now the movement was really snowballing. Bob, however, was in conflict. "You know, Doc, I've just come through some important material for me. You might say I've broken through an intellectual cold front. The thing that I've come to appreciate is that I was lacking in the power of direct emotional response. We all care for Claudia, but to visit her definitely violates the doctrine— no outside contacts. The same, the very same doctrine that's given me so much trouble."

Here I sat, gripped by the need to make another sudden, major decision. The steady hand of leadership so necessary for the group's future life was at stake. I knew I had but a minute at best to think it over, for a longer time would be needlessly painful for them. "Are their inclinations without neurotic maneuver?" I asked myself quickly. "Was their motive to see Claudia a primary one? Would such a departure, with my approval, represent a neurotic triumph for any of them?" The answer came quickly. No doubt their expressions were signs of healthy humanity. The brief silence produced by my meditation discharged itself with a question to them. "How would you feel about having the whole group, including me, go to see Claudia rather than having you visit her individually?"

"Are you kidding, Doc?" Bob exclaimed in the manner of one who has been asked to accept the gift of a large sum of money.

"Boy, and how! I sure would!" Betty followed.

"What an idea," said Moe, slapping his hand on his knee.

"You mean you could arrange such a thing, Doc?" asked a doubting Molly.

"Let me put it to you this way. If it is possible to make these arrangements, is there anyone against the idea of our holding a regular ninety-minute session at the hospital with Claudia?"

"Wowie—if that isn't something!" grinned an exhilarated John.

"You mean we would hold a regular session just as though we were here, only it would be in the hospital, Doc?" asked Bob in amazement.

"Why not?" was my response.

"Oh, sure, it's done every day!" he said jocularly, gesturing with his shoulders and whipping his arms around while snapping his fingers in one uninterrupted motion.

"Exactly. Every day and twice on Sundays, I'm sure."

"Would we meet here and then go up to the hospital?" inquired Eve, ignoring the attempted levity.

"Perhaps it would be better if we met in the lobby of the Empire Hospital at, say seven forty-five, Thursday night.

"Of course, this is still contingent upon the necessary approval of all of us here as well as the authorities involved at the hospital. May I therefore ask if you all approve of these plans?" Scanning the room, I received a succession of affirmative nods.

"Well, then, this is what we will do. Unless you hear from me to the contrary, I will meet you in the lobby of the Empire Hospital on Thursday night at seven forty-five. I assume you all know where it is located—on the East River near the Triboro Bridge. I believe the best way to get there is to take the Lexington Avenue and then a crosstown bus. Okay, everyone?"

"Okay, Doc," they chorused vigorously.

After bidding the group good night, I called Dr. Green. "Bernie?"

"Yes, Case."

"I've got an unusual request."

"Shoot. What is it?"

"As you know, that girl of mine is a member of a group-therapy unit. After you called this evening, I spoke with them. The sum and substance of it is that we would all like to hold a session in her room on Thursday night. Do you have any objections?"

"No, none at all. I think it's quite an unusual twist, and a nice one at that."

"Okay then. Do I have your permission to speak to Dr. George, the hospital administrator, about the matter?"

"Sure, go right ahead, Case, and tell him that I'm for the idea."

The following morning, before the arrival of the day's first patient, Dr. George and I had completed the details. At first he was somewhat taken aback by the idea, but, following some gentle

179

assurance that we would not disrupt the hospital's tranquillity, and that it would be only one time, he was able to see the human values involved. As a matter of fact, his concluding remark caused us both to laugh. "You psychiatrists and your continuous love affairs with your patients never cease to amaze me."

13. *The Visit*

When Thursday evening rolled around I found myself feeling somewhat buoyant. I had decided not to drive to the hospital, but to take a taxi instead, and as we drove through the snarled streets cluttered with traffic and people, I was glad that I had gone by cab. It gave me necessary time to think over the approaching meeting. The progress reports on Claudia had been mixed. The preoperative inflammation of the veins in her legs, despite the use of anticoagulants, eliminated the practice, so widely followed today, of getting the patient up and out of bed the day or two following surgery. However, the laboratory confirmed what Bernie's educated eye had discerned. Namely, a teratoma of the ovary.

These were not, however, the principal thoughts in my mind at the moment. The night was chilly and damp; the noises emanating from the foggy river brought back memories of the loneliness of the members at the beginning of the group sessions. How unfortunate it would be, I thought, not only for Claudia, but for all of us, if anything went amiss. We had made such progress, had just begun to appreciate the importance of being important to one another. Could such a calamity conceivably do untold damage to these gains? I wondered. With further thought, I felt that, though such a loss would be a tremendous shock to all of us, we would have to learn to accept the cruelties of life as well as the joys we so recently had come to experience. It also dawned upon me that I had to guard against such an overprotective, pessimistic attitude. After all, Claudia had come through the operation well and was steadily improving. At that point, a deep gratitude toward Bernie came over me for having managed Claudia's complicated case so capably.

My thoughts slowly swung over to the particular session we were about to hold. I would have to be careful that our kindness to Claudia did not feed her feelings of omnipotence. I knew that physical illness causes emotional regression at times. We all tend to "baby" ourselves when ill.

With the rest of us sitting around Claudia, the tendency to duplicate the setting of infancy must be resisted. Somehow or other, I must manage to maintain the sense of equality. The avoidance of excessive commiseration could perhaps be forestalled by stimulating the others to talk about themselves. It then occurred to me that I had confidence in them and that I was mighty proud of my group. They had profited well by their association with one another. They were well on the road to normal relatedness, and perhaps my fear that this session would make them regress, individually and collectively, to their infantile, self-pitying mold was groundless.

When the cab driver turned and said, "Here we are," I was prepared. Clustered together in the far corner of the lobby was my brood. A peculiar sensation swept over me as I sighted them. I was more happy than usual to see them. Although only the normal length of time between sessions had passed, it seemed considerably longer. Meeting them was like a railroad-station greeting of a relative whom one had not seen in several years. Perhaps, it was because they had on coats and hats, but more likely because our family was meeting away from home.

Smiling broadly, I said, "Hello, everyone. It's nice to see you. I'm glad you all made it."

"Good evening, Doctor," came back a warm, but more than usually dignified response.

Immediately I sensed its meaning. They were happy to see me—their father, but I was in the house of medicine now, and their calling me "Doctor" instead of "Doc" signified an awareness of this. In addition, it symbolized their realization that the family was outside its sanctuary—home, and the intimate emotions which come so easily within the protective shelter of the home do not flow so readily outside its confines. It was analogous to a child's calling his father "Daddy" at home, but "Father" away from home.

"I've made arrangements for us to go ahead immediately," I told them, "so if you'll all follow me, we'll take the elevator to the twenty-first floor." On the way up Moe asked the elevator operator if he had had a good day today, or had he had his usual ups and downs. Moe's bulk dissuaded the operator from punching him in the nose. This bit of byplay broke the tension for all of us.

Miss Cunningham, the head nurse, in her starched uniform, came out of her office and greeted us in a friendly but restrained manner. No doubt this procedure had breached some rules of nursing protocol. She promptly led the way to Claudia's room. Eve, entering first, swooped over to the bed and embraced Claudia, and then kissed her. The rest of us stood hat-in-hand in slightly awkward manner, waiting to greet the patient. Claudia, raising herself up on her elbows after the embrace, was the first to speak.

"Oh, I'm so excited. Nothing could make me happier," she cried, then, suddenly smitten with social consciousness, directed, "take off your hats and coats and hang them in the closet. Please make yourselves comfortable. Everything is ready."

With this accomplished, we all returned to the center of the room. Claudia motioned to us to sit in the circle of seats already arranged.

"How are you?" asked Bob, with deep affection.

"Fine as wine. In fact, just stellar."

She showed the physical effects of her surgery. She had lost weight, and her lacy bed jacket revealed a hollowness around her neck and collarbones. Despite this loss of weight and the ordeal she had been through, her morale was excellent. Her dark eyes danced. Her long page-boy hairdo glistened—obviously the result of repeated brushings. Her pallor was not sickly; rather it enhanced her femininity in contrast with the glistening coiffure.

"May I tell you something?" she asked as she allowed herself to fall leisurely back into the pillow and stretched her thin arms

183

playfully in front of her, catlike. "I've always loved my bed. I never minded going to sleep as a child. My mother would get a big kick out of the fact that I would get into bed, stretch out comfortably, and say that it felt soooo good. And after I had snuggled in, I would vow, 'I can't wait 'til I grow up, but, Mother, I still love to cuddle in my bed.'"

It was obvious that some regression had occurred, but not of an unwarranted variety. The childhood associations revealed her conflict. The age-old fantasy is one in which infancy represents the epitome of omnipotence when the world is at our beck and call. Maturity, its counterpart, although sought after, is not strongly pursued, as it represents a shrinking state of power over others, and a diminution of our grandiosity.

"But really," she went on, "I don't want this session and your visit to center about me. It reminds me of the time recently when I was sick with my menstrual period, and my boy friend was with me. I was naturally concerned about my discomfort, but I think I rather exaggerated it so that he would be oversolicitous of me."

"Yes, I know what you mean," Betty said. "I've done the same kind of thing at times myself."

"What woman hasn't?" asked a forgiving Eve.

"I haven't," Molly said sternly.

"I hate to break this mood, but may I say I'm glad you're doing so well?" commented Moe, now more relaxed.

"Oh, yes," came the chorus, "glad you're coming along so nicely, Claudia," in the manner of dinner guests giving the proper response a moment or two late.

"It's my babbling that's at fault," responded the gracious hostess. "I never gave you a chance, did I?"

"Oh, well, as long as we're all here and clicking along, that's what counts," Tom remarked glibly.

"Yes, I agree, Tom," I said. "It's certainly nice the way this has all worked out, isn't it, group? We're really fortunate to have such wonderful co-operation from the hospital and from Claudia's surgeon."

"Yes, we are; it's really remarkable," observed Bob.

"It's things like this that renew one's hope in people and in institutions," added Moe.

"I don't know about that," John said.

"Okay, don't get started again on any of your pet theories," crackled Molly. "For a change they are all making sense. Quite honestly, when this idea was suggested last week, I thought the Doc was out of his mind. I thought there could never be a sillier idea, and besides, I was sure no general hospital would allow a collection of screwballs like us to hold a seance within its precious walls."

"Did you really think that?" questioned Claudia curiously. "When Dr. Green told me about it, the idea seemed as natural as could be."

"I know I'm changing the subject, and if somebody objects, I'll drop it, but I just want to say this is the first time I have ever been in a hospital when I haven't been scared out of my pants," declared Tom. "I swear these places always give me the creeps; even the smell is enough to put fear into me. It carries me back, that smell, to the time I had my tonsils out as a kid. I remember how worried I was. Some doctor snuck up behind me and put something over my face and the next thing I knew I was choking to death. I remember raising so much hell, screaming and kicking, that I broke his grip, and bit his thumb. I can still hear him calling me a little brat. I suppose I was, but I was sure scared."

"Come to think of it," broke in Bob, "I was supposed to be a heart case as a kid, and I'll never forget those visits to the clinic of the hospital. They are indelibly fixed in my mind. All those doctors and nurses in white uniforms with their mumbo-jumbo, and my mother standing next to me while I sat in the carriage—it's all so vivid—and I'll tell you this, I didn't like it for one minute."

"I have my feelings about hospitals, too," said Molly. "That old bitch of a mother of mine used the doctor as the bogie man. Whenever I had been particularly bad, she would say, 'And if you keep it up, I'm going to take you to the doctor, and he'll wrap you in a bandage and that will keep you out of trouble.'"

"Gee, I guess I'm lucky. I never had horrible experiences like those," said Betty. "I liked doctors and hospitals. Our family doctor was a wonderful old man. He used to tie ribbons made of gauze in my hair, and gave me tongue depressors to play with, and lollipops. A visit to his office was always a big occasion for us. When my sister and I went for our periodic physical checkups, it was always an occasion to look forward to. Although he never knew it, the dear old doctor and I were married in my make-believe. I used to imagine that his office was our home, and that he was my husband and his nurse our house servant. The doll I played with in his waiting room was our own child, and it was the doll who was coming there to be treated as a patient, not me— Ah!!! childhood!!!"

"Speaking of dolls," Claudia spoke up, "when I was five, an aunt gave me an incubator doll. I went outside excitedly with it to play with two friends. I was furious because they insisted on play-ing the parents to the doll, and left me out. And I remember some-thing else also in connection with this. I was playing with a neigh-borhood boy and we were pretending to be doctor and nurse. All I can recall is the smell of the rubber mat that I was lying on, and for some reason, I felt guilty."

"That reminds me, Claudia," said Tom, "I don't know how it started or exactly when I stopped believing it, but talking about babies and where they come from, this is what I used to believe. You see, my mother and father never gave us any education or information on this subject, and so it was all left up to our imagi-nations. Well—I finally figured out that the baby grew in Mother's stomach and that when it was big enough it came out her behind. And you know, because of my unwillingness to be friendly and co-operative—when people used to say that I was a shit—it all seemed to fit, because I knew that was where I had come from, just like that other stuff. Once when one of the fellows in the sixth grade said to the gang that I always looked so sloppy and messy, I felt it was quite all right because I knew I was the product of a bowel movement, and therefore, shitty in my appearance."

"That's awful," exclaimed Betty.

"It certainly is," echoed Eve, "but it explains so much about you that I couldn't understand before."

"I only hope, Tom, that some difference in your opinion of

yourself will be reflected in your personal appearance as a result of your understanding this," I said.

"I hope so too, Doc," he said in low tones.

"I had a funny idea about childbirth, too," grinned Molly, somewhat embarrassed. "I used to feel that I would become pregnant if I let a man kiss me. Also that because my belly button was just a slit, I couldn't have children like everyone else had. It took me years to come to the realization that babies were not born out of the belly button."

"This all reminds me of an amusing episode in my life," Eve said. "I was fourteen and a half and had not yet menstruated. I was considerably concerned and felt that I would never be able to have children. It was Columbus Day, and I had gone to the movies with a friend. When I returned no one was at home. I went to the 'john,' and there it was. I was thrilled. I ran to the phone and called this friend. We were going to a dance, so she, from her more experienced pinnacle, wisely advised me to wear a tight girdle in addition to the napkin. She reasoned that this would give me more comfort. I had a particularly good time at the dance that evening and believed it to be because of my newly acquired womanhood. The next day, I told my mother of the occurrence. When she offered to tell me the facts of life, I blithely dismissed her with, 'It's not necessary, Mother, I know already.'"

My earlier concern that this hospital setting might produce an excessive preoccupation with self-centered bodily infancy material was now dispelled. The associations produced by the setting and the circumstances had caused a recall in the patients but remained on a person-to-person level. It seemed that everything they were discussing was related to people and events in a pertinent way instead of a "poor me" attitude. I was pleased with this turn of events, for the circumstances had proven a stimulus to let down the bars of reticence. The group's conversations made it quite clear that they had carefully harboured these memories and felt concern as they dealt with their relationships with their parents, illnesses, as well as distortions of sexual knowledge.

In an anxious but controlled voice, Betty started on her pent-up associations. "It happened to me when I was ten. I had had no preparation. I was sitting on the toilet seat when all of a sudden I let go with this gush of blood. I was scared to death and started to cry. I even wondered what I could have done that was wrong. As if that wasn't bad enough, I tried to conceal what had happened for a while. After I took my panties off and washed them, I put on a fresh pair. You can imagine my panic when, within a half hour, I discovered they were again full of blood. I realized then that I had to tell my mother though I didn't know what to say to her. It wasn't only embarrassment—I was convinced that I had done something wrong. My mother attempted to treat the matter lightly, which only made things worse. Her attitude was most noncommittal. This thoroughly confused me. I expected punishment, and not receiving it, I merely became more bewildered. She went to her closet, produced a sanitary belt and napkin without further explanation than to tell me to put them on, and to change the pad whenever necessary. This I construed as being a bandage applied to girls when they had been wicked. I suppose I'll never forgive my mother for that. Today I realized she was trying to be kind by treating the whole affair in such a blasé manner. All it did was to convince me further that I had been a wicked daughter. But I know this—if ever I have a daughter, I will certainly see to it that she gets the proper approach to the problem."

At this point Claudia came back into the conversation. "Speaking of female secretions, a story suddenly comes back to me that I haven't thought of in years. I was spending the night at Cousin Leslie and Mark's house, since my parents were away for the weekend. Cousin Leslie was at the movies. Mark, aged twelve, entered my bedroom and with perfect composure proudly displayed his penis to me. I was embarrassed, as this was the first time I had seen a penis. With this, the realization that men were different from women suddenly took on deeper meaning. He proceeded to tell me about wet dreams, and for a year or so after, when my girl friends were talking about having their periods, I thought it was the female version of wet dreams."

Here John seemed to feel the urge to hold forth. "When I was twelve or thirteen, I suddenly developed a severe case of acne.

I've always been a rather shy and self-conscious person but this was really the end. I stayed in my room. I would only come out for school and meals. One Saturday, my dad called me down into the parlor. He was trying to be fatherly and helpful. In his typically clumsy but highly intellectual manner, I think he was trying to have a man-to-man talk about the birds and the bees. It was all rather gruesome as I recall, but when he turned to the subject of my pimples, I could have died. He implied that they were a result of my playing with myself. The warning imparted to me was that if I expected to get rid of the pimples, I had better stop that activity. Up to that time I had always harbored a fear that bodily harm would occur to me as a result of my masturbation and this proved it. Now when I feel the urge, I carry it out without feeling degraded."

"I know what you mean about that kind of a fear," Moe broke in. "My father once even threatened to cut it off if I didn't stop, after having caught me at it. That bastard didn't stop me, although I always did wonder if it would affect me in any way, until I got to college and read some hygiene books on the subject."

"I always had the fear that I'd never live long enough to grow up and go to bed with some woman," said Bob, attempting to be just a little too casual about the whole affair. "In any case, I used the idea as rationalization, and kept masturbating for years. As a matter of fact, it's only since Eve that I've stopped it."

Last came Tom. "Fellows like me have to! Girls just don't go for me. My mother always tried to give us the impression that paying attention to your body in any way was sinful. So when I did do it, it just added to the rest of my feelings of being shitty."

"All this business of unworthiness and bodily destruction was sure aroused this past week," said Claudia. "It's quite an ordeal, signing your name on a piece of paper which gives them permission to cut you up. The surgeon had warned me that there was a possibility that some of my female organs might have to be removed. And, boy, if you think that wouldn't give you a scare, you have another think coming. As you all know, I have labored under feelings of not being feminine enough as it was, without the helpful loss of some female organs. I assure you it's no joke, but I'm glad I didn't wind up sterilized."

Without flinching, Eve picked up the thread. "One day when I was about fifteen, while coming home from high school, my girl friends and I went into a lingerie shop. A woman and her husband were examining the lingerie. When the woman picked up a bra, her husband turned to her calmly, and said, 'You can't use that, you don't have two any more.' I realized he was saying that she was missing a breast, but I was still shocked and puzzled. I went home and told the incident to Mother. Mother explained that some women get cancer of the breast or some other malady, and must have the breast removed. I remember hoping this would never happen to me. The fear I associated with it was that a man would never want to love me with such a deformity."

"Exactly," interrupted Claudia, tensely. "I had all those fears myself. You can't imagine what I went through when I was pregnant. At times I would see myself thoroughly mutilated by the experience, with all my innards torn out of me. At other times, I imagined my breasts disfigured by nursing. I also imagined bleeding to death on the delivery table with all the stories of mothers dying in childbirth flashing in front of me like scenes in a movie. And as if this wasn't enough—the concern and worry I engaged in as to whether my child would be physically normal was constant. Would it be a Mongolian idiot, be missing a limb, or would there be too many normal parts, like two heads or something? You can't imagine, girls, what goes through the mind of a girl who is about to become a mother for the first time."

"Oh, yes, I can," retorted Betty, "and without ever having been pregnant."

"Let me tell you this," Molly interjected aggressively, "I can understand what you're talking about, Claudia, but I have a bigger fear. You see, when I was born my mother was taken away to a mental hospital. She had exactly the kind of worry that you were talking about before. She was deathly afraid something would be physically wrong with her baby, and when I developed a case of yellow jaundice soon after being born—that did it. The doctor later explained to us that this seemed a justification of her fears that she had been less than a virtuous woman during her life. The actual truth was that she had been as straight as an arrow. I, too, must confess that I am afraid of childbirth because of the fear that I might do harm to my baby. I've always had this fear—afraid that I might go off my rocker and do some atrocious thing to the baby."

When Molly finished speaking, she turned and looked at me, as did all the others. Taking the cue, I said, "I knew this session would be unusual. I knew there would be some reminiscing and recall of a variety that we had not previously experienced. If therapy is to be successful, I feel it's necessary for this type of recall to occur, in terms of what may be translating the There and Then into the Here and Now. It takes real security for this to occur and it's a pleasure to see you people demonstrating this security. I'm sure, if you'll stop to realize—you've lived with these words and their disturbing images far too long, but have never felt safe enough heretofore to discuss them openly with another person. It's this new-found security that permits your openness with this so-called dangerous material. Of course, you realize it's all unrealistic and couldn't really happen to you, and I'm sure you're beginning to suspect that, with greater maturity, these thoughts will disappear like melting snow in the presence of warm sunshine. The thoughts would not have been there in the first place, in fact, had your childhoods been otherwise. Indeed, it's been a very fortuitous development—this coming to the hospital at this time. I suppose these fears of ours would have come out sooner or later, but present events have hurried them along a bit."

"I understand what you mean, Doc," Bob said gratefully.

"And that goes for me, too," said Molly.

"And to say the least—me," followed Claudia.

"Well then, people—before I call the session to a close, may I extend to each and every one of you my heartfelt wishes for a prosperous and healthy New Year."

With echoes of, "The same to you, Doc," still ringing in his ears back at the office, a tired and spent psychiatrist closed the door feeling that the year had been a notable one.

14. *The Old and the New*

The evening preceding the first group session of the new year found me conducting a silent recapitulation of the group's history. And as I sat eating my dinner in a restaurant, I asked myself the germane question, "Were the conflicts being resolved?" The recollection of the patients' stymied emotional status came back to me. The pictures of their excessive acting-out in life away from the group flashed before me. These two conditions had been properties of their conflict. Certainly, I thought, there could be no doubt about the group in this respect: it had helped unsnarl these problems considerably. The action in the group had given them real experience in the true psychological sense of the word. I, alone, had been unable to be a whole family configuration to them, but the group had fulfilled the family function. No longer would they engage in fruitless and disturbing pursuits with respect to their relations to others. Such actions were now almost completely within the boundaries of the group structure.

And when I returned to my office with fifteen minutes to spare before the group met, I sat down behind my desk with the same thought process continuing. But before I had gone much further, I found myself smiling and wondering whether I was beginning to take myself too seriously in relation to these events. In fact, I was glad that I could laugh at myself as a target—since I had come to realize that it is so easy to take one's self too seriously.

Encouraged by my own willingness to laugh at myself and thereby feeling that I had not lost perspective, my survey with its associations went on more comfortably. And I realized that there are periods when we all must reminisce and deeply communicate with ourselves. Perhaps the most common of these periods occurs at New Year's—the New Year's resolution often representing the result of such activity. However, I was hoping not to conclude my internal communication in the form of any resolution. To me, such a process as turning over a new leaf means incomplete self-communication and often leads into the faulty belief that will power is a greater force than reality would indicate. If anything, our group experience had shown that growth is a slow process, one in which the person cannot "will" himself into maturity.

Then as my horizon broadened to include all of my professional experience, it became clear that the neurotic is often characterized by an inability to have something new happen to him. He may travel near and far, become rich or poor, marry and divorce, but he still thinks, speaks and behaves in the same stereotyped manner. It is as if he were saying, "Look what it's doing to me," rather than "Look what's happening."

In keeping with these thoughts, I was reminded of an incident, not even related to therapy. The setting was a medical convention that I was attending. A brilliant, young physician had introduced an intriguing and startling concept. After the usual applause, the chairman opened the meeting to discussion. The first to speak was a conservative-appearing physician who suggested by his mannerisms one of the pillars of the profession in his community. He began to attack the new concept in a most methodical and logical manner. However, it was near the end of his criticism that he spoke the words that made the greatest impression upon me. He said, in effect, that in all of his thirty-two years of experience, he had never seen any of the phenomena mentioned by the speaker and furthermore, he did not see that these young and aggressive ideas were accomplishing anything other than disrupting matters. When he concluded, another member arose and said, "Perhaps the criticism of the distinguished doctor's inability to accept and under-

193

stand the viewpoint presented in the speaker's paper arises from the fact that he has had one year's experience times thirty-two." And now in retrospect, I felt that I understood the depth of the "quip" that at the time had appeared only as a defense for the new idea.

Another area that came into focus was the relationship between immaturity and morality. The group's experience had led me to see that they were not as closely related as I had thought them to be. As a result, I could see them as being two separate and distinct entities. The cries of good and evil seemed present only when there was an absence of the deeper understanding of human behavior. When the individual can say to himself, "I am I," he has arrived at a state not only of being familiar with himself but a state where he understands the meaning of the relationships in his environment. In fact, at this point of growth the need for self-deception is absent. His existence has been established. Time follows existence—that is, *Being* predominates over all other factors in the environment. And often when such understanding was inadequate, it led to a preoccupation with morality in place of the normal occupation with *Being*.

Certainly, as the group had grown in stature, they seemed less concerned with evaluating their behavior on a single dimension of morality, but instead, were increasingly concerned with whether what they did produced constructive results. It was as if they trusted themselves and therefore had no longer the need to dwell upon the childish concern of good and bad.

Here again, the New Year's resolution caught my attention. Its meaning struck me as being quite different from the understanding that the group was developing. It occurred to me that the use of this easier way out—the use of the resolution and other fixed childlike formulations—produced a blinding rigidity. Mainly, the memories of people thinking, "If I become a good boy or girl, I will no doubt be rewarded and good things will come to me." By contrast, I was pleased to realize that the group was showing evidence of "If I can understand my neighbor's behavior and accept it, perhaps we will both be better off for the experience." Even further, I felt their growth could be seen in their need to depend less upon my opinion as an authority-figure who in the past they had wanted to have praise them if they practiced unfeeling moralistic self-control.

In marked contrast, I felt that now they were increasing their enjoyment of being people who were imperfect and would never be otherwise, but to whom it was no longer essential to be perfect to have the pleasures of life.

The unspoken atmosphere of the group seemed to point up the fact that imperfection and adjusted living were not antagonistic but could live side by side without conflict. The group seemed to have acquired one of the comprehensions that is most difficult for people—that the main trouble between themselves and others arises out of this formerly irreconcilable clash between perfectionism in one's own eyes and one's constructive relationships with others.

In the remaining few minutes before the group started, I thought of Eve and Bob. Eve no longer found it necessary to play the part of a "Lorelei." She had gone one step further—she had accepted the role of motherhood in her relationship to Claudia with humility. Bob, in turn, had certainly revealed considerable growth. His external arrogance had disappeared as he had gained internal stature. One could easily tell by his behavior that he felt the value of emotional relatedness. His increased masculinity revealed itself in the absence of the Don Juan byplay.

There was no doubting it. I was happy to be a part of our group. And looking into the adjacent room as they were assembling, seeing them individually, the feeling that we, as a group, had traveled a long way brought about a sense of worth-whileness that I felt belonged to all of us.

The final object of my internal communication was myself. This group experience had affected me deeply. My own family relationships had improved. It had always seemed strange to me that some people believed that, because a person was a psychiatrist, he automatically qualified as a good mate and a parent. I held no such beliefs. Despite all my training and experience with patients, I knew that I too had to live through the necessary adjustments in these roles, at home. There was no doubt in my mind that I had gained in this sense through our group's experience.

Of somewhat less immediate concern, I began to consider that perhaps it was time to start another group in my private practice. I reasoned that I had enough patients who needed this and it might be a dereliction on my part not to give them this opportunity.

The first session of the new year opened in the same mood which had consumed me in the time that I had been alone before the session started.

"Let's see now, we've been going at this since April," said Bob. "For my money, it seems in many ways as if I've just begun to appreciate living. I want to tell you about a 'pipe dream' of mine. You know, one of those fantasies we all have and sometimes carry around with us all our life. You all know, of course, that I'm a psychologist, or soon will be. I've often asked myself why. Why did I become a psychologist? I think the reason is only now becoming clear, as I speak with you. My mother was a sort of philosophical woman. You know—the kind that all the other women in the neighborhood would come to for advice and tell their troubles to. And, as you may remember, my father was supposed to be the head of the household, but it was Mother who wore the pants. My daydream encompassed the ambition of so many little boys—to be better than Father. But in my case, of course, Father was Mother, and therefore it meant being better than Mother. This, then, to my mixed-up way of thinking, had narrowed down the choice of a field of operation to human relationship or clinical psychology. In a sense, it also explains why I felt so extremely hostile toward the Doc. In the early days, I bitterly resented the group. This embitterment was based on my desire to destroy his accomplishments as the masculine mother. For a while, he was my mother in pants—but now he's a father-figure and masculine to me in every sense of the word.

"In this pipe dream, I was preoccupied with seeing myself as a designer. That is, a designer of a new personality test. My fantasy saw me acting in a superlative manner. All sorts of decorations and honors were bestowed upon me. This would signify that I had outmatched my masculine mother. It now also occurs to me that my taking over the group in the beginning, as I did, was more of the same thing. But getting on with this fantasy of mine, I've come to another realization—that people's emotional structure, as seen by the various psychological tests, doesn't explain adequately what they are really like in terms of function. At school and in the clinic, they are now doing group therapy, too. I've had to test many of our patients. Later on, seeing these very same patients' behavior in a clinical group, I appreciate what the Doc has said, 'There's more to the human personality than the one-to-one human contact.' By this I gather he means, as you and I have heard him say, 'People are born into a group, grow as part of a group, develop through a group, create as a member of a group and in death leave the group. So why try to understand the human being in terms of single one-to-one responses.'

"This realization, with the acceptance of the group and the Doc, has enabled me to speak of my fantasy, and I guess I'm ready to give it up now."

"Honey, you're really catching on," Eve said with warmth. "As you were telling all this about yourself, I couldn't help but say to myself, 'That's my Bob—he's my man.' Bob, I'm going to let you in on a secret. If you'll have me, I want to marry you."

When the roar died down, Bob was finally heard to say, "It's okay by me, baby." However, there was a lack of definiteness about the remark. It was done in an air of conviviality, as was Eve's proposal. The group, equally, did not respond as though they felt the exchange had been a serious one. This horseplay was a by-product of their new-found security. No longer did every word have to be of dire consequence.

"Speaking of daydreams," said Eve, "I have one of my own. It concerns being a career woman. I was going to become some sort of woman executive who was consulted on business decisions in the publishing world. I saw myself coming to New York and within a year's time taking a penthouse apartment overlooking the East River. But, alas, just like yours, it too has gone down the drain. Now it's marriage, white picket fence and all, for me. I've seen too many cold women of high-fashion who, beneath it all, are suffering from extreme loneliness. It's just not my cup of——"

"Huh," interrupted Molly. "That's kid stuff compared to my

dreams of glory. You see"—and as she spoke, she actually seemed to believe in what she was saying—"I have talent as a writer." On and on she went with detailed description of her abilities, her forehead furrowed and eyebrows drawn to emphasize the seriousness of her mood. After about five or ten minutes of this self-possessed enchantment, she had to admit a few discrepancies. Moe ascertained that she had never really had one piece of her work published. And when Eve inquired as to how she went about her writing, the truth came out. "Actually," she said, "it's all in my head, and I just don't seem to be able to get it down on paper. During the day, at work, I have these great ideas, but on the few occasions that I do sit down to write, I've only done a page or two, at best." In anguish, she turned to me and asked, "Why is it, Doc, that I have such an exalted opinion of myself at one moment, and the next I am nothing more than a complete and utter nincompoop?"

"Why do you think?" I returned her question.

A baffled look spread across her face. In a moment she said with strong query, "Is it because I can't accept the real me?"

Taking her response and turning to the fast-growing oldest son of the group—"Bob," I said, "Bob, how does that strike you?"

"That's it exactly." The words gave me a momentary feeling of a young self-assured fast-striding two-year-old colt. "Whenever there is a deficiency of self-acceptance, the human being turns his imagery into grandiose fantasies, and the resulting forces simultaneously further reduce the self-acceptance."

"Well, I'll be God damned!" John was heard to say in annoyance. "It may all be true, and I didn't hear the Doc saying it wasn't, but let's not get too smug about it, Bob, old boy."

John, I feared, was becoming jealous of Bob's progress. It was true that Bob's manner of speech was too erudite for the occasion, but it was not so condescending as it had been in the past. This time Bob's security was adequate. He acknowledged John's comment with a nod of his head, but did not jump for the bait. Silently he lit up a cigarette and waited for the action to continue.

"Well, if you don't mind," Moe said in a rather apologetic

tone, "I would like to register my hopes for the new year. I'd like to get a better job and find myself a girl friend."

"Good for you!" John remarked amiably.

"Yes, I'm dissatisfied with my job. I see no room for progress or advancement. I need something at work that is more challenging. There was a time when all I asked of my job was that it would not be too taxing and would pay well. Now I find myself saying each day that I wish something new would happen at work. As I sit at the drawing board, I find myself sketching plans of things which have nothing to do with my job. I'm beginning to suspect that maybe I have some inventive talent instead of just being another run-of-the-mill engineer. Now as to the matter of a girl friend —well—I'm over the major part of the hurt at the loss of my wife. The group experience here has taught me one thing with respect to this problem. Life goes on no matter what. It's no use for a fellow like me to mope around. The Doc says self-pity is a destroyer. I say it stinks. I'm sick and tired of feeling sorry for myself. The only cure for loneliness is for me to get off my lazy ass and find a girl friend. I've started to notice them in the subways again, and I think I'll accept an invitation to a party an old buddy of mine is throwing next weekend. So we'll see what cooks with that."

"If only I could stop hating people," Tom grumbled. "That's all. I get so damned tired and wornout by hating that I never have any time left over to do anything else."

"Yeah, I know what you mean," said Molly. "You and I are birds of a feather. We are both so God-damned busy hating the world because it won't love us on our terms that we might as well not be here." Molly turned to me. "Doc, how do you stop hating?"

"I'm afraid that's a leading question, Molly, but what do you think, Betty?"

"I'd say you've got to give," she responded.

"Give what?" barked Molly.

"Oh, you know," Betty said, annoyed. "Just give—love somebody, take a chance and love somebody."

"But I can't," retorted Molly. "I can't seem to love anybody, because every time I start to, I begin to feel so vulnerable. I feel I'm going to get hurt. And yet that's not it exactly. It's more that I feel I'm going to lose something."

"Yeah, I know what you mean," was Tom's remark. "You'll lose the love you have for yourself."

"What do you mean?" asked Molly irritably.

"You know what I mean," he said. "You and I don't love people simply because we don't feel anybody could love us as much as we love ourselves."

"You know, maybe you're right," she said with an air of resignation.

"Look, on this I *know* I'm right," he finished up the exchange.

"Okay, so it's the truth," Molly started anew, "but how do you go about changing it, Doc?"

Betty, leaning forward in her chair to such an extent that she was almost off it, spoke. "I can't understand why you don't see it, Molly. Not that I'm saying I'm a prize example, but if you'll just see what's gone on here in the past months you'll have the answer. Take Claudia, for example. She's improved and loves people, isn't that true?"

Silently, Molly nodded her head in agreement. "Well then, all she did was to begin to talk to people here as if they were people. She didn't spend session after session merely bellyaching to the others as though they were professional listeners. She got interested in others and made herself interesting to them, and you know what, the first thing we all knew, she became a happier person."

"What you're saying is perfectly true," said Molly in a martyred tone.

"Doc, what's the last bulletin you have on her condition?" Eve inquired.

"Why, I heard from her surgeon today that the inflammation in her legs had subsided, and that she probably would be permitted out of bed for the first time today. I was also told that her parents have been down to visit her, and are staying in New York until she leaves the hospital."

"That certainly sounds fine," she responded.

"It'll be good to have her back. I've missed her this session," Moe's cheery voice rang out.

"You know, that was some session we had in the hospital last week," said Tom.

"You enjoyed it, eh?"

"Yes, I did, Doc. It made me feel for the first time in my life that people really do care for one another."

"I'll tell you this, Tom. I'm enjoying what you're saying at this moment." Whereupon I received the first smile I ever had from him.

Carried away by the success of the moment, I suppose I went a bit overboard in a philosophical way. "Isn't it a pity that so frequently it takes a human tragedy to bring out the humanitarian qualities that otherwise lie dormant within us? It's always been a source of wonder to me as to why this is true. In fact, the feeling is somewhat akin to our Christmas spirit. I mean, it takes an occasion for man to practice good fellowship. It's almost as if he couldn't do it otherwise. Sometimes when I walk around the streets of New York and see the callousness of people, I actually shudder. I'll never get used to the sight of passers-by in Times Square ignoring a drunk lying in the street or sometimes even stepping over him as if either he wasn't there or else was a misplaced curbstone. Yet, I feel if you took the same group of people and showed them a movie of the man's life story, they would probably pick him up, and give him a room in their own home. Tom, it's a peculiar world you and I live in. I don't know the answers any more than you do, but it would be nice if we could all be kinder to one another without needing tragedy as the stimulus."

"You know, I've never thought about it, Doc," he said, looking me in the eye for a change, "but I like what you've said. It makes me feel that it's high time I began to take care of me."

The silence that settled over the room following these last words of Tom bespoke each person's identification with the matter.

The profundity of the moment and the silence were brought disturbingly to an end. The door opened and two somber people plodded toward the group, their hats and coats on, their arms drooping at their sides. They came to a halt when they reached the outer edges of the circle. They peered at us and the suspense rose higher and higher. At last the eyes of the group turned away from them to me. Although no one spoke, all the patients' faces were crying out, "Who are they?"—"What are they doing here?"—"We don't know them, do you?"

These events, which seemed to take an eternity, actually occurred within a matter of seconds. Suddenly, I realized that these strangers were unable to speak. "May I help you?" I finally asked, my calm words belying the tension of the occasion.

The question caused the woman to turn to the man and then back to the group, and after a moment more of painful silence, she spoke. "She asked us to say, 'It was wonderful.' "

When no further information followed, I said, as gently as possible, "Who?"

"My daughter, Claudia."

"Oh," came a response from several of the patients.

"You are Claudia's parents?" I asked as I stood up and walked across the room to shake hands with them.

It was more than a moment before Claudia's father realized that I had made a gesture to welcome him. Slowly, his hand rose and met mine. "I'm happy you could stop in to see us. Won't you please sit down and join us?" I turned to Moe and said, "Moe, be a good fellow and get two extra chairs from the closet behind you for Mr. and Mrs. Evans."

They sat down, still in their hats and coats, and I asked, "How is she?"

Again, a pregnant silence. This time, however, the mother found the necessary energy to speak. "We are here, because she asked us to come. Her dad and I came down from New Hampshire to visit her while she was still in the hospital. We were so delighted with her progress and she'd been telling us in such glowing terms about all you people—the time you came to visit her at the hospital made such a difference to her. We never received a letter from her which didn't mention the fun she was having with 'Her Group.'

"Today, when we went to visit Claudia, her poor appearance shocked us. A minute or so before we arrived, she was getting out of bed for the first time with a nurse's assistance. She suffered a severe, stabbing pain in her chest and collapsed back onto the bed. As we walked into the room, she seemed to be in great pain; her breathing was labored; her head, stomach and everything seemed to hurt. She started to choke and turn purple. Dad ran out into the hall calling for a doctor. I could only hold her and pray. For a moment she appeared to improve. She looked up at me and smiled—the most beautiful smile I've ever seen—and she said, 'Mother—I love you —and please tell them all—the group—it was wonderful!' "

Mrs. Evans continued, now berating herself laboriously. "Why, even when I said that I thought she would get better because of the improvement in her color and breathing, Claudia again knew better. She shook her head calmly and said to me with a smile that it would be all right now, Mother, and that I wouldn't have to worry about her any longer. In addition, she made me promise not to interfere with her child, who is growing up without knowing who her real mother was. She said that the child is now part of a happy family and shouldn't know about her background. Of course, I promised, and I intend to keep my promise, just as I have carried her final words to you people."

"Oh, my God, no, it can't be true!" screamed Eve, through her tears. She cried until the misery seemed to enter the marrow of her bones.

Bob rose, walked over and put his arm around her shoulders. "Now, honey, take it easy—take it easy—but let it out—it's better that way. I know you've had a tremendous shock and no doubt the loss is greater to you than to any of us—you two were so close. But, honey, just stop and think how much worse it is for Mr. and Mrs. Evans—don't add to their already heavy burden. It will take a little time for us to realize the fact that Claudia is gone. These things are always that way. Death is so resolute and so one-way. Its finality is what makes it so tough to take."

Despite my own grief, I couldn't help but look up from my seated position to Bob—and he caught my glance of pride in him as a maturing young man.

Mrs. Evans spoke again. "In the bedside table, I found eight letters—some barely legible. On different nights she had written on a hospital pad. The note that made me saddest was addressed to one of you here, called Eve. It made me realize in what way I had not been the mother I should have been, but it seems as if she forgave me with her last few words. . . ."

"Yes, just as I came back into the room," Claudia's father said haltingly, "I also heard her words. Her mother and I feel so deeply grateful to you people. I suppose we'll never understand the full impact of what she meant by 'Tell them it was wonderful.' However, sitting here at this moment with the full realization of the loss of our only child hitting us, it makes it more tolerable just to be here—so perhaps I do feel a little of what it must have meant to her."

"It is impossible to tell you the sadness I feel at this moment. We all know what your loss is, Mr. and Mrs. Evans—for you see—in a way of speaking—it's an equal loss to us. It's hard to explain, but Claudia was our baby, too," I ended.

"Of this, there can be little doubt," answered her father.

"I realize the truth of that, Doctor," said her mother, "and it pleases, but also pains me, to know it was so."

"Now there, let's not be so hard on ourselves, Mrs. Evans. You actually did your best; and if you must make a reckoning, it isn't what we've done or have not done in terms of wisdom that counts, but rather, in terms of love."

She looked at me and almost managed a small smile.

Eve had her face buried in her hands on her knees. Her bobbing head showed that she was still sobbing. Bob had returned to his seat. Eve was sitting next to me and my hand fell on the back of her neck and brushed the strands of her long page-boy bob.

"Is that Eve?" inquired Claudia's mother.

I nodded.

"Yes, that's Eve," Bob said strongly. "As you've probably gathered by now, Mrs. Evans, these two girls were very close."

"Yes, I know, and it had always been my wish that my daughter and I could have been such friends."

Betty, who was sitting on the other side of Eve, spoke. "Eve, say something; it will be better for you if you do."

I had now taken my hand from Eve's head and a moment later, she sat up. First she turned and looked at Betty; then she glanced at me. Finally, looking in Mrs. Evans's direction she said, "Mrs. Evans, have you your daughter's note to me with you?"

"Yes, I have." Fumbling through her handbag to find it, she hesitatingly held it, looking at Eve.

Eve looked at her questioningly.

"I guess it's best if I read it to all of you." In a tone indicative of her need to free herself, Mrs. Evans began to read.

" 'To Eve. Were it not for you and your concern for me, I would never have known the comfort of love. In the past, this love was known to me only with the crippling features of restraint. We have known each other nine precious months—the length of a pregnancy. These nine short months of knowing you have meant more to me than any other nine months of my life. It's not that I believed my mother didn't love me, but rather, that she was unable to show it when it counted. It's through knowing you and the others of the group that I have felt the pulse of life. Only your kind of demonstrativeness seems capable of rendering this. It became so easy to understand my own mother after finding all of you. It is my intention to tell her now that I understand and can at last appreciate her in her own setting. You see, Eve, I believe the only difference between you and my mother is the ability to relate.

" 'You may wonder why I've written these notes to you and the other group members. It's very simple. I've had the time and the inclination to tell you—and the others—the importance of our emotional communication. Love, Claudia.' "

Eve walked over and picked up Mrs. Evans's gloves that were lying at her feet. She was in full possession of her dignity as a young lady as she returned the gloves, saying, "I'm sure these are yours." She placed them in Mrs. Evans's lap, then clasped her hands within her own, and finished the sentence with the reassurance, "And these are my hands for you to rely upon."

Mrs. Evans, looking up into Eve's face, replied, "Yes, perhaps you will be my daughter, now."

"Of course I will."

Moe, who had a seat next to Mrs. Evans, got up and gave it to Eve. He went over and sat in her former chair.

"It's truly a fine thing that exists here," said Mr. Evans in a subdued voice. "You've made it so much easier for us. We don't know anyone in this big city—we're just small-town people from New Hampshire. The only things we know are family life and neighbors. In a sense, you've supplied them both to Claudia and in this strange and confusing city you are now supplying the same to Mrs. Evans and me. We didn't know whether to call you or not. I simply said to my wife, 'Emily, let's go to his office and deliver Claudia's last words to him personally.' I never expected to find her group here. I can see now how much worse it would have been for Emily and me if we had had to take that long lonely train ride home without first speaking with some kind people—especially people who knew our daughter so well."

"Yes, of course, Mr. Evans, I know this situation all too well myself," Moe answered. "Several years ago when I was in Korea, my wife died, and when my captain told me the news, I had no one to turn to. It's only those of us who have been in this position, and have not had friends or neighbors to turn to when death struck, who can appreciate this kindness."

"It's a funny thing to hear you say that, Moe," said Tom, "especially when the Doc had explained to me earlier this evening how often tragedy brings out the otherwise non-active humanity in people."

John, joining the sentiment, then spoke. "Of course, it's true, but let's not forget, it's a terrible price——" and he stopped abruptly.

Picking up the loose thread, Molly said, "The place will never be the same without her. Even her death means more to me than most people do, living. She's given me hope—hope and promise."

"Mr. and Mrs. Evans," Bob broke in, "perhaps you have an idea now what your Claudia meant to all of us. Just in case it's not clear, let me say that Claudia was our barometer. As she went, so went this group. When she began to love others, the group began to love as only people can love. She never would have cared to admit this, but she gave more to us than we gave to her."

Mr. Evans looked at his wife and then at Bob and said, "We thank you."

A decisive nod of acknowledgment came in return from Bob,

while the group at last showed some signs of release from their severe tension.

At this point, I turned to the group, to bid them good night, long past the usual time. Each member, with deep communion, shook hands with Claudia's parents. Most did so in silence. I asked Mr. and Mrs. Evans if they cared to remain and they did. We went into my inner office.

It turned out that they had not had time to think about any arrangements. Since they were strangers in New York, I offered my help, which they accepted. I was glad they did. When these preparations were taken care of, it seemed that their shock began to lift. We parted company some two hours later, very much spent people.

Two days later, the group and I went to a chapel on the West Side to pay our last respects. This choice of locality was made by the Evanses in acknowledgment of the close attachment between the group and Claudia.

After that last meeting, we saw Mr. and Mrs. Evans off at Grand Central. They took their girl home to rest in the country, under the same maple tree whose shade had protected her playful childhood hours.

The day following Claudia's death, I saw Bernie. He was not a happy man. His first words were, "What a terrible break!—and she was just the 'pet' you described."

"Yes, Bernie, it was—she meant a great deal to all of us. The shock of it is almost unbelievable. I had never given much thought to its possibility—it seemed too remote. When I heard about the tumor, the idea of death did flash before me, but when you told me postoperatively that the capsule was intact, I relaxed and felt the storm was over."

"It's a strange thing, Case—but these emboli cases [a loose blood clot brought by the blood current from one organ to another organ and which obstructs the circulation] are most unpredictable. Sometimes I believe that despite all we know and do in terms of preventing the formation of clots with anticoagulants, it simply isn't enough. We need something better. . . .

"By the way, we did a 'post' [post-mortem examination] and her lungs were full of emboli, as we had suspected—there simply wasn't another thing we could have done for her."

"Yes, I know that, Bernie. However, I want you to know that I deeply appreciate your management and especially the way you gave her the personal reassurance you did."

"Thanks, but let me say this: although I knew her but a short time, it was easy to see why you people felt the way you did about her. . . . She got me, too!"

Friday evening, we gathered for a regular session. Perhaps in your lifetime you have seen the interior of a henhouse. That is what I thought of when I entered the room. The chairs were closer than usual. Absent was the usual noise. In fact, it was the first time I had ever walked from the inner office into the group room that I had not been greeted with the usual buzzing-bee impact. Why, even the radio had been turned off. I took the seat left for me, which placed me between Moe and Bob. The men and women had again segregated themselves. There was, however, a difference. I was not serving as a fulcrum this time. Instead, they had placed me in the middle of the male section. This implied they wished their leader, in ritualistic manner, to sit as a tribal chief among the men as the leader of their community. The usual salutation, on my part, was unconsciously omitted; instead I said, "Shall we begin?"

The silence which followed finally registered with me. This was their way of letting me know that leadership from me was necessary. The flock was somewhat bewildered—it needed guidance.

I began, "People, would you care to know how it all happened?"

"I think it would be better that way," Moe said in a somber voice.

Looking about the room, I saw no objection and so I went on. "Well, it was like this. You know, Claudia was bedridden because of the inflamed veins in her legs. This made it impossible for her to receive the early ambulation procedures practiced in modern surgery. However, everything known to modern medicine for alleviation of this condition was done. Despite this, she postoperatively developed some clots in her blood vessels. In operations involving the pelvis, this occurs fairly frequently. Typically, this mass or clot may be released from its original location upon sudden bodily movement and come to rest in a narrower passage of the blood stream, often having traveled some distance—for example, to the lungs. This happened with Claudia. However, in her case, there were several, or a whole shower of emboli. They caused a condition known as pulmonary embolism or a state in which the lungs are affected by the embolism.

"So much of her lung tissue was involved that a massive collapse occurred and life became incompatible with the condition. Such things are practically unpredictable and when they strike in the manner in which they did with Claudia, there is really nothing that can be done."

I had spoken in a rather low voice, attempting to be reassuring. I felt that this was what they needed—the remainder of the information. It was the desired help, for their lack of information fostered their insecurity.

"Do you think she suffered much?" inquired Betty.

"Not really. After all, the conversation she had with her mother at the end couldn't have occurred if she had." She actually had suffered, as most victims do who are stricken with this condition, but I thought that to be truthful at this moment would be painful.

"You know, Doc, I felt truly sorry for those people," said a strangely tender Molly. "I can't explain it but I felt a warmth toward them. It really must be a terrible thing bringing your only child back home in a box when she is at the peak of her youth."

"Yes, Molly, I understand, and furthermore I have a great deal of respect for them. Those people have a life that you and I don't quite appreciate. We're so impressed with ourselves in this big-city life, and yet it's their simplicity that makes me wonder if they're not the richer people. It's going to be this simplicity with its humility that will soften the blow for them. It removes the sting and the pain."

"I can see what you mean, Doc," she continued. "You could

see the roots of that love of people in Claudia—I guess that's why we all cared so much for her."

"Yes, Molly, that's it all right. People do tend to miss such neighborliness and its often-seen companion, kindness, when they practice so much isolationism."

"Wasn't it nice that she forgave and understood her parents before she went?" chimed in the friendly voice of Betty.

"Indeed it was," I answered. "After all, they were really nice people and had done their best."

"You know, Doc, in a way, after meeting them it's kind of difficult to understand Claudia—if you get what I mean," said Moe.

"Not at all," Bob responded. "Claudia had to rebel—it was her way—it was this or be a hopeless, dependent cripple."

"Bob's right, Moe. You see, people like her parents have all the wonderful friendly qualities in the world, but so often are unable to let other people, and especially their children, live their own lives."

"Naturally, I see it, but I guess, because my family life was just the reverse, it's difficult for me to understand," Moe concluded.

"It's true that I was very dependent upon my mother," Bob broke in, "but, unlike Claudia's family, ours never had that cozy, warm friendliness which seems to be the subject of our admiration this evening."

"Oh, I see what you mean," responded Eve and continued, "You might say, Bob, the same was true in our home. It was also very one-sided—all mother and little else. My mother attempted, at least on the surface, to be friendly and neighborly, but it was nothing more than social climbing of a deft variety. There could be no mistake about it—she was a despot and friendliness became a casualty."

Moe, turning toward Tom, said, "Tom, I don't know how to say this to you, exactly, but it did my heart good, for your sake, to see you cry at the chapel."

"I guess I understand," Tom answered with mild embarrassment. "I never realized that she had crept into my being as much as she had, until I saw her at the chapel. In the beginning, I had always thought of her as a pathetic and aimless child, but in these last few months, at times she actually made me feel so much—what I felt couldn't be expressed as one thing, but as many. Sometimes, I was jealous of her progress and on other occasions her progress encouraged me and, at still other times, she reminded me of my sister. In case some of you don't remember it, I have a sister—and she always managed to be more successful at everything than my brothers or me. So, when Claudia made her remarkable improvement, it came to me as no great surprise. I'm used to having the girls in the family show up the fellows. What is new, however, is this—Claudia didn't take over Eve's position here. You see, that's what happened at home. When my sister grew up she replaced my mother and I am the helpless victim of that—for my sister is my mother, but my mother isn't my sister."

"Well, well," Moe exclaimed, "you really got quite a load off your chest, didn't you?" Before Tom could speak again, Moe continued. "Now I can see why you and I are so close here—we're real brothers. You're my younger brother and I'm your older brother," and as he spoke these words, a light seemed to go on in his face. "Ah, I get it all clearly now. Bob and Eve are my parents, the Doc is my grandfather, and you, Tom, are my younger brother. The rest of you are like brothers and sisters, but not exactly. You're more of what I would think of as the brothers and sisters I had at school, the places where I worked and the fellows in the Navy."

"You know, Moe, that's the way it is for me, too," answered Tom. "I can see each one of them actually as clearly in those roles for me, as if they really were these people. I can't make up my mind whether the Doc picked the rest of them to fit or we've done this molding."

"What's the difference?" snapped Moe. "It's clear that it is a reduplication of our families. Each one of us apparently sees his or her own family as they sit here in this circle."

"All this is true, what you two have been saying," came the somewhat patronizing voice of Betty, "but I think you are becoming very engrossed in something we all have known, more or less, for some time. And as a result, you, especially Tom, are succeeding by this maneuver in denying the strong feelings you had which Moe noticed in you at the chapel."

"I didn't think of it that way, Betty, but I guess you're right."

"Well then, how about it?" she said, persistently sticking to her objective.

"Oh, hell, I don't know what to say," Tom answered with a shrug of his shoulders.

"Yes, you do," Molly rejoined.

Confused and disturbed, Tom looked at Molly. He did not answer her. He lacked the mature ability to communicate further.

Sensing his 'brother's' inadequacy, Moe picked up the ball. "Let me ask you this," he said turning toward Molly, "What did you feel while you were at the chapel?"

"Well, I'll tell you—it was the first time in my life that I'd ever been to a funeral. Quite frankly, I was scared stiff. It was the first time I'd ever seen a dead person, and it frightened me. It made me remember the time I had the dream—the one in which I saw myself being buried alive. If it had been anyone but Claudia, I swear, I never would have gone." As she finished her last sentence, a notable amount of embarrassment had crept into her speech.

"Molly," I said, "there's no need for you to be ashamed of your feelings and especially under these circumstances. It's not uncommon to be afraid of the dead and your dream of being buried before you are dead is seen frequently with this fear. I feel it means merely that you're afraid your life is passing you by. Perhaps when therapy is successfully concluded, and you are really living, your fear of the dead and of dying will have passed. Remember that those of us who are really involved in living have little time to dwell upon death."

"You mean it's as simple as that, Doc?" she inquired in childish tones.

"Yes, I do," I answered without hesitation. "I have often felt that so many of us spend so much valuable time of our short and precious lives in preoccupation with death, that it might be said that we are the living dead. In fact, many of us are so busy defending ourselves against new experiences while seemingly engaging with life, that actually in effect we produce this living-dead state."

"Say, Doc," the adolescent voice of John broke in, "that's some concept you have there. At first, when you began to speak to

Molly, I thought you were kidding, but I see you mean it. And now, as I give it some thought, I think you've got something there. It just strikes home with me. I mean—I guess—you might say—it certainly applies to me, as well."

The idea caught fire. Slowly, one after the other addressed themselves to the newly erupted concept. Each, in his or her way, began to see his life in a new perspective. The perspective was devoid of self-pity. Almost for the first time in their lives they were able to understand life without the crippling self-pity. The liberation took the death of Claudia out of the realm of a needless and untimely tragedy and placed it in a constructive and meaningful setting for them. It gave substance where emptiness had dwelled. It replaced immaturity with courage. And last and most basically, it was humanity in action.

By the time this tremendous session had reached its end, the group leader had been carried to recall a fragment of a poem, in the midst of his conversation. He was speaking to Molly in summary when the immortal lines of "Thanatopsis," by William Cullen Bryant, came forth:

> "So live, that when thy summons comes to join
> The innumerable caravan which moves
> To that mysterious realm, where each shall take
> His chamber in the silent halls of death,
> Thou go not, like the quarry-slave at night,
> Scourged to his dungeon, but, sustained and soothed
> By an unfaltering trust, approach thy grave,
> Like one that wraps the drapery of his couch
> About him, and lies down to pleasant dreams."

Upon my completion, Molly brought the session to a gracious end by saying, "Doc, I just want to say to you—thanks—just plain thanks."

15. *Substitution, Not Replacement*

In our next session, the following week, the atmosphere was cold and filled with isolation. Near the end of the session we had another interloper. This visitor was a young man in his thirties, neatly dressed in grey. He rang the doorbell, and when I investigated, he stood in the doorway and said, "Are you Dr. Beukenkamp?"

"Yes."

"Well, I have a little note here for you——"

"Might I inquire who you are, sir?" I asked.

"Oh——" he replied, "I guess you don't know me by sight. I'm Bill, Claudia's boy friend."

"Well, I'm glad to know you, Bill," I said, shaking his hand. His firm grip impressed me. I thought to myself, "Weil, young man, you've certainly held up well under this ordeal." His verbal response was in keeping with his handshake. "I was out of town on an assignment for my employers when it all happened," he continued. "I just got back yesterday to learn the sad news from Claudia's landlady. And after I spoke to her parents on the phone last night, I realized I, too, wanted to express myself to her group. And so, I've written a little communication for them which I hope you will accept. I realize it's somewhat audacious of me—but you people meant so very much to her and she meant so much to me, that I felt compelled to express my feelings to you."

"Of course, Bill, I'm glad you've come to us—to those of us

who cared—to unburden yourself. And I do understand. Won't you come in and meet the group and share your communication in person?" I offered.

"If it's all the same to you, Doctor, I'd prefer not to. I'd rather just hand you the message and let you read it to them. I'm afraid the whole situation is still too fresh and painful for me to do otherwise, but thank you, anyway."

"Of course, Bill, I appreciate your sentiments completely." I accepted the extended envelope; our hands and eyes met, and he was gone.

I took my seat, told the group what had occurred and inquired about the advisability of reading the message to them. From several quarters, especially from Eve and Betty, I was urged to do so.

The envelope contained a poem entitled, "On We Lived."

If one were to ask me,
The reply would be:
I've never before lived and loved
With the knowledge
That this was not forevermore.

A little mature, you say.
Perhaps—though its sweetness
Was beyond the real.
We held each other and ourselves to such an extent
That each transcended and was no more.

Gone now,
Leaving its blue-grey memory mist,
The rhythm
Still holds the sought-for promise
Of immortal bliss.

Tears of loneliness which really never came
Ended with the blank of stare.
Our hearts, it seems, always knew
What we had not been acquainted with,
And yet, on we lived.

215

Eve was the first to respond. "Please read it once more," she pleaded with pain in her voice.

I read it again, and again Eve was the first to speak. "I think it is a very beautiful expression of his feelings for her."

"I agree!" resounded from all corners of the room.

"The only thing that made me wonder a bit was his remark that it was not forevermore," interjected Bob.

"But, honey," asked Eve, addressing Bob, her own lover, "didn't you know?"

"Know what?"

"That he too probably has been to a psychiatrist and thus realizes apparently that he is flesh and blood? Gone is the adolescent philosophy that love is 'forevermore.' Flesh is more fragile than the 'Rock of Ages.' It certainly sounded to me as if he knows that humans are mortal."

"Oh," said Bob, enlightened, "I see. He really is a mature person."

"Of course he is," stated Eve definitely. "Remember, those of us who carry on so hysterically at weddings and funerals are frequently not feeling emotion for the parties involved, but are lamenting our own image loss. It takes real maturity to have his viewpoint and adaptability—and to ride on after as severe a blow as he's had."

"I'm beginning to see what you mean," said a more sober Bob. "I once read that death is the equalizer; now I know what that means."

"All these events of the past two weeks certainly have left their imprint upon me," said Moe with resignation. "Why, even when I was in the Navy and saw people killed on both sides of me, I always felt it could never happen to me—that it could only happen to the other fellow. I appreciate the truth now—that I'm not indestructible."

"This isn't a very pleasant subject," Tom broke in, "but it's sure doing me a world of good. I, too, felt I was one of these indestructibles that Moe refers to. Do you know that ever since this Claudia business, I actually watch myself crossing the streets?"

"Well, I'll tell you one," Bob remarked lightly. "I went so far as to have a will made up during the last week."

"You did?" asked an amazed John.

"Yesiree! I sure did. I haven't got much, but what little I have, I want to go to the right places," he answered firmly.

"Well, as a matter of fact, I've been thinking about it off and on myself," confessed John, "but I have so little property that it hardly seems worth while."

"Listen, brother," Bob said, "a will isn't a thing based solely upon property. It also has an importance in such matters as where and how you wish to be buried, merely to mention two other items. Then, too, a will is a good place to register your own epitaph. I think I'd like to be able to say in mine—'I lived, I laughed, and I understood!'"

"You know, I never thought of it that way before," was John's serious reply.

"Let me tell you something else," Bob persisted. "I have stipulated in my will that when I die, my eyes are to be willed to the eye bank. After all, I'll no longer need them and they might mean a new lease on life for someone else."

"You have?" said Betty, awed. Before anyone else could say anything more, she went on, "Gee, that's wonderful. I think I'd like to do that, too."

"As I was sitting here, looking about the room with its one vacant chair, I suddenly realized that I have feelings of rejection," the somewhat dejected voice of Molly was saying. "Furthermore, it's the same feeling I got when my father died while I was still a little girl. You might say I felt cheated. I know nobody—or very few—die deliberately; nonetheless, it makes it damned tough on those of us who are left. I know I would have had an entirely different life if he had lived. Not much of a worth-while relationship existed between us, but when he went, I was in a terrible fix. I know it's irrational—but I can't help the feelings I have—I feel somehow I've had a dirty trick played on me. Now, I don't want anyone to go and tell me all about the stupidity of this—I just wanted to get it off my chest."

"I don't find it so stupid," John remarked. "To children, the absence of a parent or parents does seem like punishment. Remember, children depend on parents, and if parents are gone, children feel the absence is based upon the fact that they've done something wrong."

"Yes, John," I said, "I agree with you. It takes quite a mature person to appreciate the meaning of death or divorce. Even more maturity is required to avoid fantasizing that somehow or other he, the child, is not linked and therefore not responsible. Lastly, let's not forget that we always remain someone's child and have some childishness normally within us."

The last few minutes of this session seemed almost to belie the earlier part. For after I finished my words, a lighter air was discernible; the old time joviality re-emerged and great interest developed when I made an announcement.

"I feel it is best for all of us that we keep the membership of our group up to its quota," I suggested. "It increases its potentiality of relating. Therefore, when the proper patient appears, I shall ask him or her to join our group." This statement brought some light-veined comment, which could be understood in essence as being analogous to the reaction of a child who has been told that he is going to have a new brother or sister.

As usual, Molly was the most vociferous. She attempted to berate me by saying that she felt there were enough present and it was hard enough to get attention without having still another mouth to feed. The rest of the group took the announcement much more in stride. It seemed as if the sex of the new patient was more interesting to them than the fact that a new arrival was to come at some future date.

Later that winter, Abigail came into our lives. She was a mulatto. Furthermore, the word "beautiful" might have been coined just for her. About five-foot-four inches of queenliness, she stood before me. When we shook hands the first time, I was acutely aware of her gentle manner. Her brown knit dress augmented the tones of her velvety skin and subtly revealed her warm curvaceous body. She wore her jet-black hair in a strikingly attractive upsweep. This seemed to accentuate her remarkable facial characteristics: the flat cheeks with their high bony structure, set off by a dainty sensuous mouth and small chin. The nose appeared almost as an artist's afterthought—its turned-up quality suggested beguilement.

Abigail was called Abby by most. She was twenty-eight and an excellent schoolteacher. Her entrance into therapy came about in a hurried fashion—in a self-propelled manner. It didn't take many individual sessions for me to hear her complete and distressing story.

Abby was an adopted child, born in Charlotte, North Carolina. At the age of three months, she was a doorstep foundling. Examination of the basket in which she was lying disclosed a note pinned to her bunting. It stated her exact and tender age, explained that her name was Abigail, and thoughtfully attached was a copy of her formula. She was of sound health and the family upon whose doorstep she was left unhesitatingly welcomed and adopted this tiny charmer.

Upon finishing high school, she had decided to take up a profession. This brought her to New York. Having been an excellent student, it was comparatively easy for her to go on and receive her master's degree.

Like so many of that day, the wonderful family that adopted her failed to tell her she was adopted. This painful information drifted to her ears all too shockingly from her playmates. It wasn't that she then became resentful. Instead, it merely spurred her on to greater independence. In reality her adjustment might have been termed quite adequate, for she was bright, well liked, polite, gracious—in other words, every inch a poised young lady.

At Teachers College of Columbia University, she met another mulatto, an industrious and enterprising young man. It was not strange that they were drawn to each other. For over a year they dated. They were in love and the time finally came for her to meet his family. The dinner was festive and exciting, followed by reminiscences in the living room.

Somewhere during the course of the evening, Abby mentioned unabashedly that she was an adopted child. This was no longer a sensitive area for her, nor was it upsetting for her fiancé's family. However, by the time that the family albums were being circulated, Abby did mention a most interesting fact. Precisely: the story of the "note" and its details flowed forth. These facts took their toll upon her fiancé's mother, who recognized her own daughter and felt duty-bound to tell her so.

It seems that the family's fortune, not long after leaving Abby a foundling, had greatly improved, not only materially, but also emotionally. However, it was too late, and Abby was lost to them. The family had two more children, both of them boys. To escape unpleasant memories, they had moved to New York, and as irony would have it, out of eight million people in the area, the person with whom she became involved would have to be her own brother, the older son.

Yet, was it so odd? For if you stop and consider the facts closely, the improbabilities do not loom quite so large. They were both mulatto, and although they lived in a city the size of New York, the chance of meeting was thus increased, not only because they were in the mulatto minority, but also because of their cultural and intellectual drives. Even the fact that New York served as the common meeting ground is not really such an oddity, for New York is known as the world's 'melting pot,' and absorbs minority groups with far less tension than most other places. Then, if you realize further that at Teachers College they would quite naturally be thrown together as part of a normal routine—the meeting of these two unusually attractive people of like endowment is not so strange.

Abby had entered my office, a disillusioned and somewhat embittered young woman. Yet her politeness and fine characterological endowments prevailed. She may have been down, but she was determined not to stay there.

Seldom had it been my experience to see such emotional courage. Mixed in with her confusion was the battle best labeled loyalty. In one split second, not only did she lose a man about to become her husband, but now she had two families instead of one. Which way was she to turn? Back to the biological family, or to those who had raised her lovingly? She felt a kinship to both. Such monumental decisions required therapy—not advice or counseling.

The day following the dinner party which tumbled Abby's world, she came in to see me. It seems that she learned about me through her roommate, a social worker, who knew me professionally. Upon hearing the news, the roommate, with Abby's full approval, had arranged the appointment.

Two days after the beginning of Abby's therapy, I received a call from George, the older brother, and her former fiancé. He had attempted to reach Abby, who refused to answer the phone. However, the alert and more objective roommate did speak with George. She told him that Abby was seeing a psychiatrist who could best answer any questions. George called to question me about what damage had been done. His concern for her ran deep and dealt with natural and obvious guilt. We spent some time on the phone, during which I attempted primarily to reassure him. I gave, and he accepted, the name of a colleague so that he too might have some necessary therapy. Although we never talked again and probably will never meet, that contact and the memory of the occasion will not readily be erased from my mind. It is at pivotal points such as this, when a psychiatrist holds the delicate balance of a patient's future life in his hands, that his maximum commitment in terms of maturity and wisdom is called upon. Every word is taken by the patient and weighed on a scale, you can actually see the patient rising or falling with each of them. When I put the receiver down, I felt I had been through one of life's major experiences. No doubt, it was a mutually satisfying contact, which I'm sure enriched the lives of both of us.

Many weeks passed, during which the bitter tears of loneliness and despair flowed over Abby's golden cheeks. When at last I felt that she had accepted me as a dependable father-figure, I broached the subject of group therapy.

At first, and quite typically, she balked at the prescription, but unlike the patients of the group, her resistance had a different content and manifest. They, as you recall, had resisted out of fear of losing their preferred status as the "only child." Of course there were other elements involved, such as fear of exposure and dread of the unknown. However, had not Abby had the unfortunate incident of falling in love with her own brother, probably she would not have needed therapy. Since this was the case, she was not as vehement and vociferous as the other patients had been. Nonetheless, she had cogent and valid arguments to offer. The episode had been so personal and unusual that the humiliation of discussing it with total strangers could be understood. Equally valid was the other issue she raised. She had no desire to suffer further rejection as a result of being mulatto.

My management of these points followed these lines: With respect to the humiliation, I pointed out that it wasn't necessary to divulge the information as such, for I had learned that therapy is not as intimately bound up with facts as has hitherto been suspected. Instead, therapy which is geared for growth requires participation. And in her case, it was necessary to relive and relate, in terms of participation, the turbulence of the experience, without necessarily revealing the specific episode. Through this participation, she would unconsciously undergo the normal emotional upheaval in re-forming a family configuration which she otherwise would have to experience with her biological family. The only difference would be that the issues would seemingly vary. The emotions would be vented and resolve themselves upon the new issues instead of the old.

Rest assured that this displacement does change the underlying issue and attitude, even though not expressed. Perhaps an old and familiar example may best serve us at this point. We all know, I'm sure, of the husband who comes home after a rough day at the office with a cantankerous boss and "takes it out on the wife and kids."

With respect to the issue of racial prejudice, I began with recognition of the facts.

"Of course, Abby, I would be the last one in the world to attempt to say that such prejudice does not exist. However, one cannot live long in this world without discovery of a very fundamental fact, specifically, that everyone to varying degrees is a victim of some overt persecution. For example, some people don't like Jews, others don't like Negroes, and still others don't like foreigners of any sort. Some don't like mothers, others don't like children, and so it goes. Thus, you see there isn't a soul alive who isn't hated and objected to by someone.

"Abby, I'm not trying to dismiss this lightly. I fully realize that mulattoes, for example, are the subject of more intolerance than some others of the human race, but my point is this—since all of us are bombarded with prejudice, isn't it obvious then that we cannot escape it? Furthermore, isn't it clear that we have to learn to adjust to this reality? In fact, the problem of prejudice is not simply what it does to us, but of equal importance—how we respond to it. If we can cope with the prejudice we all receive, it implies our emotional adequacy. Perhaps on those occasions when we can't, thè unconscious problems represent an overwhelming fear we possess. For example, when 'A' attempts to restrict or injure 'B' because of religion, color, sexual behavior or otherwise, it may mean that 'A' sees 'B' as possessing the same unconscious conflict he has within himself. This conflict is usually in partial repression. The sight of it in 'B' makes 'A' react against it—or fills him with self-hate and intolerance of himself as he finds himself in another human being. In some situations 'A' does not find the conflict in 'B,' but what he does see ignites what he fears he may possess and is afraid will become active in himself.

"However, if 'B,' in response to 'A's' prejudice, behaves in less than a mature manner, it implies that 'B' is using the same mechanism, or is obviously practicing prejudice also."

With this explanation, I naturally consented to her request for a few days to think it over. At our next meeting, she accepted the idea of group therapy for herself. "I realize that if I'm to be helped I must rely upon you as I would any other medical doctor. Mind you," she said, "I do this, not on blind faith, but rather because I trust you as a physician who knows what he is doing."

Now I was sure of it. This girl was basically at a greater level of maturity than the usual new patient. This fact served us well. That is, our group structure was at such a critical point that a newcomer would have to be of greater maturity than the usual patient at the beginning of therapy. By this, I do not mean that therapy groups cannot have replacements, but rather that the timing of the new arrival should be at opportune or uncritical stages.

When the group met for the first of its twice-weekly sessions in that particular week, I reminded them of my earlier announcement. As I recall, I chose a lull in the middle of the session to speak. "Group, a few weeks ago I mentioned that when the proper time came and right individual appeared, I would have someone take Claudia's place—not as an exact replacement of Claudia, of course, but rather as someone to bring our group quota back to eight. That time has arrived." There was no visible change other than a brief moment of reflective silence. Tom was the first to speak.

"Doc, I didn't get whether you meant the person was a man or woman."

"That's right, Tom, I didn't say, did I?"

"Is it your plan, then, not to say?" inquired Moe.

"Yes, that's it, exactly."

"Why?" inquired Moe.

"Moe, there's an inequity that exists in therapy. I, as the therapist, can ask you such a question, but for your benefit, I can refrain from giving you an answer on medical grounds. Of course, I realize you can always refuse to answer a question, but it wouldn't be on the same grounds, would it, Moe?"

After a moment of meditation, he answered slowly, "Yeah—come to think of it, Doc, I guess you're right, much as I hate to admit it."

At this point, Bob spoke up. "Doc, if I guess the reason why you won't tell whether it is a male or a female—if I guess correctly, will you confirm it?"

"I'm sorry, Bob, I can't enter into deals, but I'd welcome your guess."

"Okay, smarty pants, he called your bluff," John interjected.

"Well, then, here goes," Bob said in a nonchalant semisophisticated manner. "As I see it, the Doc and all of us think of this group as being a reliving and a family unit—right?"

Several heads nodded in the affirmative.

224

"Since this is apparently so, the idea of bringing a new member in is like having a baby born into the family."

"That's right," said Betty, with marked spontaneity.

"Well, glad you agree with me," Bob nodded. "And it seems to me that one does not know the sex of a baby until it is born."

"Right again," agreed Betty.

With this, Bob took a swift turn, looking at each of us individually to gather the consensus by visual, nonverbal poll taking. He seemed assured of his findings. He felt he had been correct. He didn't ask for my opinion, he merely looked in my direction and I felt it incumbent upon me to speak.

"Bob, I wish to answer you. Not because you questioned me, and not as a result of any of the preliminaries, but rather because you worked it out with participation. Bob, I'm proud to see you no longer launch into highly opinionated soliloquies as you formerly did. This was a job well done. You worked as a member of the group and thought with them as an integrated whole—you weren't exhibitionistic or 'know-it-all.' And so I'm going to tell you. You were absolutely correct—those were the precise reasons."

"New baby or no, I don't like it," Molly said. "You can all go to hell, for that matter, with your highfalutin theories and ideas. All I know is that the Doc is squeezing another patient in here, and it will make it that much more difficult for me again."

"What do you mean, 'again?'" inquired Eve in a diplomatic but assertive voice.

"Simply this: Claudia was all right and all that sort of thing, but she sure did get a lot of attention around here. I swear, at times I thought I was in the wrong place. When she died I was sorry, but I wasn't sorry that there was one less of us here, and now old moneybags is gonna bring in somebody else."

"Be reasonable, Molly, no one here is preventing you from getting well, and another patient is necessary, as the Doc has pointed out, since eight patients have proven to be the ideal number," said Eve.

"Be reasonable, hell!" Molly snapped. "All I know is that I always have to fight that much harder to gain the floor."

225

"But that's exactly the point," John interposed, "no one has the floor here, really. The idea is, as the Doc just showed Bob a while ago, that participation is expression, whereas holding forth and talking about your own problem doesn't produce anything new or different. You've got to live with people to be an adequate person, as the Doc has said, and I for one believe him."

"Oh, go to hell, I do as I damn well please here," said Molly.

"Molly, you have every right to do as you please while you are here," I said to her. "In fact, were it not so, then this couldn't be called therapy. So go ahead, find your way out and do what you need to, but let me add this. John's interpretation of my idea was right."

This seemed to soften Molly a bit, and after a moment or two of thinking the matter over, she passively commented, "I guess, Doctor, the trouble is—my sister. She was always my father's favorite. In fact, he even preferred her to my mother. I simply can't help it; I just don't like the idea, especially as the new patient will probably turn out to be a female. You see, my sister was younger than I."

"Exactly, Molly. I wouldn't be a bit surprised if you were one hundred per cent correct in what you've said, and I further realize it's extremely difficult for you to behave otherwise, but maybe if you make an effort in this setting where all of us are treated justly and fairly, you'll be able to work out and live down these unfortunate past experiences."

With my words, she smiled, which was most unusual for her in situations of this type, dropped her head to one side, and in a lowered tone said sheepishly, "I'll try."

It was a cold wintry night. Washington's birthday had recently come and gone, when Abby made her debut. To say that she was the center of attention would be an understatement. This was not just because she was a new patient, but because she was so strikingly beautiful as well. She wore a yellow cashmere cardigan sweater set with a charcoal black skirt. Her hair was in its usual, neatly upswept fashion. A creamy white single strand of pearls adorned her lovely throat. I thought, as I looked at John, that he

226

seemed to have entered into a world of ecstasy. Moe, also looking in John's direction, cracked, "John, close your mouth, you're drooling."

Too embarrassed to respond, he looked away in irritation. Eve served as hostess, although I had joined the group early in order to be present when Abby arrived. Immediately following my introduction, Eve took over as head of the reception committee. Come to think of it, her actions weren't so strange after all. To begin with, Eve had lost her most valuable feminine companion when Claudia had gone, and she was obviously in search of a replacement. Secondly, Abby, every bit the lady, appealed to Eve's sense of culture and propriety. These two lovelies truly enhanced the beauty of the setting. The feeling I received, as I listened to the tête-à-tête between them, was that Eve was "looking up" to Abby. It was as if she sensed Abby's maturity almost immediately and realized it was somewhat more than her own. Although the admiration that Claudia had for Eve might serve as an example, there was a difference in degree in that Eve did not have as far to reach as did Claudia. The grace and tact with which Abby handled this new situation immediately commanded the respect of the group. In fact, at one point, Betty inquired, "Gee, Doc, are you sure that she isn't 'planted' here to serve in some therapeutic manner? She certainly doesn't seem to be in need of therapy."

Abby took the compliment with a gentle nod and soft-spoken thanks.

It was hardly necessary, but nonetheless I reassured Betty and at the same time took pressure off Abby, by saying that the new-comer was indeed a patient.

Tom's reaction to Abby was characteristic. Finding a new, strong feminine figure, he attempted to make of her another mother-figure. The timing worked an advantage in his favor. That is, Abby had no protocol on which to rely and therefore was compelled to some degree to comply with Tom's pedestal-placing maneuvers.

Throughout the course of the evening, Molly just stared at our newest member. To say that she was calculating would be underemphasis. I think, as I recall it now, that she had been

227

prepared to attack another demanding infant and that on discovery of a much more mature, feminine figure, the threat was absent. Yet, she was unable to converse with Abby. The discussion with Molly at our previous session had borne fruit.

It seemed to me that Bob had two important reactions to Abby: her maturity relieved him of exerting the excessive guiding influence which Eve at best had been able only to placate; and, of course, there was an out-and-out admiration for her beauty.

Thus the evening proved truly successful for all. Abby had found a medium in which she could work out her calamity. The group had not been burdened with another screaming infant—it had found its mother instead.

16. *Something Blue*

When the Yankees had "slaughtered" the Brooklyn Dodgers in their preseason series at Ebbets Field—according to Moe's accounts, anyway—spring notified us with bursting energy that our first anniversary had passed. Little attention was paid to the occasion other than a brief comment by Tom, who noted that he was able to find his way to my office these days without getting lost in the subway.

Abby had gained the affection of all. Hardly could anyone remember the fact that she had not been a charter member. Her position was so solid and secure that the ravages of her experience were beginning to be obliterated. She had made no attempt to tell the group of her former relationship with her bother, George. Seeing it worked through in accordance with what I had told her in preparation for the group, I decided it was no longer necessary for her to have individual sessions. She accepted this without protest. I made no comment on the fact that she had not discussed the incident for some time.

As is the natural custom with so many of us when an anniversary comes and goes, I couldn't help but engage in reflection. I suppose, to be more accurate about it, one might not call it reflection, but rather a review of our progress.

Eve had really become the young lady that she had merely appeared to be. Her relationship with Bob conveyed respect for the male being. Gone were her needs to compete with men and her sufferings because of alleged male supremacy. Similarly, her clutching dependencies upon the opposite sex, with destructiveness as their usual motive, were no longer evident. Her former inability to receive affection with comfort from an older woman had likewise disappeared. For this latter improvement, Eve was indebted to Abby.

Molly, ever since the arrival of Abby, had also shown signs of improvement. It would be a mistake to attribute this solely to that event; Abby's coming merely precipitated the improvement. Actually, it had taken close to a year for Molly to develop the security necessary for her to trust the fairness of the environment.

The equitable reception of Abby's addition to the group finally destroyed her idea that life was made up solely of a series of betrayals.

John, apparently fully recovered from his loss of fatherhood, was showing signs of having a better work record. His studies at school and his ability to get along at his part-time job had improved decidedly. This improvement was brought sharply into focus by his comment, "I no longer need my boss's constant approval." And another comment, to the effect, "When the professor is lecturing, I don't fantasize that he is just talking to me any more."

As for Moe, his degree of participation was so obviously improved that he had grown to be our psychological repairman. His witty remarks had removed rough spots for us time and time again. I, like the rest of the group, felt a warm spot indeed for Moe as a result of his many kindnesses.

Betty had left her babyhood and was an up-and-coming adolescent. There was less of a time lag in her putting into effect her usually wonderful creative ideas. Her designs showed more firmness and stability, even in the sketching stages. There was a flair and boldness about her patterns. Her painting had gone from the primitive into the portrait class. Granted she painted women far better than men, but the improvement was immense. She was one of us and, significantly, she realized it. Gone were her feelings of not belonging. Instead, there was courage based upon security.

230

Of course, Bob, the oldest son, was ready for the manly road that lay before him. It had taken a ferocious fight to break through his intellectual façade, but once his defenses were down, he made tremendous progress. His ability to reason and not dictate was refreshing. The absence of the need to be tied parasitically to a mother's apron strings had increased his acceptability to all those about him. I sensed in myself a freedom concerning Bob. No longer did I hold my breath when he launched into a new enterprise; I felt with sheer relief his ability to discriminate and not to employ subtle hotilities. There could be no doubt, he was a joyous son.

And not to be forgotten in this array was the therapist. How had I changed through this experience? Perhaps, for one thing, I had become more patient with myself. My silent internal dilemma in struggling with these very same patients had contributed to an intolerance of myself. With resolution under way, it then became obvious that I too could afford the comfort of comparative success.

The May Day session is clearly etched in my mind. It was on this occasion that Bob and Eve had come in with a detectable air of suspense. That something exciting was afoot was shown by the fact that they sat next to each other. This they had not done since the time they merged their households. He looked at her with a warmth which penetrated both their beings. We had all seen him look at Eve in the past when admiration and sensuousness were the driving forces, but this was far more encompassing. It had a quality of completeness and conveyed a sense of durability. Absent was any feeling of erratic bravery. In fact, there was not a trace of the former attitude of calculated flaunting.

She, in turn, was quite poised, but not with coolness—far from it. Her calm was a reflection of an inner joy. This particular feeling that a woman in love experiences is different from that of a man who is in love. It comes from the realization that a man, in keeping with her own emotional maturity, has become passionately united with her. No longer does she need to struggle against a sense of incompleteness—for now there is the satisfaction that his love and hers are one. Utter contentment is involved, and yet, this does not completely express the feeling. Perhaps it is peace with fulfillment, benevolently large and full. Men are often lonely and unsure of themselves, but are not as likely to translate this into the realm of incompleteness.

As a matter of fact, as expressed later in Eve's own imagery, "The emptiness of snug harbor is at last gone—a ship has come to rest at its moorings."

After the customary friendly exchanges of the first few minutes, Bob, in a deeper voice, asked if he might have the floor. As soon as the hubbub of chatter had died down, he began, "Eve and I wish to announce that we have set a date—a date for our wedding." A smile came over his face as he turned toward Eve and she toward him. An aura of light emanated from each of them as they clasped hands. The rest of us were still. We were drinking in the happiness that was theirs. When this loving moment settled and its overtones grew dim, I spoke. "Bob and Eve, I'm overjoyed."

Still holding hands, and in most gentle voices, they responded simultaneously, "Thank you—we both owe you so much."

"And I, you—for you have brought me more than a step closer to happiness." The three of us smiled at each other and the glow spread as the group expressed similar sentiments. Best wishes and congratulations poured forth in unabashed flow. After some of the excitement had subsided, it was Betty who started inquiries concerning particulars with, "What date have you chosen?"

"Saturday, July second," replied Eve. "First off, the Fourth of July holiday makes it a long weekend," she continued. "This will make it possible for our families to travel less hurriedly to and from the wedding, which, by the way, we intend to hold here in New York. We'll use one of the smaller and quieter hotels for the affair. The idea is that we both feel we'd prefer not to have our respective families dominate the scene—which they already show signs of attempting to do. Of course, we'll permit them to exercise all the privileges they would normally have on such an occasion, but they need to be reminded of the fact that this is our wedding. We're not hostile, but we do know that they haven't changed."

"Yes, that's it," echoed Bob.

"Are you going away?" Abby asked.

"I think so—but we're going to save our big trip for the time when the Doctor leaves on his annual vacation—later in July."

"That way it works out better all around," Bob commented. "You see, I will have just gotten situated in my new position with Amalgamated, in their personnel department, and I could hardly expect them to wait any longer for me than they already have."

"Are you going to continue at your job, Eve?" Molly questioned dryly.

"Yes, I am. I wouldn't have to if my family had their way about this—but, as I mentioned before, I believe we'd be better off paddling our own canoe."

Molly gave no answer; she just nodded silently. It was obvious to all that she had certain misgivings. However, whatever they may have been, she didn't have the security to express them.

Betty was annoyed with Molly's attitude. "If you don't like it, why don't you say so?" and her words were flung toward Molly the way an angry waiter shoves an order at an irritating customer. Molly, still without courage, just glared back. This served only to heighten Betty's wrath.

"Holy smokes!—I swear, you slay me, Molly—there you sit like a vulture about to swoop on carrion. The bodies aren't even dead and you're circling above in anticipation. Can't you find it in your heart to be happy for someone else?" Now Betty's voice had reached the screeching stage. It had all happened so rapidly that for a moment it seemed anachronistic, for the beautiful setting of but a few moments before had not merely been spoiled by this acrimonious display, it was as if a regression, atavistic in quality, had occurred.

Betty's last accusation released Molly. "Listen, you fairy princess, get your head out of the clouds. Remember, these two did break every rule in the book, and you can't expect me to sit and cheer them as if they were the great conquering heroes."

"Aren't you ever going to drop that line? It looks to me as if you're still grinding the same old axe. Won't you ever get off the dime?"

"Oh, go soak your head."

"The trouble with you, Molly, is you're downright jealous,

so damned jealous you can't see straight—it stirs the venom that lurks in your dirty old bones."

We had never seen Betty so angry, but after all, the sanctity and purity of marriage were at stake and she loved Eve. As a matter of fact, the group had become so imbedded in Eve's life that Molly's attack seemed to be one that struck at its very foundations, and therefore Betty's own struggle for survival was in jeopardy.

"Well, all right!—maybe I am jealous," retorted Molly resignedly, "but is that a crime? I'm only human—is there any need for you to hit me and treat me as if I were dirt?"

"That's your problem," snapped Betty with extreme disdain.

"Now—wait a minute here," came in the resilient voice of Moe. "Don't you think you're being a little too unreasonable with Molly?"

"Yeah," parried Tom, "boy, you're really tough on her."

Eve and Bob were uncomfortable, but tactfully remained quiet. In the midst of all this, I stole a quick glance at Abby. She sat with interlaced fingers resting in her lap, her gaze fixed upon them. This bitter exchange was alien to her previous experience and she seemed totally shaken by it.

Now John joined the fracas. "I don't want to sound complicated, of course, but nevertheless, let me say this—I have mixed emotions."

Moe could not hold back. He burst into laughter at John. This only succeeded in making John even more serious. With brow furrowed, shoulders set as if he were walking into a March wind, he plowed forth. "No, really, I mean it; I'm not kidding—I feel mixed up about all this. Before Molly began, I was happy and now I don't know—I don't know. Betty seems to have struck a right note when she said that Molly was jealous, but yet, there's something else cooking. I don't know what it is, but it has something to do with my feelings toward Eve. I'm glad she's getting married, but there's also something sad about it for me—I swear I don't know."

"Maybe you're sad, John, because it reminds you of your own near marriage," were Moe's words.

John slid back in the chair, his shoulders drooped, and there was a silence. Several moments passed, and then, straightening up, he spoke. "Moe, you're quite a guy—I think you've hit it right on the head. Of course, that's what it must be—what else? I know I haven't gotten over it. I'm really happy that Bob and Eve are getting married—I think they're well suited to one another—but it does remind me of my own failure. I so wanted to be married and to be a father.

"Funny thing, but just last week and quite by accident, I ran into Angela. At first, I didn't know whether I would even stop to speak to her, but our meeting occurred in such a way that we couldn't avoid it. We said hello—and exchanged the usual 'how are you'—and then she mentioned that she hadn't gone through with the abortion after all. She had gone to a home for unwed mothers and given our child over for adoption. Somehow—it seemed to make a difference—I don't know why it should, but it did. I know I will never see the baby; it was a boy, but I guess I do realize—it was because he wasn't destroyed, that something which once was beautiful and good still had a vestige of existence."

"John," ventured Abby softly, "I never knew this story, as you probably are aware, but naturally it has some personal implications for me. You see, I'm an adopted child, and although the circumstances concerning my parentage were different, I understand your feelings so well. I've never minded being an adopted child— my foster parents were wonderful. In fact, it's only recently that I've come to realize just how wonderful they were. A while ago when several of you were fighting here, it dawned upon me that I had never seen such bitterness in my own family. Now, mind you, I'm not condemning, nor am I being boastful—it's simply a testimonial to my foster parents. So, John, please do revel in the fact that your son has been adopted, for it can be a blessing."

"What can I say to that?" sighed John, and tons of grief melted from his drooping shoulders. "Abby, I don't know how you came here—I don't know why you're here—but all I can say is I'm glad. I never depended on anyone to restore my losses, but you are the most wholesome, wonderful human being I've ever known. I'm not in love with you. I don't admire you as a beautiful Grecian goddess. It's more that I feel your kindness and protection, which make me feel more pride in myself. It's very hard for me to say this, but you are the only person I've ever known who is beautiful through and through. Your beauty is comfort."

"John, you're a wonderful boy. I've known a few like you—the way you express yourself is endearing and I want to thank you for your kind words."

"You've made it possible for me at long last, Abby, to put aside these painful memories—in knowing you and seeing you, I've attained some peace within myself. It makes it possible for me to feel that perhaps my son will be all right, and somehow or other that I, too, will turn out well."

Now the flavor of the setting changed again in this momentous session. The tension of the battle between Molly and Betty was broken. And who else but Moe could have helped bring it about?

"I always said that every child should come equipped with a mother—in fact, I'm all in favor of it!" he joked.

"I'll say," chimed in Betty.

"Yeah, she's quite a gal," Molly rejoined.

"You know, it's simply amazing to me to see what we've experienced here," Bob said for the first time since the discussion began. "I've been sitting back and watching this, but not in the way that you might think. I've been very much a part of it and yet I've been able to see it objectively. What's appealed to me so much is seeing two people, like Abby and John, find themselves through such common need—they both seem so much better off as a result. The thought that comes to mind is best expressed by two words—which have been repeating themselves over and over in my mind—fortunate strangers."

"What a wonderful expression, Bob," his wife-to-be said admiringly, and she repeated it to herself in a stage whisper, "fortunate strangers."

"Yes, that's exactly what we are, we're fortunate strangers," said Abby, "for I couldn't agree more with what Bob has said. John's comfort, rest assured, was not an isolated thing; I gained, too. You know I'm sure that we, as people, cannot survive unless we're kind to others, thus I'm feeling freer and happier. We were all strangers and when I think of strangers, I feel the emotion of loneliness. But now we are no longer lonely, aren't we truly fortunate?"

"You really said a mouthful there, Abby," Moe remarked. "The whole idea of being fortunate is a pleasant relief for me—it gives me hope. I've been thinking, 'Well, if Bob and Eve can make it, why can't old Moe do the same?' The truth of the matter is, I've been doing a little dating for the first time in years—it hasn't been easy getting back to courting. When I was going with Ruth, and when we married, I thought I'd never be doing these things any more. In a way it makes you feel at 'that age' again, which is a good thing in itself, for who wants to be older? But on the other hand, dating and courting a girl seem so childish and adolescent to me. I wonder and say to myself, 'Moe, are you getting to be an old man before your time, or what?' I don't know how it's going to end, but I sure wish I'd meet some girl close to my own age, maybe a widow or someone like that would help—yeah, that's it!—maybe a widow . . ." And these last words were spoken with almost monotonous, but painful, slowness.

"It's strange to hear you speak this way, Moe," said Eve. "I always thought that men preferred their women to be young, naïve little girls, but apparently that's not so."

"What Moe is saying is true," droned Tom in his flat tones. "At our age, who wants to play any more?"

"You see, Eve," Moe added, "a man in his thirties really doesn't want a little girl for his wife. He may become infatuated and want to play with them, but when the time comes for settling down, it's stability and reliability that count. Mind you, I'm not against frills, in fact, I enjoy them—such things as lace curtains and ruffles on the bedspread really do count with a rough-and-ready guy like me. I don't think I'd like being married to a woman who didn't go in for some frills—it's part of her femininity. Women often get adolescent silliness mixed up with femininity—and helpless adolescence is never a substitute, in my eyes, for dainty femininity."

"Say, Moe, you really know a lot about women. I don't think I've ever heard a description like that before of what a man wants in a woman," Eve remarked seriously.

237

"Moe's words make me feel, for the first time in my life, that it would be an honorable thing to be a woman," said Molly.

"I'll string along with that," said Betty. "I think that he'll make a wonderful husband."

"Well, thanks, girls, I hope so," Moe answered modestly.

After a pause, he spoke again. "I've been thinking of my work lately—and I've just about concluded that I'm in a rut. There's no room for advancement in my present job and I'm beginning to realize it—I guess I've known it for some time, but this is the first time I've allowed myself to admit the truth."

Tom had been moved to speak. "I know that you people all think I'm just Moe's shadow around here, but I can't help it if I have to agree again. The only difference is this—what he's said about his job goes double for me. I've come to realize that I expect to get paid just for showing up at work, not for working. Whenever I do accomplish something and the boss doesn't recognize it with a pat on the back, I forget completely that I'm not there to be praised, but that he's paying me to do that work. I've got to stop being a little boy playing Tinker Toys with Daddy in the living room on a Sunday afternoon."

"Absolutely!" Molly agreed. "The same goes for me, too, but where I'm beginning to see the light is right here in this group. It's so—oo mixed up. On one hand I'm jealous of Bob and Eve getting married, for what right have they to grow up and get ahead of me—me, such a big shot—while on the other hand, I'm jealous at the idea because I don't want anyone to get better and out of here, because that would really show me up as being the dependent infant that I am. It seems I never can strike a happy balance—I'm either the big deal—the know-it-all, who doesn't need anyone else—certainly better than anyone else—or so helpless that I resent the other people's being here because I need the Doctor's help and they're in the way. I'm either the best of the lot or the worst—but never me."

"Sure, I know that feeling, too, Molly," responded Moe, "but it has a different effect upon me. I'm always afraid of being a burden on people, therefore, I never know exactly what my place is with them. Also, I have some confusion concerning Bob and Eve—

238

it's sort of on a morality basis—I don't mean that I'm an old-fashioned Joe, but I guess I've been seeing too many Hollywood pictures, where the guy who gets the girl has always led an exemplary life. But here in real life, Bob, who was a wise guy, gets the girl. Well . . . I tell you it just upsets the whole applecart. He starts out as a wisecracking smart aleck—commits the unpardonable—breaks rules—and still walks off with all the glory. It isn't that I don't feel he's worthy, it just crosses up all my old values, in a sense."

"But, Moe, doesn't this show you, once and for all, that morality is not a complete and comprehensive way in which to measure or determine how to choose your friends, mates, associates, or for that matter, to evaluate human behavior?" I inquired. I continued to develop this theme. "It's not that I'm forsaking morality; it's just that I feel it isn't complete enough to allow us to comprehend ourselves and others. Too often morality interferes with our ability to accept love."

"There's no doubt about it, Doc—you're right, but remember, that viewpoint takes time to digest."

"I appreciate that, Moe, however—keep working at it. O.K.?"

Moe nodded. His willingness to encounter these areas made me realize that I had been, recently, quite an active participant. But now, contrary to my former beliefs, I realized that such active participation, on the therapist's part, was beneficial. In a way, I now understood my previous passiveness to mean that I was afraid to become too deeply involved with the patients' emotions. In my new-found security, it was relatively easy to engage in give-and-take. And this had proven encouraging to the patient as well as diminishing my own trepidations about becoming overly invested with them. In a sense, it demonstrated that some of the arbitrary values of the doctor-patient relationship had been a hindrance rather than a help. The freedom in this newer emotional climate made all the parties more willing to explore areas that otherwise they were most reticent to develop. In addition, the concern I had on the other side of the coin had been in a measure lessened. Mainly, I had asked myself on many occasions whether I was perhaps too strong as a leader. With a sense of comfort, I had grown to a level with my patients where almost by "second nature" I could converse with them without becoming excessively enmeshed or thwarting their desires to explore the areas they held to be vital.

Molly picked up the trend. "While you and Moe were talking, Doc, I was thinking—I have the same attitude Moe does, but the difference lies in the fact that I'm the prisoner of my own penal system. I mean, I hate myself. Where Moe finds it difficult to reconcile his feelings toward Bob, I find the same difficulty within myself. When I stop and think of my own sexual behavior, I become bluer than the most strait-laced moral standard bearer—it's difficult to live with one's self, feeling the way I do. I have been repulsed by sex and yet feel normal enough to want it. Intellectually, I'm a vegetarian with respect to sex, but actually I'm a gluttonous mutton eater. You know, sex is sex; virtue is virtue and I can't make them meet."

These views were so understandable. They actually were an addiction to morality as an outgrowth of her inability to handle her own anxiety. This pattern represents an often-seen underlying operative in people who cannot cope with their own behavior. The morality addiction then becomes the easy way out and suggests defeat—defeat in the sense that they choose this rigidity in place of the flexibility of the effort and anxiety required to become adult. With this in mind, I sought to help her.

"Molly, I know how this plagues you; however, sexual behavior isn't really your problem. Instead, it's the lack of meaningfulness in your relationships. When you are finally able not to be a jailer for your own emotions and refrain from the severe judgment of them, then your investment with others will give you the pleasure you need and deserve."

Molly smiled at me, as did Moe, and this milestone session finally ended.

The weeks rolled by swiftly. May turned to June almost imperceptibly, and when the dog days of July neared, the controversy over the wedding within the group appeared to be resolved as far as one could tell.

Bob and Eve had moved into a new apartment, and were now

busily engaged in adding new furniture, planning the wedding and the thousand and one other items involved. This had served to heighten the ever-rising tide of male and female identification for the others. For example, Eve's plans were eagerly awaited and shared by the other girls. Discussions before the sessions centered on curtains, sales, trousseau and other feminine doodads. Bob, in addition to talking about his new job, was also the center of male attention with humorous discussions of wedding bells knelling the death of his freedom, and the usual ball-and-chain jokes. On one occasion, even Tom had cracked a mother-in-law joke.

It was now the last session before the wedding. It started out pleasantly with a note of gaiety, but underneath ran a current of anxiety. Had any casual observer been present, I feel he would not have realized that this was anything but a friendly group gathered for a social evening.

After approximately fifteen to twenty minutes, Bob and Eve, with Bob as spokesman, turned the tenor of the evening to a more serious vein.

"Doc, we've had a problem, precisely this—what to do about you and the group in terms of our wedding invitations. Eve and I have lain awake hours discussing it, attempting to see if we couldn't be mature about it all, but we've only gotten entangled more deeply and become more confused. You probably know that the problem is this—we want you and the group to attend. After all, we met here. This group represents the soil in which we grew, and in many ways has been more of a family to us than our very own. But there's the axiom about no outside contacts. I've certainly learned my lesson on that score by this time. I respect, at last, your authority and the authority of the group. As I say, we just don't know what to do about it."

"That's right, Doctor, we've talked this over again and again, and it seems such a pity that those people who mean so very much to us and are so responsible for our getting married are to be denied. What are we to do?" Eve pleaded.

"As you well know, it is not my function as therapist to advise and so I feel that this serious problem should be discussed by the group. Therefore, group, I ask you to consider the matter."

John was the first to speak. "I don't know—maybe this is the exception that one always hears about. I can't see, offhand, what harm it would be if we did go to their wedding; after all, the rule they broke before turned out all right, didn't it?"

"Yeah, it did, but does that mean it always will?" asked Molly sharply.

"Of course not," responded Moe, "but this might, as John says, be the exception."

"I don't know, I can't seem to make up my mind, because one minute it sounds good, and the next minute it doesn't. I like the idea of going—I want to go—badly, in fact," Tom added hastily, "yet it's difficult to see the grounds on which we can."

"Boy, this really is a doozey!" said Betty, with smothered giggles. "It would surely be fun going to the wedding—I always did love weddings," she went on, carried away by the infectiousness of the occasion.

"Come to think of it, I don't mind weddings myself, as long as they're someone else's," Molly quipped.

"The more I consider, the more it appeals to me," said Moe, "but I'm still not able to feel free about it."

"What do you think?" I asked Abby.

"To tell you the truth, Doctor, I find myself in an apparent minority. I hope it won't sound condescending although I can see where it might easily be taken that way."

"Okay, okay, we believe you," said Molly impatiently, "go on."

"Very well, I shall. I got the feeling as I was listening and watching that you were a group of little children responding to the news that you'd just been invited to a party—also, I feel that your jubilation is a bit shallow. It is not clear to me why I feel this, but there seems to be a false note in it.

"It's not that I believe you aren't truthful in your wishes, but that your first flush of emotions are misleading you. To me, it seems that you're over-reacting and in so doing, denying some of your doubts and beliefs concerning the serious elements involved. I'm thinking of two areas. First, whether or not, as individuals, you, personally, have accepted that Bob's and Eve's wedding represents an emotionally sound decision. Secondly, you don't appear to have gained from their experience. It strikes me that you seized upon this occasion with almost complete disregard of the fact that you are entering into the same type of behavior which you held as grounds for Bob's and Eve's relationship getting off to an unfortunate beginning. I'm sure you know what I mean by this but just in case you don't—is there truly any difference between their taking a segment of the group's behavior away from these confines and your attending this wedding? Personally, I feel that it's healthy that they are getting married—but our going to their wedding seems to be behavior of the acting-out variety which would also be taking place away from the therapy setting."

"You really think that?" inquired Moe.

"Do you believe it?" John asked Moe.

"Christ! I don't know, but she's naturally so darned smart and intuitive that when she says something I always sit up and listen extra carefully."

"I guess you're right, Moe; somehow or other you know beforehand that whatever she's going to say will make sense."

"She's the oldest and wisest still-young woman I've ever seen," commented Tom.

"You certainly have an idol, don't you?" blared Molly.

"Oh, come off it," Betty defended, "and while I'm at it, let me say this. I must agree with what she said—we're all a bunch of little chickens about this thing and I make no exception of myself."

"Well, I agree," said John after a pause.

"And that goes for me, too," Tom added.

"Yep, that's right—Abby's got the right pitch," said Moe.

"Make it unanimous then, if that's the case," Molly chimed in, and the matter seemed to be concluded.

"Well then, since that is the group's decision, I will of course go along with it, and accept it with one comment," I said at last. "It's a pleasure to note your improvement in deciding not to contaminate group activity by outside contacts. When we went to see Claudia, we remained, nonetheless, a self-contained unit—and no outsiders influenced the setting. In the case of Mr. and Mrs. Evans, as well as the communication from Bill, Claudia's beau—these were circumscribed, self-limiting states which could not be perpetuated.

Do you realize that an issue of this magnitude four or five months ago would have taken several sessions to solve, and in the process you'd have probably beaten each other fiercely in the bargain? I don't think it's only Abby's presence that has made the difference—you seem to be able to jell more quickly on an issue than ever before—and there's your answer, Bob and Eve."

"May I ask a question?" came Eve's apologetic voice.

"Go ahead, what is it?" I said.

"Will you come to the wedding, Doctor?" she asked.

"I'm sorry, but I consider myself no different from any other member of the group. I may be its leader, but I have only the same democratic rights as any of you. Perhaps if I remind you that my philosophy concerning a psychotherapist is that he's only different in degree and not in kind, you'll understand this more clearly, and believe me, I mean it. In fact, even in my lecture courses to student psychiatrists, I say what I've said to you people previously—that the therapist is the oldest patient. I hope you understand."

"Yes, I do, Doctor; it's just so difficult for us—and especially for me because I feel so indebted to you—not to have you present on my day of days."

"I can appreciate that, Eve, but do understand that I'll be with you nonetheless. And by the way, now that we're at this juncture, would you excuse me a moment?"

"Yes, of course," she responded.

I went into my inner office and got a package from my closet. Returning with it, I walked over to the betrothed couple and said, "To you, Bob, congratulations; and to you, Eve, my best wishes." Amazement swept over the rest of the group while the recipients of the gift beamed with pleasure. I returned to my seat and felt a tinge of anxiety, wondering whether I had done the correct thing. My reasoning had been long and tortuous—but I finally realized that I had to show them, undeniably, that I believed in them. No marriage, I felt, should start with any vestige of guilt and this gift represented my contribution in that direction. The situation had required the unusual—it had been unusual from its commencement. I realized, soon afterward, that my anxiety was not due solely to my act of giving them a gift, but that more was involved. For when

I had answered in the affirmative Eve's question as to whether she should open the gift now, I noticed considerable anxiety on the faces of the others, covered somewhat during the next few moments with the bustle of the unwrapping. Finally Eve displayed the gift. It was a modernistic ceramic bowl for flowers. The card read, "May your future lives together be like this bowl, repeatedly filled with fresh blossoms."

"Oh, Doctor, how thoughtful of you; you always seem to be there when it counts."

"You're very kind, Eve."

Bob came over as I stood, and we shook hands. All he said was the one word—"thanks"—but it conveyed all the residual warmth that had been held in abeyance throughout the months of therapy. When we had returned to our seats, a painful stillness permeated the room. I looked first at Moe, who seemed the most upset, and then I surveyed the entire circle.

Probably three or four minutes transpired before Moe began to speak awkwardly.

"Christ! I don't know how to say this, but it's got to be said. A couple of weeks ago, after one of the sessions, we let Bob and Eve go off by themselves and we stayed behind in the room—you, Doc, were back in your office making phone calls. The remaining members of the group decided to give Bob and Eve a gift. We were even going to include you in on it, Doc, and they made me chairman for the occasion. Well, it's no use holding back any longer. I managed the affair so badly that we don't have any gift for the occasion." He sat dejected, his gaze upon the floor.

"Now don't take all the blame," cajoled Molly; "if any of the rest of us had been more on the ball, it wouldn't have happened, and you know it."

"Christmas! I feel like a stinker," said Betty.

"Boy, that goes for me, too; I could crawl in a hole and die," said John.

"And the funny thing of it all is," added Tom, "do you know who was the only one to contribute her share of the money? Well, I'll tell you, if you couldn't guess by yourselves—it was Abby, of course. I know this because Moe asked me to hold the money."

Abby sat motionless.

At this point, the maturing oldest son rose to hitherto un-known heights, for him. "I think it all makes sense," he began. "Wasn't it you, Moe, who, back when all this began in May, said to the Doctor, while he was talking to you about morality, that a new viewpoint takes time? Well, then—why don't you listen to your-self? You don't think you can get over a lifetime's difficulty in three short months, do you? You see, I don't take your behavior or that of the rest of the group as a personal rejection of Eve and myself—because I understand it. In fact, to do otherwise would have meant that you were behaving insincerely—you can only give with free-dom when your security permits it. I know for a fact that it would have been impossible for me to do what you've attempted to do so bravely, had I been in your shoes. So may I say for myself, I bear you no malice, I respect your intentions and they, of course, were above reproach."

Bob's words hit their target. Moe raised his head and shyly accepted the understanding given him.

"I couldn't have said it as well myself, or even understood it clearly, but my feelings are just the same as Bob's," said Eve, and she too gave each and every one of the members a broad, under-standing smile.

"All I can say after this is, that if people can be as big as that, then I'm glad to be related to them," said an incredibly timid Molly.

"How you ever managed to see that and help us, Bob, I'll never know," Betty remarked gratefully as she walked over and planted a kiss on his cheek.

"Bob, I suppose I'm not exactly the one to say this—who am I to know?—but, man, you're really a man," John said.

"He sure made it, didn't he?" said Tom, turning to Moe.

"He sure did, and he rightly deserves all the happiness now, that I wanted to be able to wish him previously."

Abby closed the session with a motherly tradition. She reached into her bag and produced an old-fashioned lacy blue gar-ter, saying, as she handed it to Eve, who sat next to her, "In keeping with the old custom, let me lend you the 'Something Blue.'"

246

17. *Self-Determination*

It was exactly six thirty A.M. and Saturday morning had finally arrived. For some strange reason I had awakened earlier than usual. Dawn had hardly broken. My wife, lying next to me, was still asleep. And as I turned my head and looked at the clock to recheck the time, it struck me: the wedding is today! But why should I be awake this early? And the answer that came back only left me more dissatisfied. It made me, at last, face the fact that two people, of whom I had grown very fond, were getting married and I regretted not being present at the wedding. Following this feeling came a disturbing association. It was as if two of my children were marrying each other. Such a dilemma, no doubt, would awaken any parent. Then my problem began to clear. My previous necessary but now not valid attitude toward them was resolving: Bob and Eve no longer needed their previous family structure. These, their gains, revealed much to me. It was apparent that the whole family would be broken up soon, for our roles had changed—certainly those of Bob and Eve had. Through their marriage, they had developed a new formation and viewed the rest of us from this vantage point. It became increasingly clear: we were two families. Up to this point, we had been one family, but in the splitting, we, the group, had become the in-law family for each of them. Bob and Eve were no longer blood relations of the original family. Instead, they were treating the group as the family of their respective mates.

247

Of significance and value was the fact that Bob and Eve saw me and the others without conflict.

Even after I arose and had breakfast, they were with me. As I drove to the hospital, I glanced at the car clock and imagined what they were doing. At noon when the customary civilian-defense siren blew, synchronously announcing the end of our seminar, I suddenly realized that they were wed. A strange sense of relief came over me. I could only conjecture about it, but they were safe now, it seemed.

Although the rest of the weekend, including the holiday, went by on a more passive note, a yearning dwelt within me. I longed for Wednesday night—I wanted to see the bride and groom. At last the evening arrived. Even the air conditioning sounded different that night. Gone was its usual low murmur. Now it seemed to be singing. The room scintillated with excitement. We were all of us, including Tom, a little ahead of time, eagerly awaiting their arrival. When they walked in at last, our eyes were filled with delight. One look fulfilled our wishes and dispersed our fears. All our wishes had materialized. Eve walked into the room without hesitation, and her bright exuberant "Hello, everyone" captivated us. Bob, a step behind, though a trifle less buoyant, walked in jauntily. For a moment all was quiet as they sat beside each other in the two chairs unconsciously reserved for them. Betty was first to speak.

"Come, come, don't hold out any longer. Tell us all about it," she said.

Eve turned to Bob with a warm smile and then turned to Betty. There was a volley of exchange between them.

"What do you want to know?"

"In what hotel did it take place?"

"Why, in the Hotel Westchester."

"Who married you? Who performed the ceremony?"

"Bob's family minister from Brooklyn."

"Who were your attendants?"

"Well, the matron of honor was my roommate from college, Grace Gordon."

"Who was Bob's best man?"

"His brother, Dick, and his other brother, Jim, was an usher. The other usher was a supervisor from Bob's school."

"I can hardly wait to hear about your gown—what was it like?"

"My gown was beautiful! It was white silk marquisette with a full ballerina skirt. The bodice was all little tucks with the tiniest covered buttons down the front and a deep neckline. The sleeves were long, of course, and were similarly tucked. I had the cutest little half-cap made to match my gown with a finger-tip tulle veil and I carried an old-fashioned bouquet of lilies of the valley and white orchids."

"Oooh, it sounds dreamy. It was a morning wedding, wasn't it?"

"Yes, it was at eleven. Bob wore a morning coat and all the usual paraphernalia."

"Whereabouts in the hotel were you married, Eve?" asked Abby, interrupting this volley.

"My mother and father had reserved a suite for the wedding. They had also taken a room for me in which to dress. You see"— and she said this in a sort of knowing whisper—"they never knew about our living arrangements. To continue the deception, I stayed at our old apartment while Bob moved into the new one, where he dressed."

Resuming the volley, Betty asked, "What did the other girls in your bridal party wear?"

"All the girls, including Grace, wore short white embroidered-organdy dresses over the palest maize with shortie gloves. Their bouquets were old-fashioned, too, made of yellow and white daisies, and they wore little bandeaux of the same flowers in their hair. My mother looked stunning in a beige linen sheath with a Venice-lace tunic top and a tiny beige straw hat and matching gloves."

"How many people were there?"

"About fifty. As you know, Bob's parents are dead, so outside of his uncles and aunts and friends, the majority came from my family. They arrived en masse from Boston by train. You know"— she smiled—"ol' Back Bay Boston—they haven't quite figured out what those new-fangled machines are doing in the sky. Our reception was truly magnificent. Daddy had got a fine orchestra, which played during and after the luncheon. You can't imagine the thrill I felt when we danced the 'Anniversary Waltz' in the center of the large room which was so arranged that the tables bordered the four walls. It's what every girl dreams of—only mine came true."

The silence which followed conveyed the emotion she stirred within us.

"Oh, Eve, it sounds so beautiful."

"Yes, it was, and may I say there was only one thing missing? You people!"

"I'll say this," said Moe, tongue in cheek, "that reception really sounded like something I would have gotten a kick out of. There's no place like a wedding reception for a fellow to find a future wife. These affairs always seem to have a contagious effect."

"That's true," said Abby. "It does seem to make a lot of engagements jell."

"I doubt whether it would ever work for me," Molly grumbled sourly.

"Self-pity!" sighed John, disgustedly. "Can't you ever appreciate anything outside yourself without identifying with it in an inferior way?"

"Look, stupid, mind your own business."

"As long as she's in love with herself, she'll never have any rivals, anyway," Tom commented.

"You two remind me of some of my relatives," said the bridegroom.

"Which ones?" asked Eve curiously.

"Those uncles and aunts of mine—the way they carried on during the ceremony was pathetic. The women, with their little lace handkerchiefs and tears—the men with their mixture of envy and timidness. Doc," he continued, "I don't know about this, but tell me if I'm wrong—when people cry at weddings, are they really sincere?"

"What do you mean by sincere, Bob?"

"Well, I remember what you said right after Claudia's death, that it was an identificational process."

"That's it, Bob. When people cry at weddings," I continued,

"frequently it's because of the feelings of loss—loss over the child leaving the family fold. Loss is equated with the fear of death, and thus they are actually crying over their own bier. When the women tearfully clamor all over the bride, it's their own shrouds they are holding."

"What about the men then? Why are they so timid?"

"That's more sexual, for after all, the wedding signals the commencement of great sexual activity, and as you know all men carry fears of sexual inadequacy. Their shyness at weddings may be attributed to their fear of failure sexually—as they identify with the bridegroom."

"You know what really annoys me at weddings, Doctor?" Eve said.

"What is it?"

"It's the comparison that goes on. Honestly, it was really awful the way my family acted at the expense of Bob's relatives. The questions about their financial status—petty questions about his family background—self-satisfied smug looks on their faces when they concluded that, by their standards, my family was far above Bob's. And then, later, after having decided that they were superior, the way they participated falsely in the gaiety. The feeling they gave me, after they had had a few too many, was that only then could they associate with the common herd. I almost died of embarrassment the way my aunts and uncles studied Bob's family's habits and made references to what they considered their lack of gentility. At one point, I couldn't help but think back to the group —how all of us never seemed to pay attention to these false values."

"Yes, I was embarrassed, too," responded Bob, "but I'm concerned about my embarrassment, for I was ashamed at some of the old-fashioned table manners they exhibited, and, in general, their lack of culture."

"But, honey, they were sweet, nice people," Eve defended.

"Yes, I suppose so, but I always wanted them to be just a little more polished."

"Bob, darling, believe me, had you come from my family, you would be better able to appreciate your own more dependable, real values."

251

"I guess you're right, Eve—class is not culture, but rather how you treat the other person."

"Where did you spend your honeymoon?" inquired Abby.

"Well, one of my uncles loaned us a hunting lodge in Connecticut where we went early Saturday evening and returned Tuesday. The lodge is on the bank of the Housatonic River in one of the nicer rural areas—Falls Village. It was a story-book hideaway. The evenings were soft and mild, and the quiet river sounds blended with the peace of the setting. At last I know why they call it a honeymoon. The second night we were there, we stayed up the entire night talking and talking. I'll never forget the sunrise. It came up, down the river a way, from behind the trees. Its scarlet set the forest aglow in a red and purple-grey paradise. I hadn't seen a sunrise since my days as a girl scout at camp and had completely forgotten how beautiful one can be. There's something so hopeful and fresh about it all—it seemed to fit us closely. We were happy."

"I honestly feel you were, and this represents the first time in my life that I've actually seen a happy person," said Molly, awed.

We all turned and looked at Molly and were equally amazed, but no one spoke for the moment.

Now it was Moe's opportunity, "I guess this is as good a time as any," he began.

"What do you mean?"

"Just a minute, Bob, just a minute." Moe got up and went to the spare closet. In a moment he was back carrying a large package, beautifully wrapped. He leaned over the back of Eve's chair and placed it in her lap, saying, "Our best wishes to you both—a little late, but nonetheless, here we are and I mean all of us."

"Oh, thank you." Eve's voice was mildly confused.

Bob was too stunned to speak at all, but in a moment recovered to say, "Yes, thank you."

It was quite obvious that neither of them had expected to receive a gift. As far as they were concerned, the incident was over and settled.

"Well, open it!" exclaimed Tom.

"Yes, do open it," said John.

Moe, turning to the group, said, "I don't think they were expecting this," and then to Bob—"Did you really think we'd not give you a gift?"

"Well, to tell you the truth, the way I figured, it wasn't necessary any more after what we went through. I knew your hearts were in the right place and that's all that mattered."

"Don't be silly," remarked Betty, "we would no more think of doing that than jumping in the East River."

By this time Eve had begun to unwrap the gift. The gold foil wrapping with its bright green ribbon had been carefully put aside. It was obvious she planned to save them and, as so many women do in later years, pull them out from the attic storeroom and relive the moments associated with them. She lifted the lid off the white box and gasped. "My, you really shouldn't have . . . it's beautiful!" She lifted out a very large silver tray and a sterling silver coffee service.

Bob, with eyes as wide as an owl's, was numbly silent.

"Do you like it?" asked Abby eagerly.

"Oh, it's beautiful, simply beautiful," raved Eve.

Finally recovered, Bob said, "I should say so!"

When some of the hubbub had died down and thanks had been expressed, the therapist's voice addressed the group. "I want the group to know that I'm indeed pleased with the way they have recovered from their previously inhibited state."

"It does make me feel a great deal better about the whole thing," said Moe in a modest way.

"Yes, I guess we're all feeling much better about this," followed Betty. "How about it, Molly, do you agree?"

"And how! You've hit it right on the head!"

With similar comments going about the room, I brought the session to a close, saying, "I would just like the opportunity to shake hands with Bob and Eve and again wish them the best of everything."

I stood up. We shook hands and it felt fine. As I turned to Eve, she said, "Aren't you going to kiss the bride?" More than slightly startled by the question, I stood awkwardly still.

"Yeah, Doc, go on—yeah, go on," pleaded everyone strongly from all corners of the room. Bob topped it with, "I'd be insulted if you didn't."

I stepped over to Eve and we kissed gently. When we parted, Moe asked, "Hey, what about the rest of us?"

"Sure, why not," Bob said generously and everyone flocked to follow suit.

The rest of the month of July is difficult to remember. The mundane trials and tribulations of the newlyweds in setting up housekeeping were followed with eagerness by all. The impression received was that the rest of the group was learning for their own future from the experience of Bob and Eve. Never before had they shown such interest in marriage and its ramifications. That the women would be interested wasn't so strange, but the men's interest was indeed surprising.

John now wore a suit that actually fitted his shoulders. Moe was the proud possessor of several new sports jackets, and to quote him he "had a few girls on the string." Why, even Tom's shoes were polished regularly, not just intermittently.

But more important than external manifestations were their reactions to the girls in the group. They were just plain polite. The women were held in more gentle respect. Gone was their earlier attitude.

There was also a change in the attitude of the women toward the men. Betty no longer saw them as gods or devils. Molly swore less, hated less, and discussed the other half with appreciation. Of course Abby's problem was different. Seeing the successful outcome of Bob and Eve's romance undoubtedly encouraged her and aided in taking the sting out of her own experience.

It was on this note that the sessions ended for the summer. And it was a tired, but pleased psychiatrist who left for his annual summer vacation.

When our sessions were resumed the day after Labor Day, the first few drifted by swiftly. There was at first an almost collegiate atmosphere. The air was filled with, "And how did you spend the time?" or, "Tell us what happened to you," in typical sophomore-junior college-student discussion. However, the depth of feeling and involvement carried greater import.

It was during the third week that Abby opened up. It seems she had gained enough strength to invite her mother for dinner in a mid-Manhattan hotel. They had a long and understandably painful talk, and we all felt, as she broke down to tell the group the whole story, that she had tacitly forgiven as much as she ever could. She had not exploited the meeting; she simply was not made that way. The potential vindictive feelings had been honestly replaced with a sincere emotional urge to know about her relationship with her family as an infant. We all admired her tremendously as she related these details. Although no one expressed it, the feeling about the room was easily discernible: How do you ever forgive your mother for giving you away?

She talked of these events hazily at first, but at last clearly. I was struck with the boldness of her attitude and utterly pleased with the development. The response of the group to this earth-shattering story had reaffirmed the strength they had welded. She spoke of the fact that her brother, George, had re-enolled at New York University, and was apparently doing quite well. She noted the similarity of her younger brother, Howard, to John; and said she intended to attempt to have a normal relationship with him, apart and separate from the rest of the family. Howard, who was twenty-four, had just finished college and was entering the army. She and Howard had spent several evenings together during the summer, preceding the dinner she and her mother had alone. They had talked about the matter at great length and found solace in each other. Abby, in a clear and nonhostile voice, told us that she had no intention of ever visiting her parents' home. Furthermore, she felt it would be wiser if she and George never again came face to face.

On one of Howard's visits to Abby's apartment, he brought their father along. Howard had, of course, received Abby's permission first. I believe that, deep down, Abby held her father to be mainly responsible for her personal tragedy, although she never put it into words.

255

One of the many effects of Abby's story was that several of the members felt they had been lucky to have been spared such tragedy. Detectable, too, during Abby's revelation was a cooling-off period in their relationship to me. It was as if they were acting-out toward me the hostility they felt on Abby's behalf toward her parents. Passively, I sat in silence and accepted their feelings.

Another effect of this epic upon them was an attitude of sobriety. A calmer and more mature respect for parenthood seemed to have developed. Bob's and Eve's thoughts were especially penetrating. They seemed to realize the responsibilities that the future held for them.

Moe and Tom, after several sessions, recovered enough to be able to remind Abby of how fortunate she had been to have such ideal foster parents. Even Molly now realized that, for once, someone else had had a more devastating tragedy than she. Betty returned somewhat to her previous flighty self at the threat of Abby's story. Her aggression took the form of resentment in a hitherto unknown coolness to me—the identified rejecting father.

It was in this fundamental and somewhat more realistic spirit that the group met on Hallowe'en Eve. The emotional trends were divergent—but not necessarily in conflict. For example, my own feeling toward the group was one of undeniable pride. And yet, their response, though mindful of my approval, remained cool. It wasn't an armed truce nor any other form of abeyance. In fact, it wasn't even rejectional. The feeling they seemed to be expressing toward me was, "We know you're here, but please leave us alone." Thus, in accordance with their wishes, I did precisely that. And this facilitated matters.

For the longest while, the conversation seemed to carry very little pertinency. It wasn't trivial, not really light. It just lacked significant substance. A quality it did seem to possess, however, was the most important one in any conversation—relatedness. They were really talking to one another with an obviously greater sense of acceptance, revealing a security level not reached previously. All this was taking place as if they were within a vacuum, with their therapist on the outside. As the session wore on, I could feel them pulling further and further away from me. However, within their own orbit, their warmth toward one another seemed to be reaching an ever greater height. This spirit seemed to lessen the tension between them and me until finally I felt as though I could have been absent physically.

At this point, the conversation swung over to the topic of marriage. Not merely from a purely philosophical viewpoint, but rather as an offshoot of the problems involved in setting up a household. This, naturally enough, led into the area that they were really preparing to discuss—leaving home.

It was approximately halfway through the session that the conversation swung from the concrete particulars of marriage into this more charged area of "How does one leave the nest nicely?" Without any of them glancing at me, and with full self-authority, a dramatic maneuver took place. It was Moe who led the men.

"I don't see why we fellows can't get together in this matter."

"I'm with you," Bob agreed.

"It's okay by me," John assented.

And without any further impetus, the men picked up their chairs and formed a new circle. The women, who had been engaged in a gabfest as the opposite half of the previously formed circle, did likewise. It was Eve who led this faction with, "That's a splendid idea, let's follow suit."

The other three girls nodded their heads in strong approval and clustered about her.

There I sat alone, between these two worlds. I continued to feel that they were doing something constructive. Occasionally I noted a furtive glance in my direction from the two areas. These glances were met with a knowing nod of support. I felt as if I had found myself suddenly in a room with two television sets turned on. Each had a major drama playing. My attention was naturally divided. I was amazed to discover that it did not create conflict. I simply "took turns" listening to that circle where the material seemed most significant. The men had been the boldest and most productive. After a few minutes they coined the phrase, "the club," for their new subgroup formation. The gist of their conversation now was their work situations. Over and over again, their relationship to the "boss" occupied their attention. Such comments as "Oh,

257

he's a good enough guy, but he's afraid to leave us alone," and "If he'd only pay more attention to his own job, he wouldn't notice our shortcomings so much," dominated their conversation. John, in paricular, seemed to have the greatest difficulty. It was obvious that Bob had come a long way. His previous maneuvering to outflank authority was practically gone. He was happy at his new job and felt secure. There was no suspicion of his employers. He had taken their acceptance of him at face value. Moe, not quite secure, but nonetheless adequate, was dissatisfied. Listening to his story, I felt his dissatisfaction was realistically founded. His bosses did have a "good thing" in him and were guilty of some exploitation. The further the conversation developed, the more reliance he seemed to gain. His feeling that perhaps he'd be better off changing jobs solidified. The others gave him support.

John still suffered from needing excessive approval. He had improved considerably, but was still wanting. In fact, of all the men, it was he who observed my reactions the most frequently to find out how this affair was registering.

Tom perhaps could best be characterized as "low man on the totem pole." Although he had conquered his lateness in coming to therapy and to many other activities, he was still about half an hour late in getting to work. He went into a long account of his problem. This, in itself, was something new for him. I saw quickly that he could present himself better in an all-male society than in a mixed one. It wasn't that he was shy or bashful of women, but rather that he needed male identification. The impression he created upon the other men by his free-flowing discourse raised their estimation of him unanimously. It was Moe, his psychological brother, who provided the recognition with, "Say, this men's club idea really does wonders for you, Tom." He smiled in a way that showed the idea had not dawned on him previously. Recovering from the revelation, Tom broke the pause, saying, "Yeah, never thought of it before, Moe, but that's right."

John asked, "Is it that you're afraid of women?"

He again paused thoughtfully for a moment before replying.

"No, it's just that I have a feeling that men understand me better."

"I see," said John.

"But did it ever dawn on you that there isn't any difference between the sexes in the ability to understand other human beings?" inquired the psychologically oriented Bob.

"Is that true?" Tom asked in some amazement.

"Yes, it is, Tom. If you want to know what I think, I'd be glad to tell you," Bob continued.

"Yes, would you help a guy out?" was the grateful reply.

"Okay, it's like this. Men think only men can understand them—as women think only women can understand them—simply because, when they're soliciting help, they're actually misrepresenting their request. When people ask for advice, they actually don't want it. What they really wish is to talk to themselves—a sort of talking out loud to oneself with another person present. The other person is really there to ward off the embarrassment of self-indulgence. In addition, to avoid the feeling of peculiarity while speaking to oneself out loud, we desire another's presence—preferably a person of the same sex. Otherwise we have an added burden to carry. I've found out that the best thing to do when people ask for advice is to get them to give their own answer to the problem and then agree with it. For nine times out of ten, they know what's best for themselves."

"Makes sense," and Tom shook his head thoughtfully.

"I don't believe I agree with you," said John. "I think women are more understanding than men."

"They have the reputation for it," Moe interjected.

"That's true," responded Bob, "but this comes from the fact that our first association with an understanding person is a woman known as mother. When men do what you and Moe are referring to, they aren't really soliciting advice or guidance, but rather appealing to their original source of love—their mother—for more love."

"Well, I don't know if I agree with you yet, but I'll think it over," said John dubiously. He was never one to accept new ideas readily. It always struck me that in the end, he would see other people's ideas, but inevitably they challenged him first. His image of himself was too ingrained to be able to accept new ideas without threat. However, he was learning fast. This was ascertained a few moments later when he returned to the subject and admitted openly that Bob's theory concerning men and their mothers was right. This approval of Bob by John cemented the last crevice in a once wide breach in their relationship. Also, it fused the male society. Bob was now fully recognized—the oldest son. Furthermore, he had made the successful jump into independence, which the other three admired without envy.

In the meantime, and concurrently, in the female circle the conversation had slipped back to womanly talk of household planning. The natural focus of attention, of course, was Eve. Betty was the most enthusiastic. She asked endless questions. As I listened to the exchange, I felt their inquiries made Eve's and Bob's apartment as clear to me as if I had been there. Everything was covered from the foyer to the bedroom and back again—the wall-to-wall carpeting, the curtains, sheets, towels, etc., etc. And what a problem television was with respect to the living room. Eve said that, without a den, one's apartment could never have a touch of dignity—especially the living room, due to its use as a theatre.

It was Abby who commented upon the change that television had brought about in many families' living habits. It seemed to her that this new form of entertainment had done something no other modern invention had. She pointed out that the new labor-saving gadgets and the modern means of transportation had tended to take the family out of the home, whereas television had returned the emphasis to home entertainment.

"Yes," Betty perked up, "it's true! Not since colonial days has so much emphasis been placed upon having a good time at home. Why, even the game room and finished basement, as part of the do-it-yourself craze, seem to carry out this return to the 'life at home' drive."

Having exhausted this subject, they drifted to the topic of fashions. At first, the comments were rather general and not designed to fit any of them in particular. At one point Eve chose a magazine from the rack to illustrate her story. The conversation ran from Dior to Balenciaga and the latest fabrics and perfumes. Finally, the women settled down to personalities. Each, in turn,

260

lamented such things as prices and those items which they liked, but which did not become them. As I hoped it would, this conversation at last reached the touchy area of Molly's clothes. Eve and Abby carried the load primarily. Molly had not always been too careful about underarm deodorants and this was the point under discussion. A short volley ensued between the load-carriers. It made me suspicious that they had plotted their course in advance. Gingerly and tactfully they proceeded with, "I don't like this brand as it's too creamy" and "such and such does a pretty good job, but simply doesn't hold up long enough."

And then Eve turned to Molly at the critical point and asked, "What do you use, Molly?"

She carried herself well and never let on that she knew the conversation was for her benefit. She replied that she used a well-known brand, but was thinking of changing to the one they had suggested. The conversation then turned more specifically toward her. The voices dropped in volume and the secretiveness of it all revealed the kindnesses involved. They urged Molly to do something about herself. They talked about stocking seams, slips showing and all the other ways in which Molly was deficient. At first she was startled, but made a rapid recovery. Fortunately, I thought, as I observed the interaction, she did not respond with an attack. It was a rare occasion when she did not engage in a counterassault. But she knew she was being treated gently and kindly. No doubt the absence of the men was an aid in the matter.

Like John, she, too, was showing the ability to accept other people's new ideas. This was no easy task for her, for despite her mode of dress, she apparently had always felt inwardly that she possessed a higher degree of feminine appeal than most. Her shrinking fantasies, and the resulting higher level of self-respect, had truly been demonstrated on this occasion.

To digress a moment, this girls' conversation, in the weeks that followed, bore its fruit. Molly's appearance became much more in keeping with the rest of the women of the group. She had her hair cut in the Italian style and lost some weight. She bought new shoes and the dresses she wore were a decided improvement.

The women did not leave their responsibilities at this point. They were quick to praise Molly's efforts. This praise spurred her on all the more. And by curious sequel, the improvement was far-reaching indeed, for the dress habits of Tom and John picked up similarly, in emulation of Molly's example.

This phenomenon, I'm sure, has been observed by many, but nonetheless is most appealing. When women become more feminine, the men in their circle become more masculine. Certainly everyone's self-respect rises.

Returning to the session where the men and women had split up and had excluded their therapist—after the initial conversation about feminine fashions and Molly's grooming, the topic of importance to the girls became—men. At first they talked about how different they are "from us." Then it moved over to male values, which amused them. They commented: "Such babies—when they're sick, there's nobody sicker." "They're never around with the car when you need them." ". . . the fuss they make over their bowling nights and other nights out." Betty introduced the inevitable subject with, "And then he wanted to spoil a beautiful evening by claiming a kiss." This served as a cue. Molly launched into the subject with great fervor. Her hostility illustrated her still-incomplete fulfillment of feminine identification. As she droned on, she received less and less support from the others until finally she began to question herself with—"Maybe it's my problem and perhaps men aren't the bastards I always say they are." This again was evidence that she had made strides. The all-female society had served her well by offering her no convenient hate object as a target. It caused her to realize that she had more of a problem than she had been willing to admit. This realization, no doubt, was aided by the increase in the girls' acceptance of her.

With a few more references to the "amateur wrestling bouts" usually involved when going out with men, they concluded they'd prefer, as is so often the case in this type of "hen" session, to have this difficulty than no male attention at all.

When the session came to a close, I had to remind them of it gently. At once they all arose, replacing their seats in the original positions.

During the next forty-eight hours, I spent considerable time reviewing the session. One outstanding fact remained with me. This group division denoted a maturity that no patient of mine had ever exhibited previously in my presence. I came to the conclusion that I would continue to support their strivings.

At the next meeting, I said nothing beyond the usual greetings, and they continued where they had left off. They picked up their chairs again and formed the two groups, as they had done previously. No insecure glances came back to me. Instead, they plowed in with gusto. In fact, the action continued for a total of five more sessions. At each session, I sat down, greeted them pleasantly, then watched them divide into their usual two parts.

At the close of the fifth session, the two who had benefited most in each group had an interesting exchange.

Molly: "Let's join the men now. They're fun to be with, too."

And John said, "Yes, I'm ready to return—life without women isn't much."

When they had reassembled the seats, it was Bob who asked the pertinent question. "Doc, what has our behavior in these past two weeks meant?"

Carefully I explained that I felt it was not based upon past recall but was, rather, a new experience. Further, that I felt it was epic-making for them and that I was tremendously impressed with their progress. I made the analogy that they were reaching the upper borders of young adulthood as a group and would soon be ready for discharge.

It was on this occasion that I told them of my feelings with respect to maturity. I expressed the idea that maturity in terms of criteria for discharge meant—the ability for self-growth. That when I saw patients do what they had done without solicitation and with complete spontaneity, I felt assured that they were nearing this point. I further said that people always had problems—and that they, too, would have them. The only difference would be

263

that they would have an inner resource to help them bear up under anxiety, help them respond to their problems with a realistic courage.

It was not my intention in therapy to engage in the endless attempt to create an ideal specimen, but to carry on to that extent where the patient with his new growth could enjoy the enjoyable. The ability to enjoy immediacy in life, with the security to wrestle with its problems, as well as the willingness to experience distress and anxiety, served as the primary goals in therapy. I felt that they had reached these objectives with their enterprise.

Continuing, I told them that I enjoyed their appreciation of the ordinary. Their departure from the neurotic was clear in this. They were able to get more out of less, rather than the reverse, so typical of neurotic structure. I elaborated on how important it was, in terms of happiness, to strive for the middle ground—that true greatness did not carry excesses with it, but was more typified by a versatile balance. The pursuit of greatness by the neurotic was tantamount to his inability to enjoy the enjoyable. His worship of the unusual and his glorification of the "large" revealed his identification with infantile omnipotence. When people can enjoy being ordinary, then, and then only, have they found peace and happiness so characteristic of maturity. It had always been somewhat of a puzzle to me, I told them, that some of us would rather be caught nude than be considered ordinary. The truth of the matter is that, in being ordinary, we are really at our best, and certainly in being ordinary, we are at that level where we can appreciate and enjoy to the greatest degree. Geniuses may do the world great service, but they very often lack the ability to appreciate their own work. True humility is not a lowered state of being—nor is it any deflated status. Humility is greatness—the greatness of life is to become ordinary within its bounds.

They responded, as most people do when hearing this for the first time, with confusion. I explained to them that their familiar usage of these terms, "ordinary" and "mediocre," prevented them from seeing that the principle behind their usage was not that which I intended. Rather, the principle was one that consisted of integrating into one's environment—not with the loss of individuality but rather with its gain. The man who can use his environment in flexible manner to complement his ability to enjoy the enjoyable has then become normal in the broadest implication of the word. Normal is what is ordinary for man to be.

"It is in such a sense that I used the word 'ordinary,'" was my conclusion.

"Yes," commented Eve understandingly, "that's what Claudia was fast becoming." The discussion brought about by Eve's comment showed that Claudia, though gone, was very much a permanent member of our group. In fact, we all agreed that we had influenced each other to such an extent that we no doubt would continue to do so the rest of our lives—even *in absentia.*

After they had left, it was necessary for me to review the meaning of these proceedings, which illustrated, of course, the strengthening of their identities. I felt that their behavior approximated closely the psychology of late adolescence. First, that they were in the process of setting up their own value-systems. In so doing, it was obviously necessary for them to set me aside, which represented expression of the attitude so typical of adolescents. The division was necessary on this basis—the old family tie too often had stood for values which were not defensible. It was as if they needed to say, "What you, Father and Mother, have held up as gospel has in actuality not been borne out. Honesty is not always the best policy." In our growth we all need enterprise, an opportunity to undergo experience for ourselves. I felt that this behavior was essentially to be found in all people preparing themselves for the propagational experience. This adolescent self-limiting psychology which leads into "new home" building is responsible for much of the pioneer spirit the human race exhibits. Therefore, we owe it much.

This higher level of human psychology which brings people to the "new home," I have labeled, arbitrarily, the third polarity. It is this third polarity, with its pioneering attitude, that the human race is dependent upon. In practice I have never seen this emerge except in therapy groups.

Between the close of the session and Thanksgiving Eve,

events flew by with almost uncontrolled rapidity. My words had kindled the spark. The stampede for higher summits was on. The group was inflamed with the responsibility of their strivings.

I invited Bob and Eve for a joint appointment. More than one consideration led me to do this. Their whole relationship had been so unusual from its inception, that the natural events that were to follow for them, as a new family, needed special attention apart from the rest of the group. I felt that a joint meeting would further reinforce their identity as a family. I hoped that the meeting with the two of them as "a couple" would foster the feelings of camaraderie between us, as married people. Equally, any undue residual remnants of their relationship that dealt with the child-parent-like relationship to me might be resolved. It also could give an added opportunity to express my acceptance of them as married adults. Then, we could focus from the framework of these positions upon the problems of homemaking and survival as adults.

Our get-together was arranged for the end of the day so as not to be controlled by my schedule. All three of us sensed that parting was in the offing. As suspected, their interests were centered not only upon the immediate but also upon a more far-reaching subject. Eve introduced the idea to me by asking me how it felt to be a parent. I gathered immediately that she was not speaking of my role as a therapist. Unhesitatingly, I said that being a parent was perhaps one of life's greatest responsibilities. That, as an undertaking with another person, it was one of the greatest that could befall any human being—and that unfortunately I felt it was the most inadequately performed responsibility in the world. No preliminary application is ever required for the job of parent—it is given whether or not one meets the qualifications. I was heartened to say that, in their behalf, I felt they were ready, and they more than had my best wishes. I told them of a story related to me by a fourteen-year-old girl whom I had treated. This little girl asked me one day, quite out of the blue, if I could recognize who was married and who wasn't in a public restaurant if I couldn't see the wedding ring. Quite intrigued, I went along with her and said that I couldn't, but could she? "Of course," she resounded brightly, "they're the ones who don't talk to each other." Bob roared and

Eve laughed so hard that she cried. When the hilarity subsided, it was Bob who was first to recognize the seriousness of the occasion with the comment, "Now I see what you mean. Since we do relate and have worked out this problem of communication between us, we will be as prepared as possible for the task we wish to undertake."

Eve's comment followed. "I guess our premarital relationship, with its struggles, made bigger people of us."

"Yes, Eve, again you see that growth has come out of a crisis and resulted in an ordinary function of life—normal parenthood."

We shook hands at the end and bid each other farewell with the knowledge that one more group session stood between us and discharge.

I had told the group during Thanksgiving week of my decision to make this their last meeting.

When the normal flow of the first ten minutes or so had abated, I took over. In turning to Molly I had my most difficult job.

"Molly, much as I'd like to, I cannot have you and Tom leave therapy at this time. What I've decided to do is this—to have you two serve as the nucleus of a new group. I doubt whether your membership in a new group will be very long, but some more group experience is necessary." Her gasp was as startled as I knew it would be, but her comment was a surprise.

"I've often thought that, if this ever happened, I'd hate you—and although it does hurt not to finish with the rest, I know that you're doing the right thing. As you all know, I've been, and still am, a free user of profanity. What I've begun to realize is that I needn't be ashamed of it since we all release some force when we feel upset. It isn't so much what we say, or whether we swear, it's all energy and motion anyway; so just let me say this with dignity —God damn it anyway!!!"

I glanced at Tom, to see what repercussions I had caused there, and the usually inarticulate Tom surprised us all.

"Doc, I've been expecting it—it comes as no great surprise. I want to say this about therapy and myself. All my life I've been living with something on top of me. It's as though I had pulled clothes over my personality—a turtle-necked sweater. I realize now I'm slowly taking this sweater off and sticking my neck out again."

"Very good," I commented, "I'm sure you and Molly will find yourselves very quickly in a group where you serve as veterans." They looked at each other with great felicity. They knew that they were together—a feeling they had seldom known previously. In their misery they felt a union, but not through despair—this was one of encouragement.

"John, you and Betty are next. You are both discharged, but I would like to spend a few individual hours with you. I feel it would be beneficial to elaborate on some of the material we have all been through. Betty, the subject of marriage needs further illumination. I want to talk with you about your reluctance to accept the earthiness of the human animal. Remember that prudishness is only one side of the coin whose other side is vulgarity. For example, it strikes me that the 'professional virgin' is to the prostitute as prudishness is to vulgarity. Man in his healthy state is neither prudish nor vulgar, but earthy.

"John, I'd like to have an exchange with you on a 'man-to-man basis.' Your often-stated views on man's pursuits have led me to this decision. You don't have to agree with me, but I'd like you to consider another viewpoint; life holds no solution—it's devoid of answers and only demands that we live it."

Betty, aroused to the point of solemnity, graciously accepted the evaluating statement. John visibly thrashed the idea about before he was able to solidify it. But when the idea was clarified, the promise of such a venture became exciting.

"Well, that brings us to Moe and Abby—it's uncomplicated here," I said. "You're both completely discharged."

A strong "Hurrah!" burst from Moe. "What a wonderful break," he said, "for I was just about to tell you I expect to get engaged next week."

We all pounced upon him with vigorous handshakes and he proceeded to give us the details. His wish had come true. He had accidentally met a former classmate who was a widow. She had lost her mate during the war years, just like himself. They had barely known each other at college, but had secretly held a mutual admiration for each other. With his new job and new girl, Moe, now finishing his therapy, was one of the brightest lights I have ever seen.

Abby, in true Abby fashion, took her discharge in stride. In the women's group she had completed the details of her story, and her adjustment was as fine as anyone could care to see. She spoke with regret that the experience was now ending. "It's been the most truly educational experience I've ever had. You see, I feel most of what I've had in school and college could really be reduced to the word 'instruction,' but this has been real growth, a true education."

"Now then, Bob and Eve, as I told you both yesterday, you are discharged as of today. I might add it's been a long and tough voyage for all of us, but I wouldn't have missed it for all the world. It's been that sort of journey."

How could it be over so soon? Maybe it seemed abrupt, but that is exactly how it was—all of a sudden most of my family was grown and gone.

On this note, we all stood up. I went around the room and shook hands with each of them and personally wished them the happiness they deserved. The last one I reached was Bob and after the exchange had ended, he handed me a very small package and said, "Doc, this is from all of us—in appreciation."

Inside was a fourteen-carat-gold key to my office door. On it was inscribed: "To Case, the man who made us acquainted with what we knew all the time."

I was greatly moved by this appreciation and my smiling, but slightly misting, countenance showed it. After I had expressed my thanks, Eve took Bob's hand and said, "I would like you all to know that there has been another member silently present this evening—our child."

A battle over and won;
Understand the unrelated ones,
Their battle unbegun.

....other best selling
NEWCASTLE books
you won't want to miss....